RESEARCH IN
GLOBAL STRATEGIC
MANAGEMENT

Volume 2 • 1991

GLOBAL COMPETITION AND
THE EUROPEAN COMMUNITY

To the memory of

Raymond Verbeke

RESEARCH IN GLOBAL STRATEGIC MANAGEMENT

A Research Annual

GLOBAL COMPETITION AND THE EUROPEAN COMMUNITY

Editors: **ALAN M. RUGMAN**
Faculty of Management
University of Toronto
and
Research Director
Ontario Centre for International Business

ALAIN VERBEKE
Faculty of Management
University of Toronto
and
Faculty of Economic, Social
  and Political Sciences
University of Brussels (VUB)

VOLUME 2 • 1991

 **JAI PRESS INC.**

Greenwich, Connecticut   *London, England*

CONTENTS

LIST OF CONTRIBUTORS

Michiel Roscam Abbing

Maastricht Economic Research
   Institute on Innovation
   and Technology (MERIT)
Maastricht, The Netherlands

Jean Émile Denis

Faculty of Administration
University of Ottawa
Ottawa, Canada

Glenn Morgan

Manchester School of Management
UMIST
Manchester, United Kingdom

Fergus Murray

Manchester School of Management
UMIST
Manchester, United Kingdom

Tony Quon

Faculty of Administration
University of Ottawa
Ottawa, Canada

Alan M. Rugman

Faculty of Management
University of Toronto
   and
Research Director
Ontario Centre for International
   Business
Toronto, Canada

Ravi Sarathy

College of Business
Northeastern University
Boston, MA

Jos Schakenraad   Maastricht Economic Research
                                      Institute on Innovation and
                                      Technology (MERIT)
                                  Maastricht, The Netherlands

Leo Sleuwaegen   Faculty of Applied Economics
                                  Catholic University of Louvain
                                  Louvain, Belgium

Jean-Claude Usunier   Ecole Supérieure des Affaires
                                  (Université de Grenoble)
                                  Grenoble, France

Alain Verbeke   Faculty of Management
                                  University of Toronto
                                  Toronto, Canada
                                              and
                                  Faculty of Economic, Social
                                      and Political Sciences
                                  University of Brussels
                                  Brussels, Belgium

Marc van Wegberg   Faculty of Business Administration
                                      and Economics
                                  University of Limburg
                                  Maastricht, The Netherlands

Arjen van Witteloostuijn   Faculty of Business Administration
                                      and Economics
                                  University of Limburg
                                  Maastricht, The Netherlands

Arthur F.P. Wassenberg   Rotterdam School of Management
                                  Erasmus University Rotterdam
                                  Rotterdam, The Netherlands

INTRODUCTION

This research volume on global competition and the European Community (EC) results from a workshop held at the European Institute for Advanced Studies in Management (EIASM) in May 1990. This workshop was chaired by Dr. Alan M. Rugman, Professor of International Business at the University of Toronto and Research Director of the Ontario Centre for International Business Studies (OCIB) and Dr. Danny Van Den Bulcke, Professor of International Business at the University of Antwerp (RUCA) and Director of the Center for International Management and Development Antwerp (CIMDA). The administrative organization was handled by Ms. Gerry Van Dyck, Program Director to EIASM.

The main purpose of this workshop was to provide a forum for original contributions in the area of global strategic management, with a special emphasis on the present economic integration process in the EC. A limited number of contributions were selected primarily on the basis of (1) their originality, either in conceptual approach or empirical content, and (2) their relevance to the practice of global strategic management. As a result, a number of excellent papers that did not fulfil these two criteria could not be included in the volume.

Each paper in this volume develops—either explicitly or implicitly— one important theme—namely the concept of entry barriers. More particularly, each paper provides insights into the impact of the economic integration process in the EC on the entry barriers faced by business firms.

The concept of entry barrier is used here in a managerial sense to indicate a constraint that prevents other companies from negatively affecting or taking over a particular firm's product market domain. A distinction can be made here between the impact of economic integration on either natural or government imposed entry barriers. The former include elements such as scale economies, cost advantages independent of scale, product differentiation, control over distribution channels, and supplier switching costs. The latter reflect tariff and nontariff barriers to trade as well as various forms of government regulations benefiting particular companies at the expense of others.

The first three papers contain conceptual perspectives on global competition and the EC. The next three papers discuss the impact of European integration on specific sectors, namely manufacturing, personal financial services, and the media and entertainment industry. The seventh and eighth papers provide detailed analyses of joint venture activity in the European Community with special reference to the effectiveness of European industrial policy programs. Finally, the last two papers discuss the impact of European integration on "outsiders," more specifically Canada and Eastern Europe.

In "Environmental Change and Global Competitive Strategy in Europe," Alan M. Rugman and Alain Verbeke develop a model aimed at assisting managers in formulating appropriate strategies when confronted with large environmental changes. In this framework, the effects of firm level strategic reactions to a new trading environment can always be analyzed in terms of a strengthening or weakening of the natural and government imposed entry barriers benefiting the company vis-à-vis foreign rivals. Their main conclusion is that changes in entry barriers always need to be considered at the level of the individual firm. Actual changes in entry barriers will primarily depend on the ability of each company, affected by a new trading environment, to generate new firm specific advantages.

The second paper, "Multimarket Competition and European Integration" by A. Van Witteloostuijn and M. Van Wegberg, demonstrates that the "EC 1992" program implies primarily a replacement of artificial, government imposed entry barriers by natural entry barriers. From a conceptual perspective they analyze the expected entry behavior of both "insiders" and "outsiders" in the different national markets within the EC. They conclude that managers should devote sufficient attention to two key elements in corporate strategy: the optimal selection of markets for entry and the issue of entry deterrence.

In "The 'European Consumer': Globalizer or Globalized?," J.C. Usunier demonstrates that the predicted effects of European economic integration are often exaggerated. In his view, many nationally responsive firms benefit from the specific characteristics of consumption patterns in their respective home countries. These country specific consumption patterns will not be substantially affected in the short or medium run, thus limiting the ability of firms to penetrate other European markets, even after the complete elimination of government imposed entry barriers. One of his core conclusions is that existing insiders within the EC should attempt to further strengthen "culture bound" natural entry barriers against foreign rivals.

The fourth paper, "The Restructuring of European Manufacturing Industries" by L. Sleuwaegen, contains a comprehensive overview of the impact of economic integration on the European manufacturing sector. This paper analyzes the combined effects of an elimination of government imposed entry barriers and the associated increased possibilities for firms to create new natural entry barriers (especially through scale and scope economies). Sleuwaegen argues that major effects can be expected in those industries previously fragmented by nontariff barriers to trade. In this respect, he also provides an analysis of the causes for mergers, takeovers and strategic alliances in the EC.

Glenn Morgan and Fergus Murray analyze strategic changes in the European personal financial services industry in "Strategic Changes in Personal Financial Services: The Impact of the Single European Market." Their main conclusion is that natural entry barriers benefiting firms in their home markets in Europe will remain strong in spite of a gradual dismantling of government imposed entry barriers. In this context the "EC 1992" program should be viewed as only a stepping stone in a long term process of increasing globalization. Although its direct effects are rather limited, it has awakened companies to both entry threats by rivals in the domestic market and entry opportunities in foreign markets.

Ravi Sarathy investigates the globalization process in the media and entertainment industry in "European Integration and Global Strategy in the Media and Entertainment Industry." He analyzes both the natural and government imposed entry barriers in this industry. One of his conclusions is that EC directives, such as those imposing local content requirements may function as artificial entry barriers against "outsiders." The author then analyzes the different strategic alternatives open to these outsiders so as to gain market share in the EC. A possibility is that U.S. production companies, with strong firm specific capabilities to develop and market products that attract large audiences, will engage in joint venture activities and attempt to get partial control and ownership of media channels so as to overcome government shelter.

In "Strategic Alliances and Public Policy in the European Community: The Case of Information Technology" by Arthur F.P. Wassenberg and "The European Case of Joint R&D Activities in Core Technologies" by Michiel Roscam Abbing and Jos Schakenraad, cooperative relationships among high technology firms in the EC are discussed. A. Wassenberg investigates the effectiveness of industrial policy programs in the EC, especially as regards the development of strategic alliances in the information technology area. He analyzes the effects of these programs in terms of the resulting ability of EC firms to create natural entry barriers against their Triad rivals. M. Roscam Abbing and J. Schakenraad provide a detailed discussion of a number of European technology programs, again especially in the area of information technology. It appears that most of the benefits, and hence most of the effects of the programs in terms of creation of natural entry barriers, benefit only a limited number of firms. Just as in the previous chapter, the effectiveness of these industrial policy programs is questioned.

Finally, J.E. Denis and Tony Quon in "Impact of European Economic Integration on Outsiders' Generic Strategies: The Case of Canadian Multinationals" assess the general impact of the "EC 1992" programs on outside-countries, specifically on Canada. In the Canadian case it appears that outsiders will be faced with high entry barriers after the implementation of the "EC 1992" program. Hence, it may be necessary for outside firms to gain access to the EC through substituting FDI for exports.

This collection of papers will hopefully assist managers in improving their ability to respond more effectively to new trading environments. In addition, this volume should provide a building block for the development of a more general theory on the significance and the managerial requirements of a global competitive environment for both managers and public policymakers.

Alan M. Rugman
Alain Verbeke
Editors

PART I

CONCEPTUAL PERSPECTIVES ON GLOBAL COMPETITION AND THE EUROPEAN COMMUNITY

ENVIRONMENTAL CHANGE AND GLOBAL COMPETITIVE STRATEGY IN EUROPE

Alan M. Rugman and Alain Verbeke

I. INTRODUCTION

The starting point of this paper is our belief that an environmental change such as the "Europe 1992" program may substantially affect the degree of globalization of an industry by inducing increased international expansion of business firms. We define a global industry as an industry in which the overall competitive position of the various firms is significantly affected by their competitive position in different countries or regions. A firm's competitive position is defined as its ability to obtain survival, profitability, and growth, relative to rival firms.

Our definition is broader and more useful than the one suggested by Hout, Porter, and Rudden (1982). They argue that in a global industry a firm's competitive position in one national market is significantly affected by its competitive position in other national markets. Their definition requires that strong interdependences exist between the firm's activities in different countries,

Research in Global Strategic Management, Volume 2, pages 3-27.
ISBN: 1-55938-277-5

either on the input side, the production side, or the output side. In fact, such interdependences may not exist at all.

For example, in the shipbuilding industry, where large firms sell their products all over the world, production is mostly performed in one country, but the competitive position of a company in one national market may be unrelated to its competitive position in other markets. A Japanese shipbuilding firm's ability to sell its products in European countries may have little or no influence on its performance in other markets, even European ones. The definition used here, however, identifies the shipbuilding industry as a global industry. In it, the overall competitive position of many firms (in terms of survival, profitability and growth) will critically depend upon their competitive position in several markets.

Our definition also implies that the distinction often made between "global" industries and "multidomestic" industries, by, for example, Porter (1986), is largely irrelevant. In a so-called multidomestic industry, each subsidiary of a multinational enterprise (MNE) may be quite independent from the others, yet to the extent that the competitive position of one or several subsidiaries substantially affects the overall competitive position of the firm in terms of survival, profitability, and growth, it would still be a global industry. Our definition of a global industry accommodates the fact that a global industry is characterized by high intra-industry trade and/or investment. Only if an industry consists primarily of firms competing on a national basis (with little or no intra-industry trade or investment), so that activities in host countries do not significantly affect the firms' overall economic performance, should the term "nonglobal industry" be used.

While we focus on the impact of local performance on overall performance, this does not mean that each firm in the global industry must have activities in different countries (either through exports, licensing agreements, joint ventures or foreign direct investment). Several purely domestic firms may be competing in a global industry in the sense that their product market domain is restricted to the domestic market. Their inability or lack of interest in developing activities abroad (a zero-activity position in foreign countries) reflects upon their overall competitive performance (especially in terms of growth) as compared to firms that develop such foreign activities. In addition, their competitive position in the home market may be determined by the level of "shelter" provided by government regulation in the form of artificial entry barriers against foreign competition (see Rugman and Verbeke 1990a).

II.   GLOBAL COMPETITION AND
THE EUROPEAN COMMUNITY, 1992

We believe that the European Community's (EC) 1992 measures will lead to an international expansion of business firms that will require two types of organizational capabilities to be developed. First, capabilities of integration, which reflect nonlocation-bound firm specific advantages (FSAs). Second, capabilities of national responsiveness, which refer to location-bound FSAs. The concept of FSAs is explained in Rugman (1981) and further developed with applications to corporate strategy in Rugman and Verbeke (1990a).

International integration at the firm level can take three forms, in terms of the configuration and coordination of the firm's activities. First, there can be a concentration of particular activities in specific countries to obtain economies of scale. In this case, integration reflects a centralized configuration of the firm's core assets.

Second, integration can take the form of transfer of know-how across borders, thus creating economies of scope. Here, integration refers to a dispersion of the firm's asset configuration combined with a specific type of international coordination of activities; the transfer and subsequent use of know how abroad, thus creating "standards" in terms of work content and processes, outputs, skills, or norms. This requires the use of similar manufacturing processes at the production side, the use of identical brand names in marketing, the standardization of skill requirements to perform specific activities, and the sharing of a common corporate culture across borders.

Third, integration may refer to the exploitation of national differences. Here, the firm is again characterized by a dispersed configuration of assets. Coordination is achieved by linking the dispersed assets of the firm so that it can make optimal use of imperfections in the markets for production factors, intermediate outputs and final products. Exploitation of national differences on the input side typically requires substantial intra-firm trade.

In each of these three cases the firm uses core skills or FSAs to be competitive abroad. These economies of scale, economies of scope, or benefits from the exploitation of national differences, result from the firm's proprietary know-how. This know-how is used across borders, that is, know-how can be "nonlocation-bound." For example, economies of scale become relevant in an international context only when the manufactured products embody characteristics which make the product competitive abroad. Economies of scope can only be reaped if the know-how being transferred gives the firm a competitive edge vis-à-vis foreign rivals. Benefits of exploiting national differences only arise if the firm possesses necessary coordination skills to take advantage of market imperfections in the international arena.

In contrast, a focus on national responsiveness means that the international expansion of a firm needs to be accompanied by the development of specific capabilities in the different countries where the company will operate. The firm's asset configuration may be centralized or decentralized, but the profitability and growth of its operations in the different countries will largely depend on its ability to adapt to local circumstances, both in terms of market demands

ALAN M. RUGMAN and ALAIN VERBEKE

Location-bound FSAs

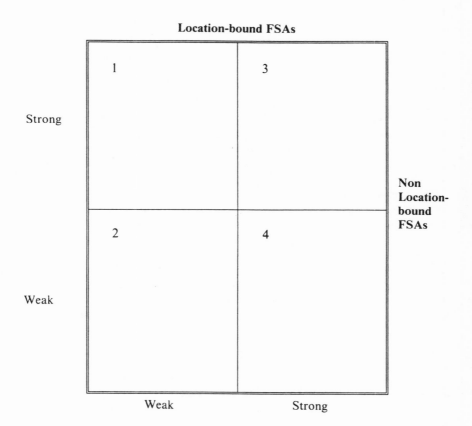

Figure 1. Firm Specific Sources of International
Competitive Advantage in Global Industries

and government regulation. In other words, location-bound FSAs need to be developed when know-how becomes of crucial importance in specific geographical areas, but cannot be used outside the area.

The core theoretical premise of this chapter, building on Rugman and Verbeke (1990a), is that the present global environment requires firms to develop dual sets of FSAs. These are the non location-bound FSAs, required to reap economies of integration, plus location-bound FSAs, required to successfully adapt to location specific requirements. In practice, given industry wide environmental opportunities for integration and requirements for national responsiveness, firms respond in different ways. The "administrative heritage" of any firm (see Bartlett 1986) may substantially influence its choice of emphasis on either location-bound or nonlocation-bound elements.

The analysis above is represented in Figure 1. Location-bound FSAs are shown on the horizontal axis and nonlocation-bound FSAs on the vertical, both with weak or strong dimensions. Quadrant 1 reflects the case whereby the possession of nonlocation-bound FSAs is of prime importance for the firm's international competitive position. Here the firm will be able to achieve a satisfactory economic performance only if economies of scale and/or economies of scope and/or benefits of exploiting national differences can be captured on an international scale.

The emphasis on scale can be found in Levitt (1983) and Leontiades (1984). The importance of scope economies is apparent in most of the economics driven internalization theory literature, recently synthesized by Dunning (1988). This can also be found in the strategic management literature, for example, Hamel and Prahalad (1985). Finally, the importance of exploiting national differences has been analyzed by Kogut (1985). The possibilities and internal contradictions associated with developing the three types of integration economies simultaneously have been described in Ghoshal (1987) and Bartlett and Ghoshal (1989), whose position we examine further after outlining the other three quadrants.

Quadrant 2 of Figure 1 describes a situation whereby neither location-bound nor nonlocation-bound firm specific advantages constitute sources of international competitive performance of a firm. This quadrant reflects the existence of firms with little potential for international competitive advantage against global competitors or uninational firms engaged in strategies of national responsiveness. Such firms face only three alternatives: (1) internal restructuring, through the development of new FSAs; (2) a form of alliance implying the external acquisition of FSAs; or (3) exit.

Quadrant 3 indicates the existence of firms which have developed both location-bound and nonlocation-bound FSAs as sources of international competitive advantage. These firms have a distinctive competitive edge compared with global rivals that have focused exclusively on the development of nonlocation-bound FSAs and have neglected to adopt specific functional activities (for example, marketing) to local circumstances. On the other hand, these firms rely on a mix of benefits related to scale, scope, and exploitation of national differences, all of which are nonlocation-bound.

Quadrant 4 contains firms where location-bound FSAs constitute a firm's core sources of competitive advantage against firms that rely more on nonlocation-bound FSAs. Typically these are uninational firms or MNEs which have focused on the development of location-bound FSAs in their dispersed operations.

To an extent, it could be argued that scale, scope and exploitation of national differences may sometimes merely constitute different perspectives on the same capability of an MNE. For example, concentrated large scale manufacturing of particular products may be useless without dispersed marketing operations sharing the same skills and brand names, and without location of the production capacity in particular countries to exploit international market imperfections. The creation of economies of scope may imply the replication of the parent company's operations in several countries. This requires a minimum size of the firm to allow replication and again means the establishment of different operations in optimal locations. Finally, the exploitation of national differences may again require a minimum scale to successfully disperse the different activities in the value chain over several countries. It also requires economies of scope, especially as regards the effective transfer of common managerial skills and internal "infrastructure" capabilities to allow the successful international coordination of the firm's activities.

It should be mentioned, however, that Ghoshal (1987) mistakenly describes the strategy of national responsiveness, which relies upon location-bound FSAs, as a subset of the integration strategy aimed at reaping benefits of exploiting international differences. In his view, national differences in output markets (for example, due to customer tastes and preferences, distribution systems, or government regulations) may lead a firm to "augment the exchange value of its output by tailoring its offerings to fit the unique requirements in each national market" (Ghoshal 1987, pp. 432-433).

Our critical point is that there is a major difference between a strategy of exploitation of national differences and a strategy of national responsiveness. In the former case, a firm takes advantage of international market imperfections, that is, its economic performance will increase as compared to a situation where no market imperfections would exist. This situation does not only occur on the input side (for example, differences in the comparative advantage of nations due to differences in the price and quality of factor inputs) but may also exist at the output side. For example, an export promotion program in a host country or the existence of a leading market for absorbing new products lead an MNE to benefit from exploiting these country-specific advantages (CSAs), which are in a way internalized into FSAs and which can thus be used across borders, that is, in a nonlocation-bound fashion.

In contrast, national responsiveness requires that a firm adapt itself to local circumstances. A firm needs to forego benefits of integration because of the requirement to tailor its activities to host country needs (see, for example, Doz 1986). This adaptation process and the concurrent development of location-bound FSAs may lead the firm to improve its competitive position ex post in relation to firms that have not developed such location-bound FSAs. Yet this remains quite a distinct strategy, as compared to the exploitation of national differences.

A strategy of national responsiveness does not permit the firm to gain benefits outside of the country in which the adaptation process takes place. No country-specific advantage is internalized into nonlocation-bound FSAs that can be used across borders. Only in the long run, and especially when related to organizational learning and innovation, can location-bound FSAs be turned into nonlocation-bound FSAs, for example, through the process of locally leveraged or globally linked innovations (Rugman and Verbeke 1990a). However, the occurrence of such an innovation process itself is conditional on the prior existence of nonlocation-bound FSAs. These require shared coordination mechanisms among the different units involved, with economies of scope. In short, national responsiveness needs a dispersed configuration of activities combined with low international coordination. It is the opposite of a strategy of integration.

III. ENVIRONMENTAL CHANGE AND FSA GENERATION

We now build upon Figure 1's classification of the relative international competitive position of any firm in a global industry as compared to rival firms. The next important question is how a change in environmental conditions, such as the implementation of the "EC 1992" program may affect a firm's need to develop new FSAs.

In our view, a thorough analysis of the seven forces driving industry competition will allow us to determine which new FSAs may be required to maintain or improve the firm's competitive position in Figure 1 and to prevent a firm from moving to the second quadrant of Figure 1 (see Rugman, Verbeke, and Campbell 1990). The seven forces include the five forces described in Porter (1980): industry competition, threat of potential entrants, buyer power, supplier power, and threat of substitutes, plus government regulation and external pressure groups. This analysis requires the creation of new location-bound FSAs, nonlocation-bound FSAs or both. In addition, irrespective of the location-bound or nonlocation-bound nature of the FSAs to be developed, we need to know the types of competitive advantage that they should generate in the market place.

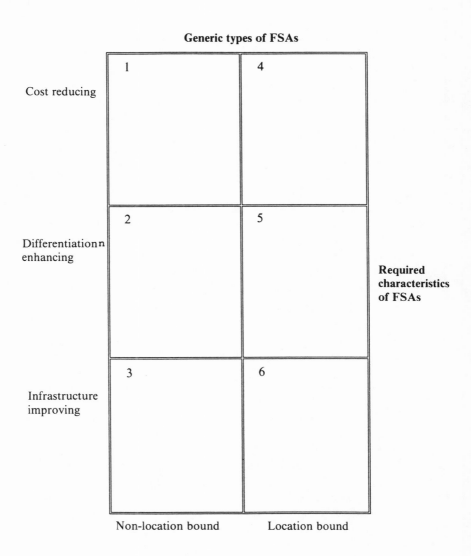

Figure 2.   Requirements for New FSA Generation

The type of competitive advantage refers to the cost reducing and/or differentiation enhancing effects of the FSAs. In certain cases, an FSA may be of crucial importance for the firm's competitiveness but it may not have a direct relation with the firm's ability to reduce costs or differentiate products; in this case the FSA in question (for example, the development of management skills) reflects an internal capability in "infrastructure."

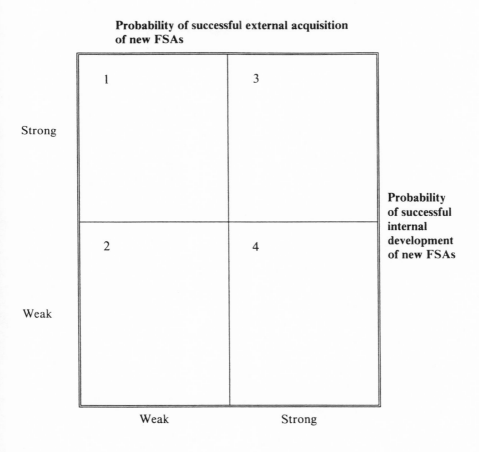

Figure 3.   Probability of Successful FSA Generation

The analysis above is shown in Figure 2 on the need to develop new FSAs Here, the horizontal axis distinguishes between the need to create new nonlocation-bound or location-bound FSAs. The vertical axis reflects the required cost reducing, differentiation enhancing or infrastructure improving character of the FSAs. As a result of an environmental change, a firm may be confronted with the need to generate any combination of the six categories of FSAs described in Figure 2. We shall discuss specific company examples in a later section.

At this stage we also need to specify the feasibility of internal creation or external acquisition of FSAs. Both of these options may have a high or a low probability of successful implementation, as represented in Figure 3. Here, a low probability of successful internal FSA generation may lead a firm to consider some type of strategic alliances. This would position the firm in quadrant 2 or 4 of Figure 3. In the case of quadrant 2, the environmental change will again lead to exit or to a sell out of the firm to another company. The quadrant 4 case implies that the necessary FSAs could not be developed by the firm but are actually available in its competitive environment. The FSA-generating process as predicted in Figure 3 only implies the potential to be internationally competitive in terms of financial performance and/or market share.

IV. ENVIRONMENTAL CHANGE AND FIRM LEVEL ENTRY BARRIERS

From a firm's perspective and given its responses in terms of new FSA-generation, the change in competitive position resulting from an environmental shock such as the "EC 1992" program can be described using the concept of entry barriers at the firm level (see Rugman and Verbeke 1990b). An entry barrier at the firm level can be defined as a constraint that prevents the firm's rivals from negatively affecting its relative competitive position (in terms of financial performance or market share) and taking over its product market domain.

There are two types of entry barriers: natural and government imposed ones. Natural entry barriers include scale economies, cost advantages independent of scale, product differentiation, supplier switching costs, distribution channels. These are the barriers normally resulting from a company's FSAs. Government imposed entry barriers include barriers to international trade and investment, government import substitution, and export promotion programs. These government imposed entry barriers, albeit often resulting from lobbying efforts of firms, are not necessarily directly related to a company's FSAs. In fact, lobbying efforts will often take place as a result of a firm's lack of capabilities to develop natural entry barriers. This may then hinder the international expansion of firms with strong FSAs and with an ability to erect natural entry barriers (see Rugman and Verbeke 1990a).

In this chapter, however, we recognize the possibility that a firm's FSAs (such as skills in business-government relations) may result in an increase of government imposed entry barriers against rivals. In other words, the FSA-generation process, especially as regards location-bound FSAs, may give a company a distinct, competitive edge. This occurs, for example, when it is able to differentiate itself against rivals through the development of know-how to be nationally responsive to government demands. We now need to know what the final impact will be of an environmental shock on the entry barriers erected by a firm against its rivals as represented in Figure 4.

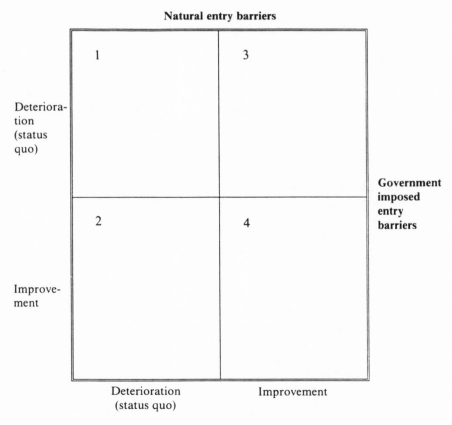

Figure 4.   Impact of Environmental Change on Firm Level
Entry Barriers Relative to Rivals

A position in quadrant 1 of Figure 4 means that the FSA-generation process has not lead to the desired outcomes. The firm faces a deterioration of both natural and government imposed entry barriers. Quadrant 1 is typical for floundering firms which could only be sustained because of government imposed entry barriers against foreign rivals. The elimination of the artificial entry barriers leads to a deterioration of the affected firm's competitive position. However, this quadrant may also reflect the situation of firms faced with an erosion of their natural strengths given a status quo as regards the impact of government regulation.

Quadrant 2 describes the situation whereby government imposed entry barriers improve whereas natural entry barriers decline. This is a case reflecting an increase in government protection to compensate for the decline of a company's natural sources of competitive performance.

Quadrant 3 represents the simultaneous occurrence of a decline in government imposed entry barriers benefiting the firm and an increase in natural entry barriers. Here the key question is whether the net impact on the firm's competitive position will be negative or positive.

Finally, quadrant 4 describes the case where a firm is able to improve its competitive position through an increase of both government imposed entry barriers and natural entry barriers.

With respect to the "EC 1992" program, the conventional view is that "insiders" will be able to improve their global competitive position through scale economies associated with the larger internal European market, in spite of a status quo or a reduction of government imposed entry barriers (see Cecchini 1988; Rugman and Verbeke 1990d). This would position "insiders" in quadrant 3 and "outsiders" in quadrant 1. Thus "outsiders," who used to service the EC market through exports, will now be faced with stronger competition in the EC. This is reflected in a reduction of the natural entry barriers they were able to erect against insiders.

In contrast, non-EC member states have frequently voiced their concern as to the creation of a "Fortress Europe" (see Rugman and Verbeke 1990b), which would position "insiders" in quadrant 4. Insiders would not only be able to improve their competitiveness through scale economies and increased control over distribution channels, but also through a rise in Pan-European sheltering mechanisms. However, in Rugman and Verbeke (1990b) it was argued that many "new insiders," switching their entry mode from exports to FDI, may be better positioned than "old insiders" to take advantage of the potential benefits created through the unified European market, thus appearing on the far right side of Figure 4.

V. IMPLICATIONS FOR STRATEGY FORMULATION

The integrated theoretical framework developed above can be used by managers of business firms in a practical manner to assist them in their strategy formulation when faced with an environmental shock such as "EC 1992." Practical application requires that the following seven questions be answered (at the corporate level, strategic business unit level or the level of a simple product line):

1. What are the core FSAs of our company? Are these FSAs location-bound or nonlocation-bound?
2. To what extent do our activities in a geographical area characterized by environmental change result from the use of nonlocation-bound or location-bound FSAs? (Classify the firm's operations in Figure 1.)
3. How will a particular environmental change affect the seven forces driving industry competition and thus our position in Figure 1?
4. Given our new position in Figure 1, following an environmental change, in the case of unchanged strategy, which position should we target as a desired position in Figure 1?
5. What are the FSA-generation requirements to obtain the desired position in Figure 1? Describe these requirements in terms of Figure 2.
6. What is the probability of successful FSA-generation through internal development or external acquisition, in terms of Figure 3?
7. Given a successful FSA generating process, how should these new FSAs affect our competitive position against rivals in terms of Figure 4?

VI. AN APPLICATION TO THE "EUROPEAN COMMUNITIES 1992" PROGRAMS

In order to demonstrate the relevance of the conceptual framework outlined in the previous sections, it will now be applied to the nine company cases contained in Quelch, Buzzell, and Salama (1990), all of which deal with firms affected by the "EC 1992" programs. At the time of writing of this chapter, Quelch, Buzzel, and Salama (1990) provided the only set of several in depth case studies on the strategic response of business firms to "EC 1992." These cases provide a diversity of firm, industry and national perspectives on the impact of the "EC 1992" programs, but all of them can be analyzed using our framework. In each case the location-bound versus nonlocation-bound FSA generating process constitutes the core of the firm level adaptation process to these significant environmental changes.

VII. CIGNA WORLWIDE AND THE INSURANCE MARKET

The core impact of the "EC 1992" programs on the insurance market is an increased requirement for nonlocation-bound FSAs in order to reap benefits of scale and scope. This occurs as a result of the EC's 1988 directive that allows firms to provide across-the-border nonlife insurance services, beginning January 1, 1990. Scale economies are expected to lead to a concentration of most of the industry's activity in the hands of 10-15 large companies. Benefits of scope, especially the sharing across-border know-how and external relations, in the form of multinational corporate clients, are also expected to increase.

In this context, it appears that the "EC 1992" programs will push Cigna from the third toward the fourth quadrant of Figure 1, unless internal strategic action is taken to correct this. Indeed, the main weakness of Cigna appears to be its limited ability to share know how across borders among the subsidiaries, thus resulting in an excessively large administrative structure and substantial cost inefficiencies. If Cigna wishes to remain in Quadrant 3, it will need to change its focus from the present emphasis on the location-bound FSAs of country organizations as the core source of competitive advantage, toward a more balanced approach. The latter would generate economies of scope through stronger coordination of the different country operations in a European head office.

In terms of Figure 2, new FSAs need to be developed in cells 1 and 3. The former refer primarily to the establishment of a European marketing information system and EC regional head office, which should help Cigna to reduce its cost disadvantages vis-à-vis large European competitors. The latter should be reflected in a more flexible reporting structure; one facilitating decision making to take advantage of business opportunities and improved product innovation skills to secure large corporate clients.

The feasibility of successful FSA generation is not entirely clear. In any case, the required FSAs, as described above, will likely have to be developed through internal efforts. The probability of successful internal FSA development appears to be the core of this case. If the management of Cigna assumes this probability to be low, thus positioning it in quadrant 2 of Figure 3, it should change its product market scope from serving large multinational enterprises toward medium-sized firms building upon the location-bound FSAs, that is, the strengths in national responsiveness, of the country organizations. It is clear, however, that the cost reducing nonlocation-bound FSA in cell 1 of Figure 2 will need to be developed in any case so as to reap the economies of scope required to compete in the large internal market. If not, Cigna's European operations will be positioned in quadrant 1 of Figure 4, with a further deterioration of the firm's natural entry barriers. Government imposed entry barriers are of little direct relevance to this company.

The two core natural entry barriers which should be strengthened or maintained are the cost advantage independent of scale (at this moment, this barrier is in fact lacking, because Cigna has a distinct disadvantage in terms of economies of scope), and the control over distribution channels, that is, relationships with brokers who currently account for 95 percent of the premiums of Cigna Europe and take price competitive packages provided by the insurance carrier for granted.

VIII. NOKIA-MOBIRA OY AND THE MOBILE TELEPHONE MARKET

In 1987, the EC Commission issued a "Green Paper," aimed as a first step toward the opening of public procurement of cellular equipment by the national publicly owned telecommunications monopolies for nonlocal manufacturers. In addition, EC wide mutual recognition of approval criteria for terminal equipment was planned for December 1990. Both of these elements mean shifting from a heavily fragmented European market with six incompatible mobile telephone systems, toward a more integrated market where firm level opportunities will arise for economies of scale and scope.

Nokia-Mobira Oy, a Finnish company, is the world's largest manufacturer of mobile phones in the world (14% market share) in 1988. In terms of Figure 1 it is located in quadrant 4. Its strong location-bound FSAs result from three elements. First, the rapid growth of the Scandinavian market, a location specific advantage internalized into FSAs in the production and marketing of mobile telephones in Scandinavia. Second, the establishment of nationally responsive production plants in several EC countries. Third, the external acquisition of location-bound FSAs in the U.S. market through the use of a host country corporation's distribution network in the United States.

However, this lack of nonlocation-bound FSAs will constitute a problem in the more integrated European market where a dominant market position will only be possible through scale and scope economies. In terms of Figure 2, new nonlocation-bound FSAs need to be developed and related to the triad of cost reduction, differentiation and infrastructure, that is, cells 1, 2, and 3. Cost reductions should come especially from economies of scope through improved coordination and learning among the different subunits of Nokia-Mobira. Differentiation advantages, the present main strength of the firm, should be renewed by extensive R&D investment. Finally, FSAs in infrastructure require an improvement of management capabilities at the Pan-European level.

In terms of Figure 3, it appears that the differentiation based nonlocation-bound FSAs can only be created through external acquisition in the form of joint ventures or strategic alliances. Indeed, as some of Nokia-Mobira's main competitors especially Mitsubshi, NEC, Panasonic and Philips are able to invest three times more than Nokia-Mobira in communication technology, it is clear that this firm will only remain a dominant player in the industry through sharing the costs and risks associated with new product development. The probability of the successful creation of these nonlocation-bound FSAs (in quadrant 3) is high, however, due to Nokia-Mobira's experience with setting up joint ventures and its reputation as a market leader in this industry.

External acquisition of nonlocation-bound FSAs with cost reducing potential will also be required, as Nokia-Mobira does not have a truly established brand name outside Scandinavia, and thus lacks a sustainable differentiation advantage.

The mere size of the resources required to generate the necessary nonlocation-bound FSAs may require Nokia-Mobira to reduce its segment scope. It is doubtful whether Nokia-Mobira will be able to acquire the non-location-bound FSAs described above without a dissipation of its core know-how in favour of rival firms aiming at increasing their market share. If such dissipation occurred, this would lead to a clear positioning of Nokia-Mobira on the left-hand side of Figure 4, reflecting a deterioration of its entry barriers against rivals.

In the case of a global segmentation strategy, it may be easier to increase the different natural entry barriers against competitors as compared to a situation whereby Nokia-Mobira would continue to compete on a full line of products in spite of limited internal resources to finance this strategy.

IX.   BIOKIT S.A. AND THE
BIOTECHNOLOGY MARKET

The "EC 1992" program is expected to have little direct influence on the biotechnology market. However, it has led to a business climate characterized by high perceived benefits of scale in this industry. Biokit, a Spanish biotechnology firm with only limited sales ($6.7 million in 1987), is characterized by strong nonlocation-bound FSAs in the form of proprietary know-how embodied in self-contained diagnostic kits, sold in the triad markets of the EC, the United States, and Japan. This positions the firm in quadrant 1 of Figure 1. However, location bound FSAs in the area of marketing, are largely lacking in this firm. In addition, no nonlocation-bound FSAs, such as global brand names, have been developed since the firm has focused on selling standardized (generic) products (i.e., only the technological basis of the product and the main part of its value added with minimal brand identification) to importers and to foreign distributors/manufacturers who would then distribute the products to end users under their own brand names. The new business environment and the trend toward large scale firms (price competition) require Biokit to develop both location-bound and nonlocation-bound FSAs in marketing, thus positioning its FSA-requirements in cells 2 and 5 of Figure 2. It appears indeed that Biokit's distributors carry too many products and also they do not push Biokit's products or provide sufficient technical information to end users. This limits the firm's growth.

A direct distribution of Biokit's own brand name is contemplated in five large markets: France, West Germany, Italy, Japan, and the United States. It appears that the necessary FSAs will need to be generated partly through internal development and partly through external acquisition in the form of ventures with foreign partners when setting up distribution channels abroad.

Biokit's leadership in product innovation implies a high probability of successful FSA-creation, thus positioning it in quadrant 3 of Figure 3. This strengthening of Biokit's marketing skills will position it in quadrant 4 of Figure 4, especially as its expansion is being associated with EC support through the EUREKA program and excellent relations with home country public agencies.

X. CHLORIDE LIGHTING AND THE EMERGENCY LIGHTING MARKET

The emergency lighting industry has traditionally been characterized by a highly fragmented market due to strong differences in government regulation across countries and heavy government shelter for local manufacturers in several national markets. The effects of the "EC 1992" programs on the emergency lighting sector will be twofold. First, the adoption of a Eurostandard in terms of product characteristics and a harmonized set of practices for the required use of emergency lighting. This means a company will only need its products to obtain the approval of the Eurostandard in one country in order to have market access to the whole EC. Second, government shelter should largely disappear due to the opening of public procurement in the EC.

Chloride Lighting is a strategic business unit of the U.K.-based Chloride Group. It has adopted a strategy emphasizing the U.K. market in Europe. In the United Kingdom, it is the second largest producer, but it is in seventh place in Europe. The strong U.K. position is partly based on government purchases, constituting 30 percent of Chloride Lighting sales in that country.

The company's FSAs are largely location-bound, building upon the well-known brand names Bardic and Security Lighting. International expansion to the European continent has been limited, as a result of Chloride Lighting's lack of location-bound FSAs abroad, especially in terms of brand names (e.g., in Germany). This problem has been exacerbated by sheltering strategies of foreign competitors, especially the French firm Saft, which, through influencing the relevant government agency in France succeeded in continuously changing the national technical standard, thus making it prohibitively expensive for Chloride to compete in France.

Hence, the U.K. division of Chloride Lighting is placed in quadrant 4 of Figure 1. Outside the United Kingdom, with the exception of a few small markets such as Belgium, its European position is close to the second quadrant with both weak location-bound and nonlocation-bound FSAs. Nonlocation-bound FSAs are presently not important in this industry, especially as no real scale economies exist in production.

In the post-"EC 1992" period, all of Chloride Lighting may be forced into the second quadrant of Figure 1, as large foreign competitors such as Saft attempt to develop brand name recognition in the U.K. market. In other words, a single European standard will lead to few benefits of scale, scope of exploitation of national differences, but it will still increase the globalization of the industry as the former single country manufacturers will seek growth through international expansion.

Hence, the core challenge for Chloride Lighting is to develop FSAs in quadrant 5 of Figure 2; location-bound FSAs of the differentiation type. This is a paradoxical situation. The creation of a Eurostandard is not creating substantial integration economies in this industry; instead it is creating a business climate in which predominantly single nation manufacturers will want to grow internationally, thus requiring each of them to develop location-bound FSAs in the countries to be penetrated. Different alternative strategies are contemplated such as the establishment of regional sales offices (or assembly/warehousing operations) in different EC countries, staffed by local nationals as well as mergers, a joint venture or acquisition. If, in this case Chloride does not engage in any of these strategies, it will be badly positioned in quadrant 1 of Figure 4, faced with both an elimination of government imposed entry barriers and a relative deterioration of its brand name image in the United Kingdom.

XI.   CANADIAN IMPERIAL BANK OF COMMERCE (C.I.B.C.) AND THE BANKING SERVICE MARKET

For the banking sector, the "EC 1992" programs represent a right of establishment and development of activities in all EC countries based on the possession of a license in just one EC country, that is, mutual recognition will prevail. This important change is supposed to increase the potential of banks to obtain economies of scope through the sharing of knowledge and external relations across national boundaries.

C.I.B.C. is Canada's second largest bank. In the pre-"EC 1992" period, C.I.B.C.'s European status was characterized primarily by nonlocation-bound FSAs in corporate and investment banking, that is, by quadrant 1 of Figure 1. However, the advent of "EC 1992" will weaken this position, partly because large EC banks will build upon their retail networks to provide both service in terms of market intelligence and knowledge of developing transactions within the EC to their customers. Hence, the real danger for non-EC banks such as C.I.B.C. lies in shifting to the second quadrant of Figure 1.

C.I.B.C. has a number of non location-bound FSAs. These include marketing expertise in targeted corporate lending areas and its dominant position in the Euro-Canadian based market in investment banking (as a result of its acquisition of Wood Gundy's nine investment branches). Which niches should C.I.B.C. invest in to generate location-bound FSAs in the EC market that would potentially strengthen its non location-bound FSAs, thus moving the bank closer to the third than the second quadrant?

At the moment this remains an open question, but it is clear that new location-bound FSAs will need to be developed, especially in the area of "infrastructure" (cell 6 of Figure 2). In addition, a careful analysis is clearly required of C.I.B.C.'s non location-bound FSAs in securing existing multinational corporate clients in the EC as well as new medium sized European customers expanding their activities in Europe. In terms of Figure 3, on the basis of the data provided in the case, neither internal development nor external acquisition is likely to occur. This means that C.I.B.C. could end up in quadrant 1 of Figure 4, with a neutral effect of government regulation but a clear deterioration of natural entry barriers, both in the area of cost and differentiation, unless FSAs can be successfully developed in selected niches.

XII.   NISSAN MOTOR COMPANY LTD AND THE AUTOMOBILE MARKET

The effects of the "EC 1992" program on the automobile industry can be classified under the headings "general" and "country" specific effects. The former enhance efficiency as a result of the harmonization of technical standards, thus leading to enhanced scale and scope economies. The latter include the removal of quota restrictions on Japanese imports, especially in France, Spain, and Italy. In France, Japanese imports were limited to 3 percent of the market, in Italy to 3,300 units, of which 750 were off-road vehicles, and in Spain to 3,200 units (the situation in 1988, but to be increased to 57,000 in 1990).

In terms of marketing, it is evident that the development of strong location-bound FSAs is crucial for successful market penetration in these sheltered countries. In each of these three countries, Nissan is in the second quadrant of Figure 1. However, the removal of quotas will stimulate the company to develop location-bound FSAs in marketing, leading to a desired position in quadrant 4 of Figure 1. This will require FSAs to be created in cell 5 of Figure 2. The firm's excellent management should ensure internal development, thus leaving the firm in quadrant 1 of Figure 3. The problem is that only limited resources are available to develop strong distribution channels in these three previously sheltered markets.

In practice, a choice needs to be made between developing FSAs in promoting a small model, the Micra, or a large car, the Bluebird. It would appear that the development of location-bound FSAs for the Micra will probably be easier, based upon the experiences of Nissan in Northern Europe. The risks faced by buyers when purchasing a car of a previously unknown brand are more limited in the case of a small car. In addition, the small car segment is much larger in the three nations. There is more potential for rapid FSA development, in terms of building up a brand name and a distribution network.

In addition, it is possible that the development of location-bound FSAs in the upper-medium segment (where the Bluebird would compete) will not be sustainable, but would indirectly give easier access to other Japanese manufacturers such as Toyota when penetrating these markets. Finally, the higher profit margin per unit of the Bluebird is in itself irrelevant for the development of FSAs in marketing.

A potential negative result associated with emphasising sales of the Micra could be the subsequent increased difficulties in developing nonlocation-bound marketing FSAs for Nissan as a manufacturer of high quality cars. In any case, focus on the Micra will undoubtedly strengthen Nissan's entry barriers of differentiation and control over distribution channels. This will position the firm in quadrant 3 of Figure 4 (since this firm does not benefit from government imposed entry barriers).

XIII. DAVID DEL CURTO S.A. AND THE FRESH FRUIT MARKET

The "EC 1992" program will have little direct effect on the fresh fruit market, but it is accompanied by a climate of protectionism against suppliers of fruit from the Southern Hemisphere. There are government imposed entry barriers in the form of quotas and tariffs. In addition, the bargaining power of buyers may substantially increase as a result of concentration in food retailing.

David Del Curto S.A., the largest Chilean fruit exporter has traditionally been located in quadrant 1 of Figure 1. Its nonlocation-bound FSAs consist primarily of technical and market knowledge on fruit production and engineering. Its main weakness as compared to, for example, South African exporters, who promote their products under the "Cape" and "Outspan" brands, is its lack of brand name recognition. Related to this problem is the absence of a long term formal/strategic partnership with distributors or retailers. As a result, the firm does not even know exactly where its fruit will be consumed. Hence, if bargaining power at the buyer side increases, this may result in increased pressure on price, especially where the firm is dependent on pricing through "free consignment," whereby distributors sell the company's fruit to the highest bidder, in return for a commission. The development of nonlocation-bound FSAs in differentiation, that is, location in cell 2 of Figure 2 is clearly required.

Unfortunately, the probability of successful generation of FSAs seems rather weak. Management mistakenly views this issue as one of creating location-bound FSAs in the E.C. market, which would lead to excessive fixed costs. In addition, a joint marketing initiative with other Chilean exporters, in the form of marketing boards is to be rejected because they would limit the firm's flexibility.

David Del Curto S.A. is located in quadrant 2 of Figure 3. An unchanged strategy will position it in quadrant 1 of Figure 4, with a deterioration of natural entry barriers, especially in terms of differentiation and control over distribution channels. David Del Curto's problem is typical for a commodity producer faced with increasingly powerful buyers who will attempt to reduce prices, unless a differentiation advantage associated with Chilean fruit is observed. This problem is especially acute as other Southern Hemisphere producers are moving toward the development of such FSAs.

XIV. FEDERATION NATIONALE d'ACHAT DES CADRES AND THE RETAILING OF CULTURAL AND LEISURE PRODUCTS

In the cultural sector any immediate impact of the "EC 1992" program is lacking yet indirectly it will decrease cross border distribution costs by 5 percent and lead to opportunities for economies of scale and scope across national boundaries. Diversified retail chains will attempt to become Pan European, building upon their existing scale advantages in financial resources. Specialized chains will attempt to gain economies of scope by reproducing their strength in home market niches abroad.

Federation Nationale d'Achat des Cadres (FNAC) is a large French retail chain competing primarily in specific niches; books, records, photographic equipment and service and consumer electronics. It is largely situated in quadrant 4 of Figure 1, with substantial location-bound FSAs in France. FNAC attempts to develop both cost and differentiation based advantages, the latter being the more important ones. Differentiation is exemplified by its distinctive, pleasant sales ambience,the provision of special services such as the sale of concert tickets, insurance against camera theft, and so forth, and its attempts to be perceived as a firm pursuing consumer interests.

It is questionable that FNAC's FSAs can be transferred abroad. Weak financial results of international diversification in Belgium demonstrate that economies of scope are not gained automatically, partly because of only limited internal transfer of marketing and procurement know-how to Belgium. In addition, international expansion does not appear to be associated with scale economies, especially where no joint purchases are possible by the Belgium and French stores, for example, because of different dominating brands in the various home country markets.

In view of the scale and scope economies sought by foreign retail chains through international expansion, FNAC needs to reconsider both the comparative strengths of its location-bound FSAs in France and the possibility to turn them into nonlocation-bound FSAs in order to reap economies of scope across borders.

In this context, new nonlocation-bound FSAs in differentiation and infrastructure in cells 2 and 3 of Figure 2 seems crucial. To date, internal FSA generation has been selected (left-hand side of Figure 3) but the probability of success, resulting in terms of an impact on natural entry barriers, seems highly uncertain. In fact, even the long term sustainability of FNAC's location-bound FSAs in France is unclear, as all its major competitors are either much more diversified (such as the hypermarkets) or less diversified (such as several speciality chains).

XV. VOLVO TRUCKS EUROPE AND THE TRUCK MARKET

The main impact of the "EC 1992" program on the truck market will likely be the indirect result of liberalizing road haulage in the EC. This will require the (partial) elimination of quota restrictions on cabotage, that is, opportunities for a trucking firm registered in one of the twelve EC nations to provide transportation services between any two points in other EC nations. As a result, the road haulage industry will be characterized by increased concentration to reap benefits of scale, scope and exploiting national differences. It will not be characterized by national responsiveness. As large buyers of trucks, these pan European trucking companies will be less inclined to purchase trucks from nationally dominating firms (such as DAF in the United Kingdom and the Netherlands; Daimler-Benz in West Germany; Iveco in Italy, Volvo in Scandinavia, RVI in France, Enasa in Spain and so forth) and they will require standardized Pan European service levels from truck manufacturers.

Within the framework of a fragmented pre-"EC 1992" market, Volvo Truck Corporation, a wholly owned subsidiary of the Swedish industrial giant AB Volvo, is strongly positioned in quadrant 3 of Figure 1, with strong location-bound and nonlocation-bound FSAs. In the area of marketing this is reflected in marketing and service activities being allocated to three layers in the firm; the European level, the level of importers in each country and the level of local dealers. For example, the European level provides the "thinking" behind marketing policies (such as a consistent Pan European approach to the use of logos, symbols, and so forth). The national level determines the actual content of the message. The dealer level is largely autonomous, for consumer personal selling.

It appears that the "EC 1992" program, and its impact on the buyers of trucks, will require Volvo to shift its emphasis toward developing new nonlocation-bound FSAs. It needs to reap economies of scope, resulting from the sharing of customers across borders. In other words, a consolidation of Volvo's position in quadrant 3 of Figure 1 requires it to shift power and autonomy from the country importer and dealer level toward the European level. This also seems to be of major importance in other functional areas such as market forecasting and after sales service. In terms of market forecasting, it appears that the lack of standardization of data gathering and processing by the different national organizations lead to errors in the estimation of total sales. In terms of service, it is clear that the inconsistencies in service systems across the EC (e.g., nonharmonization of service agreements outside the country of purchasing, differences in price for similar services, and so forth) will constitute a weakness of Volvo in the post "EC 1992" era, unless it can develop new nonlocation-bound FSAs in differentiation. An FSA in cell 2 of Figure 2 will allow Volvo to be perceived as "unique" by Pan European customers in the area of service.

Volvo has attempted to develop these FSAs internally. It can be positioned in quadrant 1 of Figure 3. Corporate management seems to be well aware of the problems associated with taking power away from the national and dealer level so as to achieve the required scope economies at the European level. This analysis obviously does not take into account required strategic change on the production side, where merger or acquisition activity may be required. Efforts in this direction included the organization of the Volvo Euro Truck Dealer project aimed at generating Euro Dealer Standards, especially in the area of service (for both the EC, Switzerland, and Austria) and a "Eurofleet" task force to allow importers to better satisfy the needs of Pan European truck fleets. As a result of this new FSA-creation, Volvo should be able to consolidate its entry barriers in the EC market especially differentiation ones, thus positioning it in quadrant 3 of Figure 4.

XVI.   CONCLUSIONS: STRATEGIC CHANGE IS BASED ON FSAs

The application of the analytical framework developed in the first part of this paper to the nine company cases has demonstrated its relevance for the strategic management problems of firms faced with the "EC 1992" program. In more general terms, seven interesting conclusions result from this application.

First, in each case, the firm under analysis is clearly confronted with globalization of competition, that is, increased international activities of rival companies.

Second, in many cases, the indirect effects of the "EC 1992" program, resulting from discretionary strategic activities of firms, are much more important than the direct effects of—and quasi-automatic firm level reactions to—the elimination of physical controls, the harmonization of technical standards or the approximation of fiscal regimes.

Third, the main benefits of integration to be reaped after the creation of the large European internal market appear to be related more often to scope economies than to scale economies.

Fourth, in spite of an increased emphasis on nonlocation-bound FSAs and integration economies, the development of new location-bound FSAs required to generate advantages of national responsiveness often remains crucially important.

Fifth, major changes in corporate strategies and the related development of FSAs are sometimes required because of an increase of bargaining power in downstream (buyer side) industries, reflecting the importance of control over distribution channels as a major natural entry barrier.

Sixth, in none of the cases do firms actually attempt to generate strong shelter based entry barriers, through government protectionism. This may seem self-evident, since the "EC 1992" program is primarily a trade liberalization effort, reducing the effects of shelter. Nevertheless, it may also reflect a bias in the selection of cases, as firm-driven protectionism in the unified EC market, especially vis-à-vis outsiders will certainly not disappear. In other words, if EC companies in the automobile industry or agriculture had been studied, then the importance of creating new government imposed entry barriers would have been much more relevant.

Finally, it is clear that the "EC 1992" program, in spite of having highly different effects on each industry, places increased importance on the need to reconsider company strategies.

REFERENCES

Bartlett, C.A. 1986. "Building and Managing the Transnational: The New Organizational Challenge." In *Competition in Global Industries,* edited by Michael E. Porter. Boston, MA: Harvard Business School Press.

Bartlett, C.A. and S. Ghoshal. 1989. *Managing Across Borders: The Transnational Solution.* Boston, MA: Harvard Business School Press.

Cecchini, P. 1988. *The European Challenge 1992: The Benefits of a Single Market.* Aldershot: Wildwood House Limited.

Doz, Y. 1986. *Multinational Strategic Management.* London: Pergamon Press.

Dunning, J.H. 1988. *Explaining International Production.* London: Unwin-Hyman.

Ghoshal, S. 1987. "Global Strategy: An Organizing Framework." *Strategic Management Journal* 8:425-440.

Hamel, G. and C.K. Prahalad. 1985. "Do You Really Have a Global Strategy?" *Harvard Business Review* (July-August):139-148.

Hout, T., M. E. Porter, and E. Rudden. 1982. "How Global Companies Win Out." *Harvard Business Review* (September-October):98-108.

Kogut, B., "Designing Global Strategies: Corporative and Competitive Value Added Chains." *Sloan Management Review* 26(4):15-28.

Leontiades, J. 1984. "Market Share and Corporate Strategy in International Industries." *Journal of Business Strategy* 5(1):30-37.

Levitt, T. 1983. "The Globalization of Markets." *Harvard Business Review* (May-June):92-102.

Porter, M.E. 1980. *Competitive Strategy.* New York: Basic Books.

Porter, M.E., Ed. 1986. *Competition in Global Industries.* Boston, MA: Harvard Business School Press.

Quelch, J.A., R.D. Buzzell, and E.R. Salama. 1990. *The Marketing Challenge of 1992.* New York: Addison-Wesley.

Rugman, A.M. 1981. *Inside the Multinationals: The Economics of Internal Markets.* New York: Columbia University Press.

Rugman, A.M. and A. Verbeke. 1990a. *Global Corporate Strategy and Trade Policy.* London/ New York: Routledge.

_____. 1990b. "Corporate Strategy After the Free Trade Agreement and Europe 1992." Working Paper No. 27, Ontario Centre for International Business, Research Programme, Toronto.

_____. 1990c. "Is the Transnational Solution a New Theory of Multinational Strategic Management?" Working Paper No. 32, Ontario Centre for International Business, Research Programme, Toronto.

_____. 1990d. "Competitive Strategies for North American Firms After 1992." In *Multinationals and Europe 1992,* edited by B. Burgenmeier and J.L. Mucchielli. New York/ London: Routledge.

Rugman, A.M., A. Verbeke, and A. Campbell. 1990. "Strategic Change in the European Flexible Packaging Industry." *European Management Journal* (September).

MULTIMARKET COMPETITION
AND EUROPEAN INTEGRATION

Arjen van Witteloostuijn and Marc van Wegberg

I. INTRODUCTION

The second half of the eighties witnessed a growing interest in European integration. The 1985 White Paper by the European Commission marked a turning point. The White Paper proposals for shaping the integration of the European Community (EC) speeded up political decision making. The White Paper presents policy measures and a time schedule for the completion of the European *economic* integration in 1992. The key objective is to abolish barriers to economic movement *within* the EC, whereas the key question is what impact this integration will have on European competition and growth. A still growing literature is directed to the latter question. This chapter complements this literature by focusing on the opportunities and threats which the European integration may impose on international business.

Research in Global Strategic Management, Volume 2, pages 29-55.
Copyright © 1991 by JAI Press Inc.
ISBN: 1-55938-277-5

The point of departure in this chapter is multimarket competition. Multimarket competition identifies rivalry among firms in a set of related (product or geographic) markets. This integrative framework builds upon contributions of both strategic management and industrial organization. The fact that firms meet (actually or potentially) in many markets, has specific implications for competition. The framework is applied to the ongoing and forthcoming European integration so as to formulate five propositions on competition, strategic opportunities and threats for international business in future Europe.

First the literature on the facts and expectations of European integration is briefly summarized. Next the framework of multimarket competition is introduced. Five key features of multimarket competition are identified. Subsequently the framework is applied to European integration. This generates five propositions on competition and strategy in future Europe. An appraisal concludes the chapter. For the sake of convenience, an incumbent firm is denoted with 'he,' whereas a potential entrant is referred to with 'she.'

II.   EUROPEAN INTEGRATION

A.   Measures and Progress

The completion of the European internal market is associated with the elimination or reduction of trade barriers between member states of the EC. The White Paper identifies three categories of barriers: physical, technical, and fiscal barriers.[1] The demolition of physical barriers involves, broadly speaking, the abolition of border controls for both goods traffic and passenger traffic. The elimination of technical barriers is said to imply, by and large, the harmonization of product standards, liberalization of public procurements, and the free movement of labor, services, and capital. The reduction of fiscal barriers is concerned with the (partial) harmonization of indirect tax bases and rates.

An impression of the nature and progress of the European integration can be obtained by undertaking a historical analysis of two important documents in the integration process: the White Paper and the Fourth Progress Report. Table 1 presents the distribution of measures over the White Paper categories. Moreover, the state of affairs in the Fourth Progress Report (1989) on the completion of the internal market is listed.[2]

An evaluation of the progress of decision making on the European integration gives mixed results. Table 2 summarizes progress on the basis of the Fourth Progress Report (1989) on internal market policy.[3]

Table 1. Categories and Numbers of (Intended) Integration Measures

		Number of Measures	
Category of Measures		WP[a]	PR[b]
A.	Removal of physical barriers	91	98
I.	Control of goods	80	90
	1. Various controls	9	10
	2. Veterinary and phytosanitary controls	71	80
II.	Control of individuals	11	8
B.	Removal of technical barriers	181	156
I.	Free movement of goods	90	79
	1. Generic harmonization	7	11
	2. Motor vehicles	6	10
	3. Tractors and agricultural machines	2	3
	4. Food law	6	25
	5. Pharmaceuticals	2	10
	6. Chemical products	1	8
	7. Construction (products)	0	2
	8. Other sectors	16	10
II.	Public procurement	8	6
III.	Free movement of labor	18	14
IV.	Free movement of services	35	43
	1. Financial services	21	24
	a. Banks	8	9
	b. Insurance	9	9
	c. Securities	4	6
	2. Transport	8	13
	3. New technologies and services	5	6
V.	Free movement of capital	3	3
VI.	Industrial cooperation	23	21
	1. Company Law	8	8
	2. Intellectual Property	11	8
	3. Taxes	4	5
VII.	Community law	4	0
	1. Transparency	3	0
	2. Competition Policy	1	0
C.	Removal of fiscal barriers	27	25
I.	VAT	17	13
II.	Excise Duties	10	12
	Total	298	289

Notes: [a]WP = White Paper.

[b]PR = Fourth Progress Report.

Source: Commission of the European Communities (1985, 1989).

ARJEN VAN WITTELOOSTUIJN and MARC VAN WEGBERG

Table 2.   Progress of the European Integration Referring to the
White Paper Classification of Measures

		Progress of Policy		
Category of Measures		A^a	P^b	I^c
A. Removal of physical barriers		37	30	31
I. Control of goods		34	26	30
1. Various controls		4	4	2
2. Veterinary and phytosanitary controls		30	22	28
II. Control of individuals		3	4	1
B. Removal of technical barriers		84	67	15
I. Free movement of goods		51	24	4
1. Generic harmonization		4	6	1
2. Motor vehicles		6	4	0
3. Tractors and agricultural machines		3	0	0
4. Food law		12	1	3
5. Pharmaceuticals		7	3	0
6. Chemical products		7	10	0
7. Construction (products)		2	0	0
8. Other sectors		10	0	0
II. Public procurement		1	4	1
III. Free movement of labor		7	2	5
IV. Free movement of services		19	20	4
1. Financial services		12	12	0
a. Banks		5	4	0
b. Insurance		3	6	0
c. Securities		4	2	0
2. Transport		4	6	3
3. New technologies and services		3	2	1
V. Free movement of capital		3	0	0
VI. Industrial cooperation		3	17	1
VII. Community law		0	0	0
C. Removal of fiscal barriers		3	18	4
I. VAT		2	9	2
II. Excise Duties		1	9	2
Total		124	115	50

Notes: ^{a}A = Proposals which have been adopted by the Commission and the Council up to May 31, 1989.
   ^{b}P = Proposals currently awaiting Council adoption (of which some are already partially adopted).
   ^{c}I = Proposals still to be presented by the Commission to the Council (of which some are already
       partly prepared or adopted).
Source: Commission of the European Communities (1989).

The overall impression is that the European integration process is irreversible
(Emerson 1989). In particular, the abolition of technical barriers proceeds
rather successfully, whereas the reduction of both physical and fiscal barriers
suffers from considerable delays. The Commission reports that "[t]he four areas
which are furthest behind schedule are (1) Citizens' Europe, (2) taxation, (3)

plant and animal health controls and (4) industrial property rights" (Fourth Progress Report 1989, p. 6). Of course, political obstacles (will) impede European integration (Peck 1989). However, the key point is that

> [t]he European program for 1992 is best thought of as a process, with the 1992 deadline being used as a forcing device, a frequent practice in Community affairs. A best guess is that Europe will not be without internal borders in the early 1993, mainly because of the intransigence of the tax problem, but that intra-European trade will be substantially freer (Cooper 1989, p. 339).

B. Distribution and Forecasts

The set of policy proposals does not influence industries symmetrically. In particular, technical barriers may have an *industry-specific* impact. Generic measures (for example, harmonization of VAT rates) affect industries alike, whereas specific directives focus on a particular industry (for example, uniform standards for chemical products). Table 3 provides an allocation of specific measures over industries on the basis of close reading of the White Paper and the Fourth Progress Report.[4]

Table 3. Distribution of Measures over Industries

	Number of Measures	
Industry	*WP*[a]	*PR*[b]
Agriculture, forestry, and fishery	67	72
Fuel and power products	3	2
Manufactured products		
Chemical products	35	36
Metal and machinery products	11	17
Transport equipment	7	11
Food, beverages, and tobacco	63	65
Textile and clothing	4	0
Building and construction	12	4
Market services		
Transport	20	16
Communication	5	6
Credit and insurance	26	31

Notes: [a]WP = White Paper.
[b]PR = Fourth Progress Report.

Table 4.   Progress of Industry-Specific Measures

Industry	Progress of Policy		
	A^a	P^b	I^c
Agriculture, forestry, and fishery	24	22	26
Fuel and power products	0	0	2
Manufactured products			
Chemical products	25	7	4
Metal and machinery products	10	3	4
Transport equipment	3	7	1
Food, beverages, and tobacco	24	22	19
Textile and clothing	0	0	0
Building and construction	3	1	0
Market services			
Transport	8	5	3
Communication	3	2	1
Credit and insurance	14	14	3

Notes: [a]A = Proposals which have been adopted by the Commission and the Council up to May 31, 1989.
[b]P = Proposals currently awaiting Council adoption (of which some are already partially adopted).
[c]I = Proposals still to be presented by the Commission to the Council (of which some are already partly prepared or adopted).

Table 3 makes clear that four industries are affected by the largest number of (intended) industry-specific integration directives (> 20 in both distributions): (1) agriculture, forestry and fishery (2) chemical products, (3) food, beverages and tobacco, and (4) credit and insurance.

Progress of the European integration also differs from industry to industry. Table 4 distributes progress over industries.

Particularly, the liberalization of the following five industries is, by and large, on schedule (i.e., $A \geq P + I$): (1) chemical products, (2) metal and machinery products, (3) building and construction, (4) transport services, and (5) communication. The completion of three markets suffers from considerable delays (i.e., $2A < P + I$): (1) agriculture, forestry and fishery, (2) fuel, and (3) transport equipment.

The number of measures aiming at an industry is not informative about the *direction* of the (expected) change: will growth and competition in the industries involved be stimulated or impeded as a result of the EC's 1992 program? Past research has pointed out that the overall effect of integration (particularly in the context of the EC and EFTA) on economic growth is positive (Mayes 1978; Baldwin 1984). The current pillar of studies considering the impact of the EC's 1992 program on European growth is Cecchini (1988), which indicates a 200 billion Ecu benefit in the years to come. However, this does not answer the question of the distribution of costs and benefits over industries and countries.

Table 5.   Results of the Sector Studies Reported in Cecchini (1988)

	Estimates*	
	Low	*High*
Agriculture	0.0	0.7
Fuel and power products	4.5	7.3
Manufactured products		
Chemical products	6.6	11.8
Nonelectrical machinery	5.4	11.3
Office machinery	1.8	6.6
Telecommunication products	3.0	4.8
Automobiles	5.1	14.1
Food	3.6	5.3
Textile and clothing	3.3	5.6
Building and construction	4.3	25.5
Market services		
Maritime and air transport services	1.4	6.9
Telecommunication services	1.7	13.6
Credit and insurance services	4.6	10.5
Other business services	9.2	9.2
Macroeconomic indicators		
Prices of products		−4.5
Level of employment		4.0
Production volume		7.0

Note: *Billions of Ecu per year.
Sources: Cecchini (1988) and Pelkmans (1988).

Sector studies have been used to estimate the effects of European integration on particular industries. Table 5 summarizes the predictions reported in the studies collected in Cecchini (1988).[5] The results are appealing.[6] Large benefits (that is, a high estimate in excess of 10 billion Ecu per year) are expected in seven industries: (1) chemical products, (2) nonelectrical machinery, (3) electrical goods, (4) automobiles, (5) building and construction, (6) telecommunication services, and (7) credit and insurance services.

Apart from industry specifics, country differences can be expected. Table 6 depicts the production structure in 1985 of the eight major EC member states in terms of the percentage industry shares in the gross value-added at market prices.[7]

Table 6.   Production Structure of EC Member States in 1985

Industry	Country[a]							
	G	D	B	E	I	F	N	S
Agriculture	1.8	5.5	2.4	1.5	4.6	4.2	4.4	6.3
Fuel and power								
products	5.2	2.5	5.3	11.4	4.8	5.7	12.4	5.9
Manufactured products								
Chemical products	3.1	1.4	3.0	2.3	1.9	2.1	2.6[b]	2.4
Metal and machinery								
products	7.8	4.6	3.4	4.8	5.5	4.6	2.9	3.7
(Machinery products)	4.9	3.2	1.9	3.2	3.1	2.7	—	1.7
Transport equipment	4.3	1.1	1.9	2.5	1.7	2.7	1.0	2.7
Food, beverages, and								
tobacco	3.7	4.2	4.1	4.8	2.6	3.4	3.4	5.1
Textile and clothing	1.5	1.1	1.8	1.6	4.2	1.9	0.7	2.5
Building and								
construction	5.6	5.4	5.7	6.1	6.0	5.7	5.3	6.5
Market services								
Transport	3.6	6.0	6.8	3.9	4.2	4.1	6.8[c]	4.3
(Maritime and air)	0.5	1.4	0.5	0.9	0.5	0.5	—	0.8
Communication	2.3	1.8	1.8	2.5	1.4	2.5	—	1.8
Credit and insurance	5.8	3.1	5.9	18.2	5.0	5.1	5.4	6.6
Total	44.7	36.7	42.1	59.6	41.9	42.0	44.9	47.8

Notes: [a]G = West-Germany; D = Denmark; B = Belgium; E = United Kingdom; I = Italy; F = France; N = Netherlands; and S = Spain.
[b]This percentage is calculated on the bais of a conservative extrapolation of the 1984 figure, since the gross value-added of chemical products in 1985 is missing.
[c]Transport and communication services are not separated in Dutch statistics.
Source: Eurostat (1988).

An index can be used to paint a first picture of the sensitivity of countries to industry-specific measures. Take the index (I)

$$I_i = \left[\sum_{j=1}^{n} s_j \cdot e_j \right] \Big/ \left[\sum_{j=1}^{n} s_j \right], \qquad (1)$$

where: i = country; j = industry; n = number of industries; s = industry share; and e = effect of integration.[8] The effects of European integration on industries, e_j, can be calculated on the basis of, for example, the number of measures per industry (Table 3) or the estimated effect of measures upon industry gross value-added (Table 5). For illustrative purposes, two rankings are determined by approaching e_j by the White Paper's measure intensity on the one hand, and the "high" estimates of the Cecchini report on the other. The first calculation gives the following ordering: (1) Denmark (27.98), (2) Spain (26.35), (3) Netherlands (23.45), (4) Belgium (22.91), (5) France (22.83), (6) Italy (22.32), (7) United Kingdom (20.66), and (8) West-Germany (20.16). The second calculation gives (1) West-Germany (12.97), (2) Spain (11.59), (3) United Kingdom (10.75), (4) France (10.33), (5) Italy (10.03), (6)-(7) Denmark and Belgium (9.80), and (8) Netherlands (9.22).[9] Probably, the second ordering is to be preferred, because the quantity of measures used for calculating the first ranking is not necessarily informative about the *magnitude* of the effects of directives; that is, measure intensity does not take account of the impact of specific measures. Apart from Spain's consistently high ranking, the second ranking differs strikingly from the first one. The small European nations are subject to the highest number of European measures (first ranking), but benefit least from the European integration (second ranking). This suggests that the economic impact of European integration, in terms of wealth, is independent from the number of policy measures taken in Brussels. Larger countries may lobby in order to shift the burden of European administration onto the smaller countries.

Although significant parts of the EC's integration program are delayed, the overall impression is that the completion of the internal market has progressed and accelerated (since the mid-eighties) such that preparation by (international) companies is warranted. Table 1 to 6 point out that this observation is particularly valid for specific industries and countries. This differentiated picture indicates that both Europhorics (overall optimists) and Eurosceptics (overall pessimists) may be wide of the mark (Daems 1989). The rankings suggest that the pros and cons of European integration will be distributed unevenly across industries and countries.[10] However, *Eurorealists* wisely opt for a well-balanced preparation in the face of the forthcoming European integration by reshaping corporate strategy while taking account of industry and country specifics (Buigues and Jacquemin 1989).

III.   MULTIMARKET COMPETITION

A.   Theoretical Perspectives

The framework of multimarket competition can be helpful in guiding strategic management in the face of Europe after 1992. Multimarket competition involves rivalry among firms in a set of related (product or geographic) markets. The European integration will intensify multimarket competition, since the very objective of the White Paper measures is to abolish international trade barriers in order to facilitate the exploitation of the opportunities of intercountry trade within the EC. This means that both entry and entry-deterring strategies are in need of modification.

The framework of multimarket competition focuses on actual and potential competition of firms operating in different but related markets. This framework integrates theories of strategic management and industrial organization. Specific sources of inspiration are the literature on diversification (Lecraw 1984), integration (Caves and Bradburd 1988), multiproduct firms (Teece 1982), multinational enterprise (Caves 1982), interbrand competition (Scherer 1980), competitive analysis (Porter 1980), transaction costs (Teece 1980), and international trade (Brander and Krugman 1983).

The key feature of multimarket competition is that *inside* (that is, from within the set of related markets) rivals are able to (relatively quickly) overcome barriers which are unsurmountable to *outside* (that is, from outside the set of related markets) entrants (Gorecki 1975; Lambkin 1988). Multimarket competition can be associated with three extreme cases. First, all inside firms may decide to enter into (a selection of) other inside rival's home markets (Calem 1988, p. 175): they develop into multimarket firms. Second, neither inside firm enters into an inside rivals' home market (Bulow et al. 1985): they remain one-market suppliers. Third, in an intermediate case inside firms maintain a foothold in (a selection of) inside rivals' home markets (Karnani and Wernerfelt 1985). Five key elements of multimarket competition underlie the outcome.

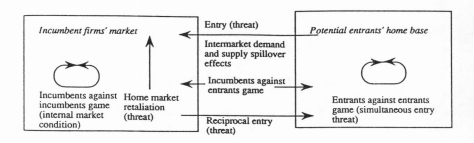

Figure 1.   Framework of Multimarket Competition

B.   Five Key Elements

Multimarket competition introduces new elements into strategy choice. Figure 1 summarizes the five key features that drive multimarket competition.

1. Competition can be associated with *three* categories of *games* which are characterized by the *focus of rivalry* that dominates competition. The incumbents against incumbents game is studied in the well-established theories of (im)perfect competition without (free) entry (Shapiro 1989): only internal market conditions determine competition. *Actual* rivalry drives competition. The entry deterrence literature focuses on the incumbents against entrants game (Gilbert 1989): external conditions dominate over internal competition. *Potential* rivalry dominates competition. The entrants against entrants game is explored only sporadically (Nti 1989): multiple potential entrants have to coordinate (implicitly or explicitly) simultaneous entry decisions. *Entry* rivalry may negate the force of potential competition: "the probability of independent entry as well as the probability of at least one entry decline with the number of potential entrants" (Nti 1989, p. 48).

2. Inside entrants can *economize on resources*. An inside entrant can divert resources from home to entry market, which, on the one hand, economizes on entry cost but gives an (opportunity) cost of entry on the other. Economized entry costs, follow from using (excess) resources in order to supply an entry market. Entry is associated with either adjustment cost in production, if the entry market good is a technical substitute, or transport cost in exporting, if the product is transferred from the home base to another region or country. Entry is easy if the entry costs are low (Calem 1988, p. 171). If firms have to operate at full capacity in order to satisfy demand in the home market, entry gives an opportunity cost in the sense of home market profit foregone by withdrawing capacity from the home market (Bulow et al. 1985, p. 172). The entry opportunity cost is zero if excess resources are employed (Cairns and Mahabir 1988) or if the resources have a public good character. Intangible assets (such as know how, consumer goodwill and management skills) have this characteristic (Teece 1980, 1982).

3. Inside firms can exploit *multimarket spillovers* (or, in the words of Yip [1989], industry drivers). Multimarket spillovers are defined as externalities between two or more markets: that is, the payoffs in market A have an impact on the payoffs in market B and vice versa. Bulow et al. (1985) distinguish supply from demand spillovers. The former include joint (dis)economies of scale or scope. Operating in two or more markets has an impact on the cost of production and selling. Vertical integration (dis)advantages are a third example (Brunner 1961). Multimarket demand spillovers cover goodwill in the home market which carries over to the entry market (Margolis 1989). The strategy of firms in market A influences the scale of demand in market B (and vice

versa). Caves (1982) summarizes spillovers in the context of multinational enterprise, whereas Teece (1982) lists multimarket externalities that diversified firms can exploit. A key argument in this literature is that (excess) fungible but intangible assets can be exploited by multimarket operation.

4. Inside firms can exert a *reciprocal entry* threat (Porter 1980; Calem 1988). This means that firms in market A are potential entrants into market B and vice versa. Three examples illustrate reciprocal entry (threats). First, incumbent firms in the entry market may decide to retaliate in the entrant's home market (Calem 1988). This strategy of counterattack is a parry to the potential entrant's entry attack (Yip 1989). Second, Watson (1982) identifies countercompetitive strategies which anticipate the potential rival's entry move: countercompetition entails actions (for example, entry into the potential entrant's home market) that force the potential entrant to tie resources to her home market. Third, hostage or foothold strategies can be employed so as to keep potential entrants in check. A local subsidiary disciplines the potential entrant's entry ambitions (Caves 1982). A foothold in the potential entrant's home market signals the ability to immediately respond to the potential entrants' entry strategy by retaliation in her home market (Karnani and Wernerfelt 1985).

5. Multimarket contact among inside firms facilitates *multimarket collusion* (Bernheim and Whinston 1990). The outcome of multimarket competition (after, for example, a series of entry and reciprocal entry moves) may well be a reduction in competition (Caves 1982). Edwards (1955) proposed the hypothesis that firms meeting in several markets recognize their interdependence and therefore may decide to tune down competition. Companies with multimarket encounters are inclined to facilitate collusion (Feinberg 1985), since the payoff of the cooperative outcome exceeds the competitive profit (Kantarelis and Veendorp 1988). This phenomenon is also recognized in the literature on international trade (Jacquemin 1989). For example, reciprocal dumping is the worst of both worlds (or, to be precise, four worlds in a Prisoners' Dilemma): if both parties agree upon refraining from dumping, joint profit is maximized (Pinto 1986).

IV. FUTURE EUROPE

A. Internal and External Barriers

The prime objective of the integration of the EC is to stimulate the European economy by abolishing *internal* barriers which impede European competition. Physical, technical and fiscal regulations that hamper movements from one member state to another are or will be demolished or harmonized. European firms, irrespective of their specific country origin, will be able to gain from a large, integrated home market with 320 million consumers. The literature shows, by and large, consensus on the issue that a significant demolition of internal barriers is under way. For example, Friberg (1989) notes that "European unification *is* moving forward—and gaining momentum" (Friberg, 1989, p. 85). A similar point is made by authors like Buigues and Jacquemin (1989), Daems (1989), Magee (1989) and Reading (1990). This justifies Assumption 1.

Assumption 1 (Internal barriers). *The White Paper integration program results in a significant reduction of the internal barriers which impede[d] intercountry trade within the EC in the preintegration era.*

However, what will happen with *external* barriers is a different issue. On the one hand, Eurobashers (Daems 1989) believe that the EC's 1992 measures install a fortress Europe that will be difficult to invade from the outside (in particular, Japan and the United States). Reading (1990) points out that

[c]onventional wisdom suggests that the completion of the single European Internal Market by end-1992, or thereabouts, will be a threat to the United States, if that market becomes an inward-looking protective trade block, and a promise if it becomes an outward-looking freely trading area (p. 28).

Similar doubts are raised by, for example, Calingaert (1989), Dornbusch (1989), Kaikati (1989), and Magee (1989). Particularly, "while tariffs are not at issue, other measures could affect the conditions of entry of goods into the EC: quotas, rules of origin and antidumping policies" (Calingaert 1989, p. 31).

On the other hand, however, opposite views are expressed by, for example, Cooper (1989) and Peck (1989). Cooper (1989) points out that

[f]or outsiders, the process on balance is likely to be liberalizing, except in the field of agriculture, for the simple reason that building a 'fortress' is not in Europe's interest. It has a great stake in a liberal trading world, has profited greatly from it, and is likely to contribute further to it (p. 339).

Assumption 2 reflects the ambiguity that surrounds the expectations about the effect of the European integration on external barriers.

Assumption 2 (External barriers). *The case where European integration goes hand in hand with increasing external barriers to outside rivals cannot be ruled out.*

An important question is what influence the likely reduction in internal barriers (Assumption 1) and the possible erection of external barriers (Assumption 2) will have on competition, strategic opportunities and threats for international business in future Europe. A first answer to this question can be provided by applying the five key element of the framework of multimarket competition (under *ceteris paribus* conditions) to ongoing and forthcoming European integration.[11,12]

B.   Focus of Rivalry

The theory of entry barriers (Gilbert 1989) predicts that immediately after the reduction of internal barriers potential competition *within the* EC will be intensified: the incumbents against entrants game gains importance. As entry barriers are lowered, the credibility of the threat of entry from other member states is facilitated. If the EC decides not to erect external barriers, the force of potential rivalry is fortified by the entry threat from outside potential entrants. Otherwise, the threat of potential entry by outside rivals is of secondary importance.

Market integration changes the rule of the competitive game (Smith and Venables 1988). Venables (1990) observes that "[e]conomic integration may . . . change the degree of market segmentation, and hence change the nature of the strategic interaction between firms in different countries" (p. 753). In particular, Porter's (1980) competitive analysis indicates that, on the one hand, incumbent firms have to reconsider their entry-deterring strategies, whereas, on the other, potential entrants face increased gateways to entry (Yip 1982).

The nature of the European integration program implies that artificial (that is, government imposed) entry barriers between member states will be demolished or reduced. This means that incumbent firms that were sheltered from international market forces through government protection will face increased potential rivalry by foreign competitors after European integration.

Previously sheltered incumbent firms may respond to intensified potential rivalry by replacing *artificial* entry barriers (through governmental regulations), if feasible and profitable, by natural barriers to entry (or, in Salop's [1979] terminology, *strategic* barriers). Otherwise, potential entrants will take advantage of the removal of the national shelters by entering the newly opened markets. For example, Buigues and Jacquemin (1989) argue that

> the capacity to resist market entrants from non-member countries . . . depends on the existence of strategic barriers to entry. The main tools for creating such barriers are the exploitation of the position of innovator and 'first mover advantage'; the use of more rapid learning processes . . . ; special relationships with customers and suppliers . . . ; control of a range of products, including substitutes, etc. (p. 65).

The Cecchini report (1988) predicts *intensified* competition after the completion of the internal market. Friberg (1989) argues that

[c]ertain to emerge is rapid intensification of price competition. In industries as pervasive as chemicals, consumer packaged goods, and financial services, there are massive price differentials between countries for the same product. . . . Price variations of this magnitude simply have no justification in the costs of raw materials, manufacturing, or logistics. They are unlikely to prove sustainable in a more competitive environment (p. 86).

The very reason for the sustainability of these price differentials, artificial barriers, will disappear after the completion of the internal market. Hence, limit (entry-deterring) prices (Bain 1956) are likely to decline.

Buigues and Jacquemin (1989) argue that the intensity of the internal incumbents against entrants game after the completion of the integration program can be *differentiated* as to environmental (industry) characteristics by applying Porter's (1985) two-criteria typology (advantages of being a leading firm versus opportunities for differentiation). Two polar examples illustrate the argument. First, specialized industries in a structural environment where nontariff barriers are significant (for instance, pharmaceuticals and software), will face intensified potential rivalry after the completion of the internal market. Second, in environments with volume as the principle feature (for example, office machinery and basic chemicals) the current market is already European, which implies an insignificant change in internal potential rivalry after integration.

After a transition stage actual entry affects the incumbents against incumbents game. The demolition of artificial barriers is likely to induce entry. *Actual* entry implies that potential rivals become incumbent firms. This changes the number of players in (and the outcome of) the incumbents against incumbents game. Market structures in the EC member states will change as a result of the EC's 1992 program.[13] For example, the German brewery industry, which was heavily protected in pre-integration times (through the *Reinheitsgebot*), will face entry by inside firms from foreign countries so that after actual entry has taken place, actual competition in the German beer market will intensify.

Proposition 1 (Focus of rivalry). *In the first instance, the completion of the internal market increases the intensity of potential rivalry (the incumbents against entrants game). Artificial barriers are replaced by natural (or strategic) barriers. After a transition phase actual competition (the incumbents against incumbents game) is fortified by actual entry.*

C. Resource Economizing Entry

The demolition of physical and technical barriers provides the opportunity to *economize on entry cost*. First, abolition of border controls reduces transport cost. Time and money-consuming border procedures will belong to the past.[14]

A telling example is the efficiency gain following the implementation of the EC's single administrative document. Second, demolition of technical barriers implies harmonization of technical product standards in the EC member states. This has the important implication that adjustment cost can be reduced considerably. For example, take the case where the regulatory requirements for consumer electronics in France and Germany will be identical. Then exporting TV sets from France to Germany or vice versa does no longer require adjustments in electronic circuits: the same TV set can be sold in both France and Germany. Expensive modifications of products can be avoided.

The reduction of transport and adjustment cost induces a lowering of the entry cost. Hence, after the completion of the internal market, entry will be *easier* (Calem 1988): inside firms can economize on entry cost. Depending on the EC's decisions on external barriers, the same may or may not hold for outside rivals. The impact of lower entry cost on potential competition varies with the *industry-specific* opportunity cost of entry (Bulow et al. 1985). Industries with excess capacity (for example, steel and ship building) or important intangible assets (for example, software and financial services) are associated with a low opportunity cost of entry. Hence, the credibility of the entry threat—and so the force of potential rivalry—in these industries will be particularly significant if entry cost is lowered after the demolition of physical and technical barriers.

The importance of reduced (entry) cost after the completion of the internal market is broadly recognized in the literature. For example, Daems (1989) points out that

> [t]he immediate effect of the 1992 project will be a decline in the costs of doing business in a European market. . . . First, the costs of shipment will go down as there will be fewer administrative hurdles at border crossings, less time will be lost in waiting for custom clearance . . . . Second, as goods and services cross borders fewer product adjustments will be necessary in order to satisfy local legislation and standards (p. 6).

Moreover, as "most sectors of the European economy—steel, detergents, pharmaceuticals, transportation, banking—are marked by chronic overcapacity" (Friberg 1989 p. 87) the entry threat will be credible after the European integration.

Proposition 2 (Resource economizing entry).   *The abolition of physical and technical barriers within the EC will provide the opportunity to economize on transport and adjustment (and so entry) cost. If the EC refrains from building a fortress Europe, this observation holds for both inside and outside rivals. Particularly, industries with significant overcapacity or intangible assets will face intensified potential rivalry.*

D. Multimarket Spillovers

The prime motivation for the White Paper integration program is that the fragmentation of the EC's market restricts European firms' capability to exploit large scale in their competition with outside rivals (Stone 1989). This immediately points to a crucial multimarket spillover that will gain importance after the European integration: *joint economies of scale*. The emphasis on the scale effect of the EC's 1992 program is spread all over the literature. For example, Magee (1989) stipulates that

> European companies have lacked a home market of sufficient size to support the investments necessary to compete with aggressive Japanese and American competitors in what are clearly the industries of the future—electronics, information technology, bio-technology, and telecommunications. . . . Today there is real possibility that this fragmented, chauvinistic Europe may disappear and a dynamic, integrated market grow in its place (p. 78).

Joint scale economies are not the only multimarket spillovers that count. Three examples can illustrate this observation. First, Europe 1992 brings the exploitation of *scope economies* within reach as product-market niches will be enlarged after the demolition of internal barriers. Buigues and Jacquemin (1989) argue that "[t]he enlargement of the market that can be served without barriers is essential, since it will have a positive impact on the dissemination and adoption of new technologies and new products" (p. 56). Second, European integration allows *distribution* to be organized on a European scale. Daems (1989) stipulates that "[i]t will no longer be necessary to build distribution organizations along national boundaries and consequently cost savings will be available" (p. 13). Third, European firms can benefit from multimarket demand spillovers by developing European *brand images*.[15] Magee (1989) points out that "it is dangerous to overestimate the force of local preference. . . . The forces pushing for pan-European markets—even in food products—are powerful" (p. 81). Quelch and Buzzell (1989) argue that "Eurobrands employing a common positioning strategy and package design will become more common" (p. 67).[16]

The recognition of multimarket *interdependencies* is crucial in strategy choice. For example, Yip (1989) points out that

> [w]hen activities such as production are shared among countries, a competitor's market share in one country affects its scale and overall cost position in all countries dependent on the shared activities. Less directly, customers may view market position in a lead country as an indicator of overall quality (p. 38).

The exploitation of multimarket spillovers is the key issue in modern global competition (Kogut 1985). This is precisely what the completion of the internal market brings within the reach of inside firms. The extent to which outside firms will be able to benefit from spillovers in the integrated EC's markets depends, again, on the issue of external barriers.

Proposition 3 (Multimarket spillovers). *Integration of the fragmented European market increases the inside firms' opportunities to exploit multimarket spillovers such as joint economies of scale and scope, and European distribution channels and brand images. The height of future external barriers determines the extent to which outside firms can benefit from intra- European spillovers.*

E. Reciprocal Entry

Global competition shows many examples of *reciprocal* entry rivalry (Caves 1982). Yip (1989) observes that

> [i]n a global strategy, competitive moves are integrated across countries. . . . [A] competitor is attacked in one country in order to drain resources for another country, or a competitive attack in one country in countered in a different country. Perhaps the best example is the counterattack in a competitor's home market as a parry to an attack on one's own home market (pp. 32-33).

Karnani and Wernerfelt (1985) describe three cases of reciprocal entry competition: Goodyear against Michelin, Maxwell House against Proctor and Gamble and BIC against Gillette. Graham (1978) reports a study of direct investments by American firms in Europe and European firms in the United States. The results indicate that an increase in the number of American subsidiaries in Europe was typically followed, after a lag, by an increase of European subsidiaries in the United States: European firms install subsidiaries as a response to entry by American companies.

European integration is likely to induce reciprocal entry competition for two reasons. First, demolition of internal barriers facilitates intra-European two-way entries. For instance, not only will French pharmaceutical firms face new opportunities to enter the German market, but besides German producers of pharmaceuticals observe new French markets. Dekker, former CEO of Philips, points out, for example, that "we will see more small companies penetrating other European markets than we have seen so far. Competition will be a little stiffer too, of course, because other European companies will invade your territory" (Stone 1989, p. 94). So, a firm from member state A entering into member state B has to take into account an increased probability of reciprocal entry by inside firms from country B (and vice versa).

Second, entry by outside firms occurs in anticipation of the erection of external barriers. Companies from outside the EC take account of the prediction that EC's protectionism will increase after the completion of the internal market. The threat of European protectionism is particularly valid for firms exporting (or planning to export) from outside the EC. Magee (1989) asserts that "[c]learly U.S. exporters should take prospect of self-interested protectionism seriously. . . . American exporters should begin now to plan and implement a strategy for maintaining access to the European single market" (p. 84). This strategy is entry before it is too late. This gives outside firms a foothold in the European market, which can be used to attack or counter-attack in the post-integration era.[17,18] For example, Kaikati (1989) argues that "[to] avoid such thinly veiled doses of Europrotectionism, non-EC firms are strongly advised to develop an 'insider' presence" (Kaikati 1989, p. 90).

A case in point is that reciprocity is even official EC policy! That is, Magee (1989) points out that

> [t]he European Community has already begun to articulate a so-called principle of reciprocity, which provides, in general, that the EC will give access to foreign suppliers on the same terms that the foreign country gives access to EC companies in the same industry (p. 83).

Dekker points out that this is an important issue for European companies (Stone 1989, p. 94). Inside and outside firms must face parity in both European and non-European markets. Implementation of the reciprocity policy further enhances the credibility of the reciprocal entry threat from inside and outside rivals.

Proposition 4 (Reciprocal entry). *Demolition of internal barriers in the context of the EC's 1992 program facilitates intra-European reciprocal entry (threats). Moreover, entry by outside firms occurs in anticipation of the erection of external barriers. Outside firms gain footholds in the European market, which can be used to attack or counterattack in the post-integration era. Outside reciprocal entry is supported by the official EC policy of reciprocity.*

F.   Multimarket Collusion

Scott (1982) points out that "when sellers meet in several markets, their recognition of the interdependence of their operations may blunt the vigor of their competition with each other" (p. 369). Feinberg (1985) complements the argument by stating that "companies meeting rivals in more than one market will be able to facilitate collusion in one or all of those markets" (p. 238). The reason is that collusion (in particular, in the form of [tacit] agreements regarding the sharing of markets) gives higher profits than fierce competition in many markets. Completion of the internal market implies the very multiplication of multimarket *contacts*. Reciprocal entry, both from inside and outside the EC, increases the number of markets in which firms operate and meet. This means that the European integration program facilitates collusive arrangements within the EC.

A second motive for cooperation can be efficiency gains. The benefit of cooperation in (or, in anticipation of) a unified Europe is recognized by, for example, Buigues and Jacquemin (1989) and Magee (1989). Buigues and Jacquemin (1989) stipulate that

> [c]o-operation arrangements, with or without the setting up of a joint venture, can also facilitate the exploitation of the new opportunities afforded by an open Internal Market. They promote synergies, avoid costly duplication, make it possible to disseminate technological information more widely, and reduce the time required to put a new product or process on the market; they also ensure that risks are more widely distributed among the partners (p. 63).[19]

Magee (1989) argues that, apart from acquisition, a "second approach open to the American company with a European subsidiary is to seek an alliance with some company in a related industry for joint R&D or cross-marketing of products" (p. 82). Moreover, this strategy can be undertaken so as to bypass the disadvantages of being an outsider. That is, "[o]ne response to Community preference [for EC firms] is for a non-Community firm to establish a joint venture with a Community firm, thus obscuring national origins" (Peck 1989, p. 297).

In line with the first and second motivation, a third argument in favor of cooperation points to collusive arrangements that can be designed to allow or deter entry. This third motivation is illustrated by, for example, Thimm (1989) for the case of telecommunications: "The very threat that non-EC telecommunication companies might derive the major benefit from an integrated European telecommunications market may have prompted the recent unprecedented cooperation among the major European IT-telecommunications enterprises" (p. 67). So, on the one hand, in the face of competition for the internal market, inside firms join activities in order to (1) agree upon sharing the profit which can be earned in the many EC markets (which implies tacit collusion), (2) capture the efficiency advantages of a large market, and (3) enter other (global) markets or create a counter-force against outside rivalry. On the other hand, apart from motivation (1) and (2), outside rivals cooperate (with local firms) so as to effectuate entry into the EC.

The EC's integration program provides for intra-European cooperative arrangements (Slot and Van der Woude 1988). The White Paper proposes 23 measures that seek to ground intra-EC cooperation in European law. For example, the "use of legal structures as the European Economic Interest Grouping . . . make it possible to set up specifically European legal entities"

(Buigues and Jacquemin 1989, p. 66). Moreover, the European Commission has installed research programs for transnational cooperation projects (for instance, ESPRIT, FAST, and RACE), which stimulate setting up technological alliances within Europe.

> **Proposition 5** (Multimarket collusion). *Completing the internal market increases multimarket contact, which in turn facilitates multimarket collusion. Inside firms join forces in order to (1) agree upon sharing the profit from many EC markets, (2) derive efficiency gains from the large market, or (3) enter other* (global) *markets or prepare for competition with outside rivals. Outside rivals use cooperation* (with local firms) *as an entry instrument. The EC's integration policy supports intra-European cooperation.*

V. APPRAISAL

This chapter integrates literature on the impact of the European integration by listing five propositions which are derived from the theory of multimarket competition. Although, of course, industry specifics cannot be ignored, five general patterns can be identified: (1) entry and entry deterrence will gain importance, (2) entrants will be able to economize on entry cost, (3) the opportunity to exploit multimarket spillovers will expand, (4) the threat of reciprocal entry will increase, and (5) multimarket collusion will be facilitated. Both inside and outside rivals have to take account of these general patterns while preparing for competition after the implementation of the EC's 1992 program.

The key *strategies* after 1992 concern entry deterrence and actual entry. The first strategy is associated with signalling unprofitable entry opportunities, whereas the second policy goes hand in hand with the selection of entry markets. The five propositions indicate factors that can facilitate both strategies. The imperatives are summarized in Table 7. Future research can be directed at identifying the ways by which firms may recognize and implement these strategies.

A related issue in the literature deals with investigating the validity of Porter's (1980) three strategies (cost leadership, product differentiation and focus) in the context of Europe 1992. The point is that none of the strategy options can be excluded (Daems 1989). First, the prime importance of scale economies after the enlargement of the European home market points to a strategy of cost leadership (Magee 1989). Second, the large European market shows increasing demand for product diversity, which implies that a strategy of product differentiation may be profitable (Geroski 1989). Third, at the same time the number of viable niches increases, which indicates the feasibility of focus

Table 7.   Entry Deterrence and Market Selection

Key Element	Deter Entry by	Select a Market
1. Focus of rivalry	focusing on incumbents against entrants game	which does not suffer from predominant actual rivalry which drives profit down
2. Resource econo-mizing entry	raising strategic entry barriers that impede economizing on entry cost	which permits to economize on entry cost
3. Multimarket spillovers	stimulating negative sillovers with potential entry markets	where positive multi-market spillovers are eminent
4. Reciprocal entry	signalling a credible reciprocal entry threat	where incumbents fail to exert a credible reciprocal entry threat
5. Multimarket collusion	showing unwillingness to collude after entry	where incumbents are wiling to collude

strategies (Buigues and Jacquemin 1989). Of course, other strategy choices are also worth considering. For example, the choice of the mode of cooperation (or entry) cannot be ignored (Anderson and Gatignon 1986; and Kogut 1988).[20] Moreover, Europe 1992 asks for reconsidering functional (marketing) strategies (Quelch and Buzzell 1989).

Uncertainties interfere with the firms' preparation for Europe 1992: to what extent will Europe decide to erect external barriers; and what will be the pace of the European integration progress? Other issues concern the lacunas in the White Paper set of proposals and the impact of the liberalization of Eastern Europe. However, the movement toward an economically unified Europe is so forceful that ignorance can be fatal. As Dekker points out, "[t]he internal market is absolutely necessary. But the internal market will also mean big shakeouts in many industries" (Stone 1989, p. 93). By taking account of likely patterns of competition in future Europe, firms may increase the probability that they will be beneficiaries rather than victims of European integration.

ACKNOWLEDGMENT

The authors are very grateful for the comments of Alain Verbeke. Of course, the usual disclaimer applies.

NOTES

1. Of course, even if these barriers are eliminated, impediments to the free movement of goods, services, capital and persons remain. For instance, Anderson (1989) points out that "[d]ifferences due to custom and culture are widespread in Europe . . . . For example, nine languages are in common use in the Community; packaging, instructions and labelling must reflect this in order to be comprehensible to the relevant consumers" (p. 13), and Quelch and Buzzell (1989) note that the "1992 reforms . . . will make individual country markets more accessible, not more identical. Most of the well-documented cultural, historical, institutional, physical, and economic differences among the EC countries will survive the 1992 process" (p. 66).

2. At least four reasons can explain the shift in the distribution of measures from 1985 (White Paper) to 1989 (Fourth Progress Report): (1) pairs of measures are combined in single directives, (2) single measures are split into two or more directives, (3) new measures are introduced, and (4) White Paper measures are removed from the agenda (for example, proposals that [in principle] need no formal decision of the Council).

3. Table 2 does not makes mention of implementation lags. After the European Council has transformed proposals into directives, member states may take time to incorporate European guidelines into national law.

4. Although the distribution is subjective in nature, it gives an indication of the allocation of integration measures over specific industries. Of course, this indicator does not take account of the *magnitude* of the impact of specific measures. The point is that such assessments would require industry-specific expertise. Note that specific measures can be attributed to more than one industry.

5. The EC studies are published in Cecchini (1988), Commission of the European Communities (1988), Emerson (1989) and in background studies. The figures in Table 5 are derived from Cecchini (1988) and Pelkmans (1988). The Cecchini report summarizes the results of a large number of different studies. For illustrative purposes, the sector figures in Table 5 present the lowest and highest estimates (in terms of billions of Ecu per year) from three calculations which are based upon different assumptions about price convergence within the EC. The macroeconomic estimates are in terms of percentage change. Dornbusch (1989) and Peck (1989) offer critical evaluations of the macroeconomic and industry estimates respectively.

6. The critique of the EC's estimates goes both ways. On the one hand, the Dutch Centraal Planbureau (Central Planning Bureau [CPB]), for example, argues that the EC significantly overestimates the effects of the 1992 program: the CPB calculates the macroeconomic percentage mutations to be -1.75 (prices of products), 0.00 (level of employment) and 2.25 (production volume). Peck (1989) observes overoptimism in the Cecchini studies by criticizing the assumptions underlying the exercitions. On the other hand, Calingaert (1989), for instance, observes that the EC's "estimates may well be on the low side" (p. 28).

7. Five remarks are in order: (1) the gross value-added at market prices is the difference between the value of the actual output and the value of the intermediate consumption; (2) Table 6 only mentions industries which are affected by the measures of the White Paper or the Fourth Progress Report; (3) the total of the shares falls short of 100%, since only the selection of industries is included which is involved in the European integration program; (4) Ireland, Greece and Portugal are not included because their statistics fail to provide sufficient data; and (5) to date, Eurostat provides statistics up to 1986, but the 1986 figures of West-Germany and Spain are incomplete.

8. This index is adopted from Van Witteloostuijn and Maks (1988).

9. The limitations of the EC statistics dictate six rules of thumb: (1) the impact on the market for automobiles is determined for the share of the transport equipment industry; (2) nonelectrical machinery, office machinery and telecommunication products are classified under machinery products; (3) the share of foods, beverages and tobacco is not cleaned for beverages and tobacco (4) the market for telecommunication is identified with the communications services industry; and

(5) other business services are excluded. Moreover, in the case of the Netherlands average values are chosen for missing variables in Table 6. The value for machinery products is set at 1.79 (i.e., the average share of machinery products in the metal and machinery sector), maritime and air is set at 0.7 (i.e., the average over the other countries), and communication is set at 2.5 (i.e., the average over the other countries).

10.   Two provisos may be needed, however. First, harmonized European statistics on member states are available only after a lag of, by and large, five years. This indicates that in the area of information gathering European integration does not (as yet) show an impressive record. Second, the fact that the impact of the European integration will be allocated unevenly over industries and countries may create political problems which can impede progress (Peck 1989).

11.   This chapter presents a general argument. Examples of case studies of specific industries, apart from sector studies in the tradition of the Cecchini report (1988), are Perrin-Pelletier (1988) on cars, Thimm (1989) on telecommunications, and Walter (1989) on financial services.

12.   The need for strategic re-orientation is well-recognized in the literature, but badly perceived by companies. For example, Kaikati (1989) points out that "[t]o take advantage of opportunities emerging in 1992, business executives should start mapping corporate strategy now. . . . Unfortunately, most are not yet prepared. Recent surveys reveal that only 15 percent of American chief executives have plans to deal with the EC in 1992, and that only 12 percent are developing such plans. A survey of French, German, and British companies reveals that that lack of preparation is not unique. The French are the best prepared: 62 percent of French companies have drafted or are preparing plans for 1992, as opposed to 36 percent of German companies and 30 percent of British firms" (pp. 85-86). An example of a positive exception is the Triplex Lloyd Group. Sharp (1990) summarizes the firm's strategy for the single European market, an important issue being to build bridges into Europe.

13.   A majority of observers expects increasing concentration together with intensified competition. For example, Quelch and Buzzell (1989) argue that "it seems clear that there will be an increase in concentration (on a pan-European basis) in many industries during the nineties, leading to more intense competition as increasing numbers of companies cross national boundaries to compete with each other" (p. 64). The exploitation of scale economies drives this result: "The view of the Commission appears to be that economies of scale are present and unexploited in most sectors, and thus that large-scale rationalization is likely to occur in many sectors, leaving a small number of mass producers operating in Communitywide markets" (Geroski 1989, p. 77). This expectation may prove to be false, however, for at least three reasons. First, entry may increase the number of competitors in the EC as a whole or in specific EC countries or industries. Second, "more noticeable and probably more important than an increase in the size of markets will be an increase in the diversity of consumers tastes that producers will be forced to confront" (Geroski 1989, p. 80), which implies increased product variety. Third, multimarket contact may facilitate collusion rather than increase competition (Proposition 5). The effect of the 1992 program on market structure and competition is, therefore, likely to be industry-specific.

14.   The following figures illustrate this observation: "Road transport accounts for 80 percent of goods movement across intra-EC borders. Cross-border delays range from 11.7 hours on the Belgium to Italy route to 1.5 hours on the Netherlands to Belgium route. The time wasted on an 18-hour trip from the United Kingdom to Italy represents 22 percent of total operating costs. Thirty-five percent of trucks on EC roads return empty from their destination. . . . [A]n average reduction of 5 percent in road haulage prices is expected" (Quelch and Buzzell 1989, p. 69).

15.   For example, to date, "(s)pecialty retailers like Benetton are marching across Europe meeting the needs of similar consumer segments in multiple markets with a common brand name and marketing formula" (Quelch and Buzzell 1989, p. 69).

16.   This goes hand in hand with an "increasing portion of advertising expenditures [that]) will be placed in pan-European media" (Quelch and Buzzell 1989, p. 70).

17.   Thimm (1989) illustrates the threat of *reciprocal* entry which may result from non-EC entry in the market for information technology (IT) by arguing that the "reverse side of a possible foreign domination of the EC's IT market are the global aspirations of the major European telecommunications enterprises" (p. 68).

18.   Moreover, Calingaert (1989) points out that presence within the EC gives better opportunities to exert influence on the EC's decision making process: "U.S. firms do have access to the EC standards-setting process. Those with subsidiaries in the EC are able to participate on an essentially equal basis with EC firms . . . . However, that is not the case for U.S. exporters without facilities in the EC" (p. 34).

19.   The recent strategic reorientation in the market for financial services reflects a telling example of the trend toward cooperation (Walter 1989).

20.   For example, Kaikati (1989) considers the entry mode issue in the context of Europe 1992 by arguing that "[c]orporate strategists should also evaluate joint ventures and strategic alliances as a means of gaining a European foothold before 1992. . . . While joint ventures and strategic alliances with Eurofirms are viable entry strategies, corporate managers should also explore the feasibility of direct investment" (p. 89).

REFERENCES

Anderson, D. 1989. "The Single European Market and the Real Economy." *Business Economics* 26: 10-16.
Anderson, E. and H. Gatignon. 1986. "Modes of Foreign Entry: A Transaction Cost Analysis." *Journal of International Business Studies* 16: 1-26.
Bain, J.S. 1956. *Barriers to New Competition.* Cambridge, MA: Harvard University Press.
Baldwin, R.E. 1984. "Trade Policies in Developed Countries. In *Handbook of International Economics,* edited by R.J. Jones and P.B. Kenen. Amsterdam: North-Holland.
Bernheim, B.D. and M.D. Whinston. 1990. "Multimarket Contact and Collusive Behavior." *Rand Journal of Economics* 21: 1-26.
Brander, J.A. and P.R. Krugman. 1983. "A 'Reciprocal Dumping' Model of International Trade." *Journal of International Economics* 15: 313-321.
Brunner, E. 1961. "A Note on Potential Competition." *Journal of Industrial Economics* 9: 248-250.
Buigues, P. and A. Jacquemin. 1989. "Strategies of Firms and Structural Environments in the Large Internal Market." *Journal of Common Market Studies* 28: 53-67.
Bulow, J.I., J.D. Geanakoplos, and P.D. Klemperer. 1985. "Multimarket Oligopoly: Strategic Substitutes and Complements." *Journal of Political Economy* 93: 488-511.
Cairns, R.D. and D. Mahabir. 1988. "Contestability: A Revisionist View." *Economica* 55: 269-276.
Calem, P.S. 1988. "Entry and Entry Deterrence in Penetrable Markets." *Economica* 55: 171-183.
Calingaert, M. 1989. "What Europe 1992 Means for U.S. Business." *Business Economics* 26: 30-36.
Caves, R.E. 1982. *Multinational Enterprise and Economic Analysis.* Cambridge: Cambridge University Press.
Caves, R.E. and R.M. Bradburd. 1988. "The Empirical Determinants of Vertical Integration." *Journal of Economic Behavior and Organization* 9: 265-279.
Cecchini, P., Ed. 19 88. *The European Challenge 1992: The Benefits of a Single Market.* Aldershot: Wildwood House.
Central Plan Bureau. 1989. "The Netherlands and Europe '92" (in Dutch). *Werkdocument 28.* Den Haag: CPB.

Commission of the European Communities. 1985. *White Paper: Completing the Internal Market.* Brussels: EC.

Commission of the European Communities. 1989. Fourth progress report of the Commission to the Council and the European Parliament concerning the implementation of the Commission's White Paper on the completion of the internal market. *COM (989)* 311. Brussels: Commission of the European Countries.

Cooper, R.N. 1989. "Europe Without Borders." *Brookings Papers on Economic Activity* 20: 325-340.

Daems, H. 1989. "The Strategic Implications of Europe 1992." *Working Paper 89-03.* Brussels: EIASM.

Dornbusch, R. 1989. "Europe 1992: Macroeconomic Implications." *Brookings Papers on Economic Activity* 20: 341-362.

Edwards, C.D. 1955. "Conglomerate Bigness As a Source of Power." In National Bureau of Economic Research Conference Report, *Business Concentration and Price Policy.* Princeton, NJ: Princeton University Press.

Emerson, M. 1989. "The Emergence of the New European Economy of 1992." *Business Economics* 26: 5-9.

Eurostat. 1988. *National Accounts ESA: Detailed Tables by Branch.* Brussels: CECA.

Feinberg, R.M. 1985. "'Sales-at-Risk': A Test of the Mutual Forbearance Theory of Conglomerate Behavior." *Journal of Business* 58: 225-241.

Friberg, E.G. 1989. "1992: Moves Europeans are Making." *Harvard Business Review* 67(May-June): 85-89.

Geroski, P. 1989. "On Diversity and Scale—Extant Firms and Extinct Goods?" *Sloan Management Review* (Fall): 75-83.

Gilbert, R.J. 1989. "Mobility Barriers and the Value of Incumbency." In *Handbook of Industrial Organization,* edited by R. Schmalensee and R.D. Willig. Amsterdam: North-Holland.

Gorecki, P.K. 1975. "The Determinants of Entry by New and Diversifying Enterprises in the UK Manufacturing Sector 1958-1963: Some Tentative Results." *Applied Economics* 7: 139-147.

Graham, E.M. 1978. "Transatlantic Investment by Multinational Firms: A Rivalistic Phenomenon?" *Journal of Post Keynesian Economics* 1: 83-99.

Jacquemin, A. 1989. "International and Multinational Strategic Behavior." *Kyklos* 42: 495-513.

Kaikati, J.G. 1989. "Europe 1992—Mind Your Strategic P's and Q's." *Sloan Management Review* (Fall): 85-92.

Kantarelis, D. and E.C.H. Veendorp. 1988. "Live and Let Live Type Behavior In a Multi-market Setting With Demand Fluctuations." *Journal of Economic Behavior and Organization* 10: 235-244.

Karnani, A. and B. Wernerfelt. 1985. "Multiple Point Competition." *Strategic Management Journal* 6: 87-96.

Kogut, B. 1985. "Designing Global Strategies." *Sloan Management Review* (Fall): 27-38.

Kogut, B. 1988. "Joint Ventures: Theoretical and Empirical Perspectives." *Strategic Management Journal* 9: 319-332.

Lambkin, M. 1988. "Order of Entry and Performance in New Markets." *Strategic Management Journal* 9: 127-140.

Lecraw, D.J. 1984. "Diversification Strategy and Performance." *Journal of Industrial Economics,* 33: 179-198.

Magee, J.F. 1989. "1992: Moves Americans Must Make." *Harvard Business Review* 67(May-June): 78-84.

Margolis, E. 1989. "Monopolistic Competition and Multiproduct Brand Names." *Journal of Business* 62: 199-209.

Mayes, D.G. 1978. "The Effects of Economic Integration on Trade." *Journal of Common Market Studies* 17: 1-25.

Nti, K.O. 1989. "More Potential Entrants May Lead to Less Competition." *Journal of Economics* 49: 47-70.

Peck, M.J. 1989. "Industrial Organization and the Gains from Europe 1992." *Brookings Papers on Economic Activity* 20: 277-299.

Pelkmans, J. 1988. "The Economic Benefits of 1992" (in Dutch). *Economisch Statistische Berichten* 73: 447-451.

Perrin-Pelletier, F. 1988. "1992: A European Market for Cars?" *Longe Range Planning* (June): 27-33.

Pinto, B. 1986. "Repeated Games and the 'Reciprocal Dumping' Model of Trade." *Journal of International Economics* 20: 357-366.

Porter, M.E. 1980. *Competitive Strategy: Techniques for Analyzing Industries and Competitors.* New York: Free Press.

Porter, M.E. 1985. *Competitive Advantage: Creating and Sustaining Superior Performance.* New York: Free Press.

Quelch, J.A. and R.D. Buzzell. 1989. "Marketing Moves Through EC Crossroads." *Sloan Management Review* (Fall): 63-74.

Reading, B. 1990. "Europe in 1992: Threat or Promise? *Business Economics* (January): 28-31.

Salop, S.C. 1979. "Strategic Entry Deterrence." *American Economic Review* 69: 335-338.

Scherer, F.M. 1980. *Industrial Market Structure and Economic Performance.* Chicago: Rand McNally.

Scott, J.T. 1982. "Multimarket Contact and Economic Performance." *Review of Economics and Statistics* 64: 368-375.

Shapiro, C. 1989. "Theories of Oligopoly Behavior." In *Handbook of Industrial Organization,* edited by R. Schmalensee and R.D. Willig. Amsterdam: North-Holland.

Sharp, J.D. 1990. "A Business Strategy For the Single European Market." *Longe Range Planning* 23: 35-42.

Slot, P.J. and M.H. van der Woude, eds. 1988. *Exploiting the Internal Market: Co-operation and Competition Toward 1992.* Deventer: Kluwer.

Smith, A. and A.J. Venables. 1988. "Completing the Internal Market in the European Community: Some Industry Simulations." *European Economic Review* 32: 1501-1525.

Stone, N. 1989. "The Globalization of Europe: An Interview with Wisse Dekker." *Harvard Business Review* 67(May-June): 90-95.

Teece, D.J. 1980. "Economies of Scope and the Scope of the Enterprise." *Journal of Economic Behavior and Organization* 1: 223-247.

Teece, D.J. 1982. "Towards an Economic Theory of the Multiproduct Firm." *Journal of Economic Behavior and Organization* 3: 39-63.

Thimm, A.L. 1988-1989. "Europe 1992—Opportunity or Threat for U.S. Business: The Case of Telecommunications." *California Management Review* (Winter): 54-75.

Venables. A.J. 1990. "The Economic Integration of Oligopolistic Markets." *European Economic Review* 34: 753-773.

Walter, N. 1989. "Implications of EC Financial Integration." *Business Economics,* 26: 18-23.

Watson, C.M. 1982. "Counter-competition Abroad to Protect Home Markets." *Harvard Business Review* 60 (January-February): 40-42.

Witteloostuijn, A. van and J.A.H. Maks. 1988. "Limburg and Europe 1992" (in Dutch). *Economisch Statistische Berichten* 73: 1090-1093.

Yip, G.S. 1982. *Barriers to Entry.* Lexington, MA: Lexington Books.

Yip, G.S. 1989. "Global Strategy: In a World of Nations?" *Sloan Management Review* (Fall): 29-41.

THE "EUROPEAN CONSUMER": GLOBALIZER OR GLOBALIZED ?

Jean-Claude Usunier

I. INTRODUCTION

"Globalization" is a controversial concept, as demonstrated in the chapter by Alan Rugman and Alain Verbeke in this book. When using T. Levitt's definition of the globalization of markets (Levitt 1983), then this concept relates primarily to demand: tastes, preferences and price-mindedness are becoming universal. It then relates to the supply side: products and services tend to become more standardized, and competition within industries reaches a worldwide scale. Finally it relates to the ways in which firms, mainly multinationals, try to appropriately design their marketing policies and control systems, to remain winners in a global competitive environment with global products for global consumers.

Globalizing then means homogenizing on a worldwide scale. The implicit assumption behind the globalization process is that all the elements above will globalize simultaneously. In practice, this does not seem self-evident. As argues Ghoshal (1987, p. 425): "'Manage globally' appears to be the latest battlecry in the world of international business." A central assumption of globalization

Research in Global Strategic Management, Volume 2, pages 57-78.
Copyright © 1991 by JAI Press Inc.
ISBN: 1-55938-277-5

is that in most cases artificial trade barriers (non-tariff, regulations, industrial standards, etc.) have kept many markets at the multi-domestic stage. If these barriers are to be removed, which is the case of Europe 1992, "insiders" which hold a large market share only in their home market, may only be protected against new entrants by culture-related natural entry barriers.

From an international marketing point of view, which favors looking at the consumer and at marketing policies across countries, the idea of globalization has been strongly challenged. It has even been renamed "the myth of globalization" (Wind 1986; Wind and Douglas 1986). Little empirical evidence has appeared on the worldwide homogenization of tastes and the preferences of a "world" consumer (Dichter 1962) for standardized low-priced/quality goods. Those interested in looking at the influence of culture on consumer behavior and the implementation of marketing policies (Usunier and Sissmann 1986; Dubois 1987) find arguments in favor of cultural resistance to the globalization process. Natural entry barriers related to culture seem to remain important in several industries (e.g., food industry, beverages, advertising, printing, and publishing, etc.).

The purpose of this paper is to show that there are neither reasons, nor evidence that the globalization process would take place on the consumer's behalf. Levitt's article remains propaganda, paradoxically even when McDonald's is opening a store in Moscow.

However, competition is globalizing (Porter 1986); therefore, companies tend to standardize their product mix. Globalization is an agenda for action, and is described in this way by several authors ("a new paradigm for international marketing" [Hampton and Buske 1987]), and practiced as such by many Multinational Corporations (MNCs). It is more a normative message than a clear movement towards a "world consumer," on which empirical evidence and positive knowledge would have gathered general agreement. It may even become an oversimplified strategic message intended at clear organizational communication in a very centralized decision and implementation framework.

This paper views the globalization process at four levels. It reviews both the conceptual literature and the empirical support at each of the following four levels:

- *Consumer behavior*—Do tastes tend to homogenize? Do cross-cultural differences in consumer behavior tend to diminish?
- *Competition*—is there a clear tendency toward global rather than regional or local competition between companies?
- *Standardization of product policies*—Are the companies' policies globalizing in terms of international marketing programs?
- *Centralization versus decentralization, organizational issues*—Are the companies' policies globalizing in terms of control systems during implementation?

We will then apply the results of this review to the fashionable theme of the "European Consumer." A relevant question is to know whether he/she even exists. Our argument is that there are some natural entry barriers related to culture that will not be affected substantially by 1992. At least this is true of the short run. The point of view that is finally developed favors the idea that there cannot be a European consumer, without some opportunity to really build a common European culture.

II. IS THE CONSUMER BECOMING GLOBAL?

There are at least three main issues under this heading:

1. What is more culture-free and more culture-bound in terms of product categories on one side and consumer behavior on the other side?
2. Is there empirical evidence showing that consumption patterns, tastes and preferences homogenize at the world level ?
3. What is the autonomy of consumers in terms of influencing the movement toward globalization?

Naturally they buy or do not buy globalized products and services. To this extent they "vote with their feet." But they also buy what is available in stores, astutely brought to them by sophisticated merchants. In this respect there could be some resistance to change, not at a product-individual buying decision level, but at a more macro-level. Here people may ask to have their "way of life" protected, especially through some kind of protectionist measures.

A. Culture Bound versus Culture-Free

It is likely that we will see larger natural entry barriers related to culture in industries that market culture-bound products or services. Consumption is tightly connected to ways of life, lifestyles, and culture. Clearly, substantial evidence, even if anecdotal in nature, shows that, especially in consumer goods, culture boundedness is strong. For instance symbolic associations linked to objects or colors may vary considerably across countries and cultures (Usunier 1985). Carlsberg had to add a third elephant to its label in Africa, because two elephants seen together are considered an ominous sign (McCornell 1971).

On the other side culture-boundedness should not be systematically overestimated. Universal appeal for quality and low-priced products exists. Culture-boundedness exists under the following conditions:

- There is a rich cultural context, around the product: shopping, buying and/or consuming it (for example, flowers, local ethnic products, etc.);
- There is an investment of consumers' cultural and often national background and identity in the act of consuming. Consuming then becomes, consciously or unconsciously, more than simply buying for utilitarian purposes (for instance the preference for "made-in" products or eating habits).

The nature of the product has naturally some influence on the level of universality of needs. Non durables appeal more to tastes, habits, and customs. Therefore they are more culture bound (Douglas and Urban 1977, Hovell and Walters 1972). Empirical evidence (Peterson Blyth Cato Associates Inc. and Cheskin Masten 1985) shows that industrial and high technology products (for instance computer hardware, machine tools, heavy equipment) are considered most appropriate for global strategies, whereas confections, food, or household cleaners, are considered less appropriate.

Last but not least, language, which is a large part of culture, remains a strong input to culture-boundedness (Carroll 1956). Whether it is for genuinely cultural products (discs, songs, TV series, newspapers, magazines, books, etc.) or for that part of any product that displays written language (packaging, brand name). In a recent empirical survey of U.S. brands as global brands, Rosen, Boddewyn and Louis (1989) have studied 650 U.S. brands, and their international scope (how many countries? age of the brand? . . .). Their general conclusion states that "despite all the talk about the internationalisation of marketing efforts, the international diffusion of US brands is actually rather limited. . . . Moreover, based on the telephone follow-up responses, one suspects that if the daunting task of doing a census of all brands were to be achieved, the finding might be that most US brands are not marketed abroad" (p. 17).

B.   Empirical Evidence of Consumers' Globalization

Eshghi and Sheth (1985) have investigated the globalization of consumption patterns with data provided by Leo Burnett Advertising Agency. They compared lifestyle-variables across four countries (France, Brazil, Japan, and the United States). Modern life-style and traditional life-style groups were contrasted in each country. Their hypothesis was that life-style contrast (inside countries) would account for more variance in consumption behavior than the national contrast (across countries). Dependent variables were six consumption variables in dichotomous form: users versus non-users, and owners versus non-owners, of: stereo equipment, soft drinks, fruit juices, alcoholic beverages, automobiles and deodorants.

Their general conclusion is the following: "The results . . . indicated that life style influences are significant in explaining consumption behavior, but the effect is not very strong. The data suggest that national and cultural influences continue to determine the consumption patterns across the four countries examined. But it must be emphasized that the inclusion of national identity as an independent variable in the analysis does not eliminate the effect of modern life style . . . , but it is not strong enough to influence consumption behavior at this time" (Eshghi and Sheth 1985, p. 144).

Zaichkowsky and Sood (1987) have looked at consumers' involvement, throughout 15 countries (Argentina, Barbados, Canada, the United States, Finland, Yugoslavia, Sweden, China, Austria, Columbia, Australia, Chile, United Kindgom, Mexico, France), for 8 "potentially global" products/services (air travel, beer, blue jeans, eating at a restaurant, hair shampoo, going to the cinema, soft drinks and stereo sets). The same questionnaire was administered to groups of approximately 50 students for each country.

The independent variables were the 15 countries, whereas the dependent variables were firstly a personal involvement inventory (PII), intended at measuring the respondents' involvement level with the goods and services, and secondly the frequency of use of each product or service over a suitable time-frame (self-reported).

The results indicate that the greatest variations in use due to country effect were found in restaurants (22 %), air travel (31 %) and hair shampoo (45 %). The largest variations in involvement due to country effect (i.e., as a variance source), were found for soft drinks (20 %) and going to the cinema (12 %). The use of stereo sets is weakly influenced by country effect (10%) and the involvement level is not related to country (1 %). It is difficult to draw simple conclusions about globalization as a whole from Zaichkowsky and Sood's findings. They nevertheless clearly show that the level of consumers' globalization is fairly different according to which product/service category is considered.

Huszagh, Fox and Day (1986) have approached empirically the consumption globalization process by addressing three questions:

1. Which foreign markets are similar ?
2. Which products exhibit potential for a global strategy by exhibiting similar acceptance rates?
3. Are there fundamental product characteristics that can explain acceptance rates?

They first clustered 21 countries, choosing 16 variables such as urbanization, consumer price index, life expectancy, or average work week. A subcluster of five countries (Belgium, the Netherlands, France, the United Kingdom, and West Germany) was finally selected as a "more homogeneous grouping in order to develop a more favorable empirical setting for a global marketing approach" (p. 35).

Penetration/consumption rates for 27 products were collected for the 5 countries, and a coefficient of variation was computed for each product's penetration rate across countries. The divergence in acceptance rates (coefficients of variation) were then plotted against three product perception scales: durable/ nondurable, household/personal, and sensory versus functional.

A rather counterintuitive result is drawn out of this experimental design: "In summary, the three plots indicate that the more nondurable/sensory/ personal a product is, the more consistent the acceptance rate. . . . However the relationships are not clearly defined." Nevertheless to some extent, these patterns do support Levitt's promise that "high touch" products are the most amenable to global marketing (Huszagh et al. 1986, p. 41).

Woods, Chiron, and Kim (1985) have looked at differences in consumer purpose for purchasing in, what they call, "three global markets," that is, the United States, Canada, and South Korea. The consumer purposes they have envisioned are: maintenance (basic necessities, convenience), enjoyment, enhancement (satisfies self image, improves appearance) and defence (protects health, avoids offending). Convenience samples of females, shoppers in shopping centers in the United States and Canada, and workers at the workplace in Korea were chosen. Respondents were asked to indicate for 16 products, one or more purposes out of 14 associated with the four major purposes indicated above.

There seems to be a larger use of products for maintenance purposes in Korea than in the U.S. or in Quebec, whereas U.S. consumers are more enjoyment, hedonist-oriented. Both Korean and Canadian female consumers are more defence oriented. Different patterns of use of products for enhancement purposes appear across the three national groups.

Finally Woods et al. (1985, p. 168) conclude that: "Taken as a whole, the findings reported here indicate that the age of universal marketing is not yet upon us. The findings do reveal that Koreans, who are members of a developing economy, are thinking about products in some of the same terms as are those in the United States and Quebec. Yet important differences are found in the reasons why they purchase products familiar to all three cultures. Women in Quebec also differ from those in the United States in the reasons they purchase products. Thus, aside from the economic differences and differences in purchasing power, cultural and psychological differences are pervasive enough to call for differences in marketing strategies."

C.   Some Arguments against the Existence of a Global Consumer

It will not be so easy to globalize consumers' motivations. International advertising people accumulate thorough experience of consumer's response to global product offers. Clark (1987), of J. Walter Thompson, argues with a large number of practical cases at hand that:

1. Consumers are not "global" themselves (national and cultural variance remains quite significant).
2. A consumer does not generally buy "global" brands or products. He does not really care whether the brand is or is not available anywhere else in the world.
3. "Since what consumers value is personal and individual, they will naturally let their individuality affect the values they place on the brands they buy. They contribute actively in this way to the persona of the brand in their own situation" (Clark 1987, p. 35).

These last two arguments are really important ones. Consumers always "construct" the identity of brands , even for "global products," and they do it on a local culture and identity base. "Global brands" might well be portfolios of local marketing assets, federated under a common lexically identical name.

From this review of literature we may conclude that the globalization process is much more "pushed" on the consumer than it is "pulled" by him. Therefore one of the main obstacles to globalization (cultural differences) tends to be neglected, although it remains significant. These natural entry barriers related to culture are influential both on consumer behavior and on the marketing environment where strategies are implemented. This explains several of the failures of overglobalizing marketing strategies. Many indicators of existing cultural differences—for example, languages, eating habits, political institutions, cultural conflicts between communities in some politically homogeneous countries, and so on—will not vanish in the near future.

Evidence is at least inconclusive about the globalization of consumption patterns. The issue of bringing convincing positivistic-oriented proofs of this process, is a difficult one. A research agenda for testing whether the consumer is globalizing or not would include such issues as: what is the pace and process of it ? In which segments ? And what are the geographically significant cultural areas ? (building on other research agendas such as Jain 1989). There are serious methodological problems involved in such a research design. These include the following:

- Which aspect of consumer behavior is studied: buying, shopping (actual behavior), lifestyle, values (psychometrics and underlying attitudes), influencing processes (in the family, word-of-mouth), and so on.
- The use of culture specific research concepts does not take into account certain differences, even when the toughest cross-cultural precautions have been taken. The concepts and theories of marketing are mostly United States culture based. Their ability to completely capture consumer behavior aspects which are specific to other cultures is questionable (Van Raaij 1978).

- Equating "national" and "cultural" variables (country = culture) hides the complex processes behind worldwide cultural homogenization. This relates to the problems of (1) clustering cultures, (2) treating subcultural variables inside countries (Hispanics in the United States for instance) and (3) questioning the relevance of geographic borders as a proxy variable for cultural borders (if any).
- Which is the relevant sample of relevant countries and relevant products, that may help prove a trend toward globalization of consumption patterns?
- Most of the studies are synchronic in design, because globalization has only recently been studied. In fact they should be diachronic and look at the pace of the homogenization process, by using at least two time periods. The best would be an annual survey, which could be regularly monitored in order to check if the process is really "en route" on the consumer' side.

The most disputable and debatable aspect of globalization is the implicit assumption that we all converge toward a "modern life-style," which more or less means "the American way of life." The true globalization of consumption patterns will occur when the "globalization-route" will cease to be a one-way traffic. Let's imagine a hypothetical example whereby U.S. consumers of pasteurized "foie gras" (made in the United States by French producers) will ask the Food and Drug Administration (FDA) to eliminate regulations, that prohibit the import of traditionally prepared French "foie gras." FDA inspectors have visited French foie gras laboratories, and refused most of them the right to export to the United States since hygienic standards were not met. If U.S. consumers really want to get global they will have to be able to import genuine french "foie gras," not pasteurized and with some innocent bacterias inside, but also with the real taste and consistency.

D. Will Consumers Resist the Globalization Process?

Another implicit assumption behind the literature on the globalization of consumption patterns is that consumers are pleased with it (low price, good quality products) and therefore do not resist the process. They might nonetheless be individuals who contradict themselves. For instance, buying P&G's Pampers for their baby, and at the same time groaning against the Americanization of society. They might resist at several levels: as citizen/voters voting in favor of protectionist governments, or as consumers/lobbyists supporting public actions (against fast food for instance). Therefore, they could possibly lobby in order to recreate some kind of artificial entry barriers which had been previously cancelled.

Global marketing can be presented as a very powerful tool to promote economic development (Cundiff and Hilger 1982). It would enhance the needs and wants of badly treated consumers who live in sellers' economies. Then marketing would favor the creation of local industries to produce consumer goods and meet their demands.

Nevertheless Belk (1988) describes a third world consumer culture, and emphasizes the hedonistic attraction to conspicuous consumption, when basic utilitarian needs have not been met. "One 'solution' under such circumstances is to sacrifice consumption expenditure in other areas . . . in order to afford payments on such luxury items as refrigerators, televisions, and automobiles . . . A reduction in food consumption in order to afford a refrigerator is more than a little ironic" (Belk 1988, p. 118).

Therefore a growing body of literature, relating to marketing and economic development, emphasizes a marketing system which "must design, deliver, and legitimize products and services that increase the material welfare of the population by promoting equity, justice, and self reliance without causing injury to tradition." (Dholakia, Sharif, and Bhandari 1988, pp. 141-142). This means clearly resisting some of the ugliest consequences of globalization, as the Nestle's infant formula problem in developing countries (Sethi and Post 1978).

There is increasing interest in the marketing literature as concerns "culture" as a variable. This has long been disfavored as compared to psychological and psycho-sociological approaches, whose implicit models were that of a universal individual (fully in line with the globalization assumptions). This is the objective of the cognitive anthropology approach (Roth and Moorman 1987), which tries to understand and explain the patterns in cognitive views of cultural phenomena, and help discover why members of a culture appear to respond to marketplace phenomena differently. This view clearly recognizes the importance of cultural group members' knowledge and beliefs on consumption patterns.

The culture of consumption is encouraging individuals to interpret their needs exclusively as needs for commodities, and people may well have a need to consume culture, which is more tailored and localized (Sherry 1987); that means consuming both local cultural products, and products as their consumption process is part of the genuine local culture. Sherry states that: "the guiding rule of such a marketing strategy, as in any ethically invasive procedure, is primum non nocere: first do not harm. In the rush to globalization, the preservation of local culture has been considered primarily as an opportunity cost. If cultural integrity is epiphenomenal to business practice, splendid; if not, social disorganization is frequently the cost of progress" (p. 189).

These are naturally two different (but complementary) issues:

1. knowing whether there are intellectual, ethical and practical reasons for protecting local cultures and consumers from the globalization of consumption patterns ; and
2. identifying if resistance mechanisms to globalization actually take place at the individual and/or social level.

This echoes Clark's (1987) arguments about false "global" consumers, buying false "global" products, with their own culture-bound motivations and purposes. It suggests that most of the resistance will be hidden to global marketers. An example will serve to illustrate this point: McDonald's in France. There is naturally a large cultural resistance against fast food and hamburgers, especially as a matter of national pride. McDonald's has succeeded beautifully with a limited number of successful outlets located in major cities of France in the very down-town places with "luxury" (high-end of the market) fast-food. Nevertheless an anti-fast-food consumer association has been established to resist the fast food movement, and nutrition specialists have clearly shown that traditional French meals (diversified food, with a one-hour length) are much better for digestion, and prevent digestive tract cancers. McDonald's is rather popular with young people, and today's children will be tomorrow's adults and parents. At the same time, it tries to establish some outlets at motorway crossings in suburbs. These outlets do not offer breakfast service: how would French people react to "Egg McMuffins?"

If a definitive lead of globalized consumption patterns over local ones, may be predicted in the very long run, the process of mixing both types of consumption patterns will be a complex one. It would be worthwhile to survey some of these processes, at a micro-level and over a long time period, in order to capture the real globalization process at work.

III.   IS THERE A GLOBALIZATION OF COMPETITION?

A.   Evidence from Macroeconomic Data

There is little doubt about the globalization of competition. Market areas do not depend mainly on consumers' preferences. Their reach is much more influenced by trade barriers, whether tariff or non-tariff (that is artificial entry barriers), and also, positively, by opportunities of economies of scale and experience effects (that is natural entry barriers unrelated to culture). Clear evidence from macroeconomic figures shows that competition is globalizing, both at a worldwide level and at a regional level.

Over the last forty years, international trade has expanded steadily and significantly quicker than the sum of the GNP's of the nations that are involved in international trade. On a common 100 basis in 1970, the index of world exports was 180 in 1984 as compared to only 154 for total world output. In addition, the index of total world exports of manufactured goods was 238 in 1984 and only 167 for the total world output of manufacturing industries (GATT 1986). This relates to a long term trend: the increase of production scales. Therefore advances in industrial productivity go along with the development of international markets and the growth of international trade. Thus, in a simple regression equation, the average worldwide industrial productivity is a very good explanatory variable for the ratio of world exports to world total output on a long period (1955-1976) (Usunier 1980).

In the very recent past the validity of this observation has not been challenged (Ludlow 1990): between 1983 and 1988, trade growth exceeds the increase in world output, generally by two or three percentage points in annual growth rate. Economic linkages between countries and therefore competition between companies continue to grow. A comparable evolution may be observed, even at an increased pace, at the regional level. Distances are less important and the move to worldwide globalization takes its roots at regional level. This is part of the message of Ohmae (1985). In Europe, the growth of intra-regional international trade has been much faster than the overall world trade growth during the sixties and seventies (Usunier 1980). Intra West Pacific trade has even grown significantly more (32% per year) from 1980 to 1988, as compared to 14 percent per year for the intra Western European trade and 16 percent per year for the intra-North American trade, for the same period (Ludlow 1990). This demonstrates a relatively slower growth as regards the globalization of competition in Europe in the beginning of the eighties.

B.   Globalization of Competition:
Evidence from Business and Industries

Many companies have been compelled to globalize their business, like Black & Decker, because of fierce competition with the Japanese power-tool maker Makita. Reasons for this are stated by *Fortune Magazine,* reporting the strategic move of Black & Decker towards globalization: "Makita is Black & Decker's first competitor with a global strategy. It doesn't care that Germans prefer high powered, heavy-duty drills, and that Yanks want everything lighter. Make a good drill at a low price, the company reasons, and it will sell from Baden-Baden to Brooklyn" (Saporito 1984, p. 24).

This trend of globalization of competition has been clearly noted, almost advertised, in business journals ("Your New Global Market: How to Win the World War for Profits and Sales," 1988). In most of these articles, which generally relate to competition dynamics in a specific industry, the vocabulary is mostly borrowed from military crafts: war, battlecries, strategic weapons, . . .

Naturally this is not to be seen so clearly in company brochures, who give a view of themselves that is more dedicated to customer service and to product/service integrity. Sumitomo Trading Company (1988) emphasizes that "the survival of the Sumitomo name for almost four centuries is testimony to the soundness of (our) business philosophy. . . . That is why we have the confidence to call ourselves Global Markets Makers. Being global implies the worldwide, long term perspective from which we build relationships and undertake business."

Michael Porter (1986) has clearly analyzed the change in patterns of international competition. At the industry level, which is the arena where competitive advantage is won or lost, there is a shift from multi-domestic industries to global ones. Porter does not consider a consumer-led globalization, but a strategic move of companies, trying to integrate activities on a worldwide basis, to gain competitive advantage vis-à-vis their competitors, at various levels of the value chain. Nevertheless this process remains conditional on the maintenance of the low barriers to trade (e.g., discussions in the GATT's framework between nation-states, not companies). Bettignies (1989) shows that the globalization of the Japanese economy is imposing some real threats to both the United States and Europe. Therefore, free trade can be maintained and expanded (to services for instance) only if a certain equilibrium of the balance of trade of nation-states permits them to maintain the environment of low trade barriers environment that favors globalization at the industry level.

IV. IS THERE A GLOBALIZATION OF INTERNATIONAL MARKETING STRATEGIES?

Competition is becoming global. Artificial entry barriers tend to disappear. But global markets remain more apparent than real, when one looks at consumption patterns (Sheth 1986). Then how to globalize products and marketing strategies under fierce pressure of the globalization of competition, but also under the constraint of consumers, who tend to resist, at least partly, the globalization movement? With respect to this question there are two major issues to be considered:

1. Standardization of marketing programs: what should be the degree of similarity in the marketing activities and policies, from one country to another?
2. Organizational issues: what is required to successfully implement a standardized marketing strategy?

A.   Standardization of International Marketing Programs: A Normative Literature

Before the classic article of Buzzell (1968), "Can You Standardize Multinational Marketing?" natural entry barriers related to culture were seen as very high, commanding adaptation to national markets and offsetting the potential advantages of scale economies. Buzzell clearly showed that with the decrease of purely artificial barriers to trade, large international companies could create natural entry barriers unrelated to culture through economies of scale. Since then there have been numerous texts telling businesspeople what to do in order to make optimal choices between standardization and adaptation of marketing policies to diversified foreign markets (for instance Ghoshal 1987;

Hamel and Pralahad 1985; Hampton and Buske 1987; Hout et al. 1982; Hovell and Walters 1972; Keegan 1969; Quelch and Hoff 1986). This literature is normative as an aim, categorizing and descriptive in nature, and oscillates between two extremes.

On the one hand globalization is seen as the new "paradigm" for international marketing (Hampton and Buske 1987). "Consumers in increasing numbers demonstrate that they are willing to sacrifice specific preferences in product features, function and design for a globally standardized product that carries a lower price" (p. 263). According to Hampton and Buske there is a shift to the global marketing paradigm because the process of adapting products to national wants and needs contradicts their global convergence.

On the other hand, globalization is seen as a necessary trend, but constrainted by the environment. The physical characteristics of a country as well as the laws relating to product standards, sales promotion, taxes, or other aspects, may affect standardization of marketing programs, especially in developing countries (Hill and Still 1984a).

In both cases, what consumers actually want in various national markets is not really considered: either differences are denied or they are treated as an external constraint. This constraint ought to be taken into account, only if ignoring critical differences in consumer behavior and marketing environment could lead to market failures (Ricks 1983).

Behind the globalization debate, there is a quite practical issue in terms of everyday life of companies: the traditional dilemma between production flexibility and marketing's tendency of customizing products to diversified needs. Factory managers would prefer to be inflexible, for low cost purposes, whereas marketing managers would favor as much tailoring to customers' needs as possible.

Developments in factory automation now allow product customization, without major cost implications (Wind 1986). New strategies have been developed to serve diversified needs, customize products, and at the same time maintain low costs as a result of economies of scale and experience effects. Modular conception of products permits the sharing of economies of scale at the components level, whereas lagged differentiation maintains a high scale of production as long as possible in the production process, and organizes cheap final customization either in the factory or in the distribution network (Stobaugh and Telesio 1983; Deher 1986).

So why maintain such a strong—"paradigm for action"— emphasis on globalization, if consumption patterns are not clearly globalizing, and if adjusting to global competition is reconcilable with tailoring products and marketing strategies to national markets?

B. Globalization as a Way to Change the Organizational Design of International Marketing Activities

The reasons for this are mostly organizational ones. MultiNational Companies that have been fast growing in the sixties and seventies on a worldwide basis achieved international expansion through allowing substantial decision autonomy to their subsidiaries in host countries. Subsidiaries were asked to replicate corporate values and organizational practices of the headquarters, but also encouraged to adjust completely to the local market (see for instance Bartlett 1983, "Procter & Gamble Europe," HBS Case 9-384-139)?

Later on, subsidiary managers have used the message of "our market is unique," to defend specific, nationally designed marketing policies. Hence they simply defended their autonomy even at the expense of sometimes rather fallacious arguments. It's probable that multinational firms needed to shift their organizational design toward more centralization in the beginning of the eighties. Headquarters wanted to have a more consistent implementation scheme as regards international marketing strategy, thus responding to the globalization of competition.

As an illustration it is worthwhile to quote what Saporito (1984, p. 26) called Black & Decker's "Gamble on Globalization": "Globalization did not go down well in Europe for one good reason: Black & Decker owned half the market on the continent, and an astounding 80 percent in the United Kingdom. European managers asked: "why tamper with success ?" But Farley (B & D's new chairman) believed that the company was treading in Europe—sales failed to grow last year—and that Makita's strategy made globalization inevitable . . . Those who don't share Farley's vision usually don't stay around long. Last year he fired all of his European managers."

My hypothesis is that the direction of causality does not go from globalization of consumption patterns (as an explanatory variable) to international marketing programs of companies (as a variable to be explained), but from real and perceived patterns of globalization of competition (exogenous) to desired changes in organizational design (re-centralization, endogenous), under constraint of, hard-to-globalize-if-not-impossible consumption patterns, and still diverging national environments (legal, distribution networks, sales promotion methods, and so on).

Most top executives probably feel intuitively that the second model is true, but for the purpose of action it may be better to express the first one. If the globalization of consumption patterns and national marketing environments is presented as an unquestionable postulate, it is much easier to "sell" the re-centralization policy inside the organization, than by presenting differences in consumption patterns as a constraint to the globalization policy. In this last case, subsidiaries' managers would have much more legitimacy when advocating their local specificities in order to resist implicitly the re-centralization policy.

If this holds true, we would predict only inconclusive empirical evidence on the question whether international marketing programs have experienced a trend toward more standardization.

Picard, Boddewyn and Soehl (1989) replicated a 1973 survey by Hansen and Boddewyn about the level of standardization of European marketing policies of United States multinational companies operating in Europe (50 usable answers in 1973, 71 in 1983). This diachronic approach reveals a mixed evolution:

- In consumers durables there was a decrease across the board in the degree of standardization of marketing policies, apart from product policy.
- In consumers nondurables, with the exception of branding, the percentage of respondents with standardized marketing policies in all E.C. countries was much higher in 1983 than 1973.
- counterintuitively, there appears to be a significant trend away from standardization of products for industrial goods. This trend toward adaptation to national contexts is true also for other elements of the marketing mix (advertising, branding, after sales service).

Hill and Still (1984a) examined international marketing policies of 19 Multinationals that sell to LDC markets. Out of 2,200 products sold by the 61 subsidiaries in the sample, 1,200 had originated either in the US or the United Kingdom. Their findings show that " . . . nearly seven changes (product adaptation) out of ten (69.4%) are marketing oriented . . . for most products, the process of managing product adaptation is critical" (p. 94). They also found that greater product adaptation was required from MultiNational Companies in rural areas than in urban areas in the LDCs (Hill and Still 1984b).

With the purpose of examining the level of advertising standardization, Ryans and Ratz (1987) exploited 34 usable responses of international advertising/marketing managers, who were participants to an international advertising conference. They self reported on their company's practices, in the framework of a questionnaire survey. Ryans and Ratz's findings indicate relatively high levels of advertising standardization, for campaign themes, creative execution, and media execution. Headquarters' managers only were interviewed, and their quantitative report on a scale may be rather far away from actual local decisions as advocated by Clark (1987). Ryans and Ratz (1987, p. 157) provide a particular interpretation of these findings: "It is interesting to observe , however, that the majority of respondents thought that usage situations for their products were very similar worldwide . . . [an] explanation is that international advertising managers have adopted the position of the globalists and assume it holds true for their products."

V.   THE EUROPEAN CONSUMER: GLOBALIZED?

At this point it has become quite clear that globalization is much more a process which takes place at the competition level (where artificial entry barriers are progressively replaced by natural entry barriers related to scale and experience) than at the consumer behavior and marketing environments levels ,where natural entry barriers related to culture will diminish more slowly and only in the long run. We will now apply this knowledge to an area that shows surprisingly high cultural diversity for a rather small geographic surface: Europe.

A.   Is There a European Consumer?

Almost thirty years ago Fournis (1962) argued that there cannot be such an individual as a "European consumer" since customs and traditions tend to persist. European countries, and cultures, are deeply rooted in the past. Furthermore, a long history of wars and conflicts has maintained strong feelings of national identity.

Diverging economic performance levels between northern and southern Europe have fed sharp income per capita differences, which, when added to differences in behavior among European consumers have been found to be discouraging for globalization (Boddewyn 1981). Naturally, European cultures share some common cultural values: the majority of them share a set of values that differentiates themselves from oriental cultures, especially as regards major events of life (birth, marriage, death). Patterns of showing emotions for instance differ widely between European and Asians; and where Orientals tend to privilege group harmony, Europeans tend to favor self-esteem and respect of individuals (Valette-Florence 1990).

Nevertheless this apparent cultural homogeneity of Europe, when compared to Asia, ceases to be so clear when we look at cultural variance inside Europe. Stoetzel (1983), who has observed public opinion polls in Europe throughout years ("Eurobarometer"), shows that there are more "European Cultures" than just one "European culture" as such. Family relation patterns, religion, every day life organisation between meals, social, family and business life tend to be rather heterogeneous.

There are huge differences in patterns of household expenditures across EC countries. For instance in 1982, United Kingdom households spent 14.7 percent of their budget on food, West Germany 14.6 percent, Portugal 37 percent, and Greece 35.6 percent. The average EC figure at the same time was 20.5 percent. Italian people consumed 152 kg per year of vegetables, the French 108 kg, and the Germans only 81. French people consume 20.9 kg per year of cheese as compared to 4.7 for the Spanish and 6.3 for British (source: OECD, year 1985). Many other examples could be given.

Marketing strategies for culture-bound products will still need substantial tailoring to each national market, or to groups of countries, even after 1992. Beer for instance is subject to differences in national tastes, in terms of being more or less bitter, foamy, bubbly, sugary, alcoholized, and according to other taste attributes. Even companies like Heineken, which is the leader for beer in Europe will tailor its products and marketing policies (distribution systems for beer also widely differ in Europe) even after 1992. Whitelock (1987) shows that standard sizes for pillow-cases differ in the various European national markets: 60x75 cm in United Kingdom, 65x65 cm in France, 60x70 cm in the Netherlands and 80x80 cm in West Germany. He interviewed textile companies that all agreed on the necessity to adapt sizes, even after 1992. Nivea Skin care cream, produced by the German Multinational Company Beiersdorff (BDF) has a leading edge in each national market in Europe. Nevertheless its consistency has to be changed and its formula has to be adapted according to its sale in Northern Europe or in Southern Europe, and 1992 will not change it (Mourier and Burgaud 1989).

B.   Europe 1992 Agenda: Globalizing Competition

From the Treaty of Rome to the Single European Act, the main European treaties have always had one main focus: to increase the size of fragmented national European markets. Custom duties have been abolished between the six founding member-states in July 1968. But the pace of integration has slowed down with the entry of new members.

Increased worldwide competition, especially coming from the Japanese and South-East Asian nations, resulted in an enhancement of awareness about the necessity to really build a large internal market (EC's White Paper, completing the internal market 1985).

The logic that lies behind the 1992 agenda, which is an appendix of the 1985 EC's White Paper, is clearly presented by the authors of the survey on the cost of non-Europe (Cecchini 1988, p. xx underlined by us): "For business and government, the two main actors, the road to market integration will be paved with tough adjustments, and the need for new strategies. For business, removing protective barriers creates a permanent opportunity, but signals a definitive end to national soft options. . . . profits which derive from cashing in on monopoly or protected positions will tend to be squeezed. The situation will be one of constant competitive renewal."

C.   Does the European Consumer Need a European Culture?

An implicit, but extremely strong assumption as concerns the treaties building the European Community is the respect of national cultures and identities. A very basic element of this is language. The original six countries had four different languages, the actual twelve have ten languages. One of them, Gaelic the national original language of Ireland is almost no longer in use in its very home country. Despite the "Tower of Babel" aspect of this incredible situation and the communication difficulties that arise from it, an army of more than 3,000 full time translators are employed in EC staffs.

The issue of a common language for Europe has never been addressed, at least publicly. It is a taboo, even an absolute taboo. In the Single European Act of 1987, the article 34 states that: "This act (is) drawn up in a single original in the Danish, Dutch, English, French, German, Greek, Irish, Italian, Portuguese and Spanish languages, the texts in each of these languages being equally authentic" (EC Official Publications, 1987, p. 574).

Language, according to linguistic anthropologists (Carroll 1956), has a strong influence on our world views, and partly shapes our individual and collective behavior. Even if this assumption in its strongest version (called the Whorfian Hypothesis) has been challenged by linguists, it remains a useful metaphor to illustrate its influence on behaviors. Europeans are committed to their language as a social and cultural asset. In most European countries there is much stronger emphasis than in the United States on grammatical appropriateness, and correct pronunciation, which is often a social pre-requisite to a number of posts.

One of the main proponents of the tabooing of the common European language issue is France. There is great pride in France about the French language. It is recognized as one of the two official languages of the United Nations, on a par-basis with English. French people have a rather defensive attitude against English, and French authorities have regularly issued during the last fifteen years official decrees prohibiting the use of English words, especially business words, in French texts (Usunier 1990).

French fears are very typical of resistance to globalization, because it is believed that through consumption patterns the whole French society and culture could be "Americanized." French people are fascinated by the American Way of Life as an exotic item. Many French, including political people, would be horrified to have it "at home." If the fears are, perhaps, legitimate, the defensive measures are certainly inadequate.

The example of Northern European countries shows that it is quite feasible to have a double-language culture. One part is the local one; it corresponds to ways of life, consumption patterns, which are not to be globalized. The other part is in English; it corresponds to international life-style and globalized consumption patterns. Television channels in English like Sky Channel and Super Channel can be seen in any Northern European countries. This is not the case in France, where the development of cable-television has been strongly limited. A few years ago the number of householders with cable television in France was half that of Ireland, a country with 15 times less population, and a much lower per capita purchasing power.

Most people believe that satellite TV in Europe, and other new communication technologies will contribute to standardize the profile of the European Consumer (Valette-Florence 1990; Usunier and Sissmann 1986). But it will be achieved in much better conditions if there is a common language to build a common European culture, sustaining new European consumption patterns.

VI. CONCLUDING REMARKS

At a micro-level companies should be very cautions about globalizing marketing strategies in Europe. Competition is rapidly globalizing, but not the consumers and the marketing environments. Therefore, for large companies willing to create scale advantages across European markets in culture-bound industries, it is advisable to proceed through acquisition of local companies that have culture-related national business experience.

The process of 1992 will be quite lengthy and European companies, whether they are regional headquarters of a non-Europe-based multinational, or a European multinational firm, or large national firms, will be highly instrumental in developing the new European culture. Those "insiders" have a capacity to create both natural entry barriers related to scale and natural entry barriers related to culture. They first need to respect that part of each local European culture which is compulsory for a marketer. The knowledge and experience of it will be an asset, inasmuch as it is costly to acquire for any new potential entrant. Then, at a macro level, their influence will be twofold:

1. They will assist in building a European management style and work ethics; and
2. They will aid in the development of a European consumer culture.

REFERENCES

Bartlett, C. 1983. "Procter & Gamble Europe: Vizir Launch." *Harvard Business School Case* 9 384-139.

Belk, R. 1988. "Third world consumer culture." Pp. 103-127 in *Marketing and Development : Toward Broader Dimensions,* edited by E. Kumcu and A. Fuat Firat. Greenwich, CT: JAI Press.

Bettignies, H. De. 1989. "The Globalization of the Japanese Economy: Implications for Europe and the United States." IBEAR, University of Southern California.

Boddewyn, J.J. 1981. "Comparative Marketing: The First Twenty-Five Years." *Journal of International Business Studies* 12 (Spring-Summer): 61-79.

Buzzell, R.D. 1968. "Can You Standardize Multinational marketing?" *Harvard Business Review* (November-December): 102-113.

Carroll, J.B. 1956. *Language, Thought and Reality, Selected Writings of Benjamin Lee Whorf.* Edited by John B. Carroll, Cambridge, MA: The M.I.T. Press.

Cecchini, P. 1988. *The European Challenge 1992*. Aldershot: Wildwood House.

Clark, H.F. Jr. 1987. "Consumer and Corporate Values: Yet Another View on Global Marketing." *International Journal of Advertising* 6:29-42.

Commission of the European Communities. 1985. *White Paper on Completing the Internal Market*. Brussels: Commission of the European Communities.

Cundiff, E.W., and M.T. Hilger. 1982. "The Consumption Function: Marketing's Role in Economic Development." *Management Decision* 20(4): 36-45.

Deher, O. 1986. "Quelques Facteurs-clés de Succès Pour la Politique de Produits de L'entreprise Exportatrice: Les Liens Entre Marketing and Production." *Recherche and Applications en Marketing* 1(3): 55-74.

Dholakia, R.R., M. Sharif, and L. Bhandari. 1988. "Consumption in the Third World: Challenges For Marketing and Economic Development." Pp. 129-147 in *Marketing and Development: Toward Broader Dimensions*, edited by E. Kumcu and A. Fiat Firat. Greenwich, CT: JAI Press.

Dichter, E. 1962. "The World Consumer." *Harvard Business Review* 40(4): 113-122.

Douglas, S.P., and C.D. Urban. 1977. "Life-Style Analysis to Profile Women in International Markets." *Journal of Marketing* 41 (July), 46-54.

Dubois, B. 1987. "Culture and Marketing." *Recherche et Applications en Marketing* 2(3): 37-64.

Eshghi, A., and J.N. Sheth. 1985. "The Globalization of Consumption Patterns: An Empirical Investigation." In *Global Perspectives in Marketing*, edited by E. Kayhak. New York: Praeger.

European Communities. 1987. *Treaties Establishing the European Commmunities*. Luxembourg: Office for Official Publications of the European Communities.

Fournis, Y. 1962. "The Markets of Europe or the European Market." *Business Horizons* 5 (Winter): 77-83.

G.A.T.T. 1986. *Le Commerce International en 1985-1986*. Genève: GATT.

Ghoshal, S. 1987. "Global Strategy : An Organizing Framework." *Strategic Management Journal* 8: 425-440.

Hamel, G., and C.K. Prahalad. 1985. "Do You Really Have a Global Strategy?" *Harvard Business Review* 63 (July-August): 139-148.

Hampton, G.M., and E. Buske. 1987. "The Global Marketing Perspective." Pp. 259-277 in *Advances in International Marketing*, edited by S. T. Cavusgil. Greenwich, CT: JAI Press.

Hansen, D.M. and J.J. Boddewyn. 1976. *American Marketing in the European Common Market 1963-1973* (Report No. 76-107). Cambridge, MA: Marketing Science Institute.

Hill, J.S., and R.R. Still. 1984a. "Adapting Products to L.D.C. Tastes." *Harvard Business Review* (March-April): 92-101.

Hill, J.S., and R.R. Still. 1984b. "Effects of Urbanization on Multinational Product Planning: Markets in L.D.C.s." *Columbia Journal of World Business* 19 (Summer): 62-67.

Hout, T., M.E. Porter, and E. Rudden. 1982. "How Global Companies Win Out." *Harvard Business Review* 60 (September-October): 98-105.

Hovell, P.J. and P.G.P. Walters. 1972. "International Marketing Presentations: Some Options." *European Journal of Marketing* 6(2):69-79.

Huszagh, S.M., R.J. Fox, and E. Day. 1986. "Global Marketing: An Empirical Investigation." *Columbia Journal of World Business,* 10(4):31-43.

Jain, S.C. 1989. "Standardization of International Marketing Strategy: Some Research Hypotheses." *Journal of Marketing* 53 (January):70-79.

Keegan, W.J. 1969. "Multinational Product Planning: Strategic Alternatives." *Journal of Marketing* 33 (January):58-62.

Levitt, T. 1983. "The Globalization of Markets." *Harvard Business Review* 61 (May-June): 92-102.

Ludlow, P.W. 1990. "Global Challenges of the 1990s: Future of the International Trading System." *Economic Impact,* pp. 4-10.

McCornell, J.D. 1971. "The Economics of Behavioral Factors in the Mmultinational Corporation." P. 260 in *Combined Proceedings of the American Marketing Association,* edited by F.E. Allvine.

Mourier, P. and D. Burgaud. 1989. *Euromarketing.* Paris: Les Editions d'Organisation.

Ohmae, K. 1985. *Triad Power: The Coming Shape of Global Competition.* New-York: The Free Press.

Peterson, B., Cato Associates, Inc., and C. Masten. 1985. "Survey on Global Brands and Global Marketing." *Empirical Report.* New-York.

Picard, J., J.J. Boddewyn, and R. Soehl. 1989. "U.S. Marketing Policies in the European Economic Community: A Longitudinal Study, 1973-1983." Pp. 551-579 in *Dynamics of International Business,* edited by R. Luostarinen. Proceedings of the 15th Annual Conference of the EIBA, Helsinki.

Porter, M.E. 1986. "Changing Patterns of International Competition." *California Management Review* 28, (2), (Winter): 9-39.

Quelch, J.A. and E.J. Hoff. 1986. "Customizing Global Marketing." *Harvard Business Review* 64 (May-June):59-68.

Ricks, D.A. 1983. *Big Business Blunders: Mistakes in Multinational Marketing.* Homewood, IL: Dow Jones-Irwin.

Rosen, B.N., J.J. Boddewyn, and E.A. Louis. 1989. "US Brands Abroad: An Empirical Study of Global Branding." *International Marketing Review* 6(1):7-19.

Roth, M.S., and C. Moorman. 1988. "The Cultural Content of Cognition and the Cognitive Content of Culture: Implications for Consumer Research. Pp. 403-410 in *Advances in Consumer Research,* Vol. 15, edited by M. J. Houston. Provo, UT: Association For Consumer Research.

Ryans, J.K., and D.G. Ratz. 1987. "Advertising Standardization, A re-examination." *International Journal of Advertising* 6:145-158.

Saporito, B. 1984. "Black & Decker's Gamble on Globalization." *Fortune Magazine* (May 24), p. 32.

Sethi, S.P. and J.E. Post. 1978. "Infant Formula Marketing in Less Developed Countries: An Analysis of Secondary Effect." In *AMA Educators Proceedings,* edited by S.C. Jain. Chicago: American Marketing Association.

Sherry, J.F. 1987. "Cultural Propriety in a Global Marketplace." In *Philosophical and Radical Thought in Marketing,* edited by A. F. Firat, N. Dholaki, and R.P. Bagozzi. Lexington, MA: Lexington Books.

Sheth J.N. 1986. "Global Markets or Global Competition?" *Journal of Consumer Marketing* 3 (Spring): 9-11.

Stobaugh, R., and P. Telesio. 1983. "Assortir la politique de fabrication à la stratégie des produits." *Harvard-L'Expansion,* (été):77-85.

Stoetzel, J. 1983. *Les Valeurs du temps Présent: Une Enquête Européenne.* Paris: PUF.

Sumitomo Corporation. 1988. *Global Market Makers. Sumitomo Shoji Kaisha Ltd, Chiyoda-ku, Tokyo.*

Usunier, J.C. 1980. "Les lois de déformation des réseaux du commerce international." Thèse de Doctorat d'Etat, Université de Paris II.

Usunier, J.C. 1985. "Adaptation standardisation internationale des produits : Une tentative de synthèse." Actes de la Conférence Annuelle de l'Association Française de Marketing, Le Touquet.

Usunier, J.C., and P. Sissmann. 1986. "L'Interculturel au service du marketing." *Harvard-L'Expansion,* 40primtenps:80-92.

Usunier, J.C. 1990. "French International Business Education: A Pessimistic View." *European Management Journal* 8(3):388-393.

Valette-Florence, P. 1990. "The European Consumer: Myths and Realities." Chapter 10 in *Europe 1992 and Beyond: Challenges and Dangers for Business,* edited by S. Makridokis. San Francisco, CA: Jossey-Bass.

Van Raaij, W.F. 1978. "Cross-Cultural Methodology as a Case of Construct Validity." Pp. 693-701 in *Advances in Consumer Research,* Vol. 5, edited by M.K. Hunt. Ann Arbor, MI: Association For Consumer Research.

Whitelock, J.M. 1987. "Global Marketing and the Case for International Product Standardization." *European Journal of Marketing* 12(9).

Wind, Y. 1986. "The Myth of Globalization." *Journal of Consumer Marketing* 3(Spring):23-26.

Wind, Y., and S.P. Douglas. 1986. *Le Mythe de la Globalisation. Recherche et Applications en Marketing,* Vol. 1, no. 3.

Woods, W., E.J. Chéron, and D.H. Kim. 1985. "Strategic Implications of Differences in Consumer Purposes in Three Global Markets." Pp. 155-170 in *Global Perspectives in Marketing,* edited by E. Kaynak. New-York: Praeger.

"Your New Global Market: How to Win the World War for Profit and Sales." 1988. *Fortune Magazine* (March 14).

Zaichkowsky, J.L., and J.H. Sood. 1988. "A Global Llook at Cconsumer Involvement and Use of Products." *International Marketing Review* 6(1):20-33.

PART II

A SECTORAL APPROACH TO GLOBAL COMPETITION AND THE EUROPEAN COMMUNITY

THE RESTRUCTURING OF EUROPEAN
MANUFACTURING INDUSTRIES

Leo Sleuwaegen

I. INTRODUCTION

A.   A Renewed European Action Plan

With the Treaty of Rome in 1957, six Western European countries—
France, West Germany, Italy, the Netherlands, Belgium and Luxembourg
—set out to create a common market known as the European Economic
Community (EEC). The Treaty was designed to create a single market for
the free movement of goods, services, capital, and individuals. However,
despite the elimination of intra-European custom tariffs and the completion
of a common external tariff by the late sixties and the creation of the European
Monetary System in 1979, the European Community (EC), in the meantime
enlarged with the United Kingdom, Ireland, Denmark, Greece, Spain, and
Portugal, remained a fragmented market. In June 1985, the Commission of
the European Community published proposals to create a Single European
Market to strengthen the Community's competitiveness in world markets. The
resulting document was entitled "White Paper on Completing the Internal

Research in Global Strategic Management, Volume 2, pages 81-102.

Market." The proposals called for 300 regulatory changes leading to a complete elimination of trade barriers and to the free movement of goods, services, capital, and people.

To achieve its goals, the Commission identified three kinds of barriers to be eliminated:

1. *Physical barriers,* through the gradual elimination of all remaining customs formalities that hinder the movement of goods and individuals. These barriers impose costs on industries by causing delays, by increasing formalities, paperwork, transportation and handling charges.
2. *Technical barriers* to be minimized through mutual recognition or harmonization. Such would ease distortions in the competitive process in the form of different technical regulations, and norms for goods and services and labor in Member States. Goods and services approved for sale in any Member State, will become freely marketable throughout the Community.
3. *Fiscal barriers* through the harmonization of value-added tax rates and excise duties. Harmonization of taxes is expected to improve the competitive allocation process within Europe.

Rapid execution of the White Paper proposals became possible by the signing of the Single European Act in July 1987, which facilitated the decision making procedures and introduced better cooperation between the Commission, the Council and the European Parliament. Complementary to the White Paper proposals, the Single European Act commits Member States to addressing important wider issues, involving: economic and monetary policy cooperation (European Monetary Union), social policy, economic and social cohesion in the EC, technological development, environmental protection, and issues concerning foreign policy. In addition to these wider issues, pressure for reforms to the EC's existing Competition Policy (mergers and acquisitions) has arisen as an essential component of a completed internal market.

B.   The Benefits and Major Economic Effects
of the Single Market

The Cecchini report on the "Cost of Non-Europe" presented evidence on the direct effect of improved efficiency following the removal of protective measures by different national governments, and estimated the indirect effects from further EC-market integration and increased competition for several industries.

Following the logic developed in the Cecchini-report, implementation of the White Paper proposals are expected to result in a lowering of consumer prices and an increase in product choice and quality, leading to substantial increases in consumer surplus and overall gains in net economic welfare for the whole Community. A schematic representation of the different effects from market integration is represented in Figure 1. Following the arrows in Figure 1, it is expected that, in the first round, the removal of non-tariff barriers will lead to direct cost reductions which will lower prices, and in turn, will lead to increased demand for the products and services concerned. Increasing demand allows producers to take advantage of unexploited scale- and experience economies. These improved cost conditions will result in further price reductions and subsequent market enlargements.

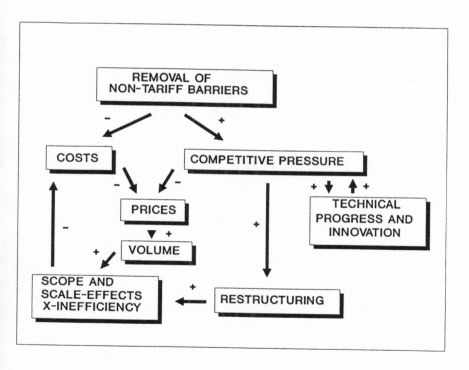

Source: The Cost of Non-Europe, EC Commission (1988)

Figure 1. Market Integration Effects

Equally important, the removal of remaining non-tariff barriers will bring about more intense competition among European companies, causing further price reductions and important industrial restructuring. More competition will eliminate X-inefficiency, resulting from the use of inferior technologies or the non-optimal use of inputs. Within this process, industry structure will change such that fuller exploitation of scale and experience economies might be realized. Improved organizations in a wider and more competitive market are expected to stimulate the development of new products and production processes, which in turn, will lead to further efficiency gains and subsequent market enlargements.

The reasoning developed at the micro economic level has been used in macro econometric simulations to assess longer term and feedback effects on the European economy. It was estimated that changes at the microeconomic level, over a period of six years, would raise Community GDP by 4.5 percent, reduce average price levels by 6.1 percent and increase employment by 1.8 million, compared to a scenario without the 1992 program.

The effects of the 1992 program are not evenly spread across industries. In a pioneering effort to measure the impact on the Community's manufacturing industries, Buigues and Ilzkovitz (1988) estimated that industries most likely to be affected by the 1992 proposals comprise about half of all value-added generated in EC manufacturing industries. According to their methodology, industries are considered particularly sensitive to the 1992 program if these industries are still characterized by high non-tariff barriers to trade. Likewise, industries with moderate non-tariff barriers are considered sensitive if they are characterized by substantial economies of scale or display a price dispersion across Member States of more than 10 percent. Industries with high non-tariff barriers are basically industries that depend strongly on national public procurement or are sheltered by different national regulations or norms that impede intra-Community trade. In industries where non-tariff barriers are moderate, administrative controls, national regulations or norms give rise to supplementary costs without fully impeding trade. The selection procedure resulted in the identification of 40 industries—out of a total of 120 (three-digit) NACE manufacturing industries—which are expected to be particularly affected by the completion of the internal market. According to the different criteria used, and in combination with the intra-European import penetration ratio (EC imports/ EC consumption) Buigues and Ilzkovitz further subdivide the 40 sensitive industries into four groups. Table 1 summarizes the basic features of the four groups. The list with all the industries is given in the Appendix.

Table 1.   Structural Characteristics of the Groups
Sensitive to the Completion of the Internal Market

Average in Each Group[a]	Group 1	Group 2	Group 3	Group 4	Non-sensitive Industries
Level of non-tariff barriers	high	high	high	mod	low-moderate
Intra-EC import penetration ratio	31.9	7.9	11.2	35.4	18.5
Price dispersion	8.9	25.3	9.7	13.8	12.6
Share of firms with fewer than 20 employees in the industry's turnover	5.0	4.6	4.7	7.0	10.4
Growth in demand between 1980 and 1985	80.4	48.3	42.6	33.2	33.6
Ratio of intra-EC to extra-EC imports	0.9	4.5	2.2	1.9	3.7

Note: [a]Average weighted by the share of output of the industries in each group.
Source: EC Commission services, as reproduced in Buigues and Ilzkovitz (1988).

According to the distinctive characteristics of each of the four groups, the consequences of the completion of the internal market turn out to be very different. Group 1 comprises industries (information technology, office automation, telecommunications, medical equipment), which are associated with public procurement and are industries in which demand is growing strongly. Many products have a high technology content. Most industries are characterized by global competition, which explains the relatively low level of price dispersion in these industries (8.9%). Because of unnatural market fragmentation, European companies cannot operate at efficient, large scales, which put them at a disadvantage vis-à-vis American or Japanese competitors. The enlargement of the market, aided by several coordination programs, should increase the technical efficiency of European firms due to greater exploitation of economies of scale and should foster technological cooperation between European firms to strengthen their competitiveness.

Group 2 comprises more traditional industries (electric boilers, railway equipment, pharmaceutical products) characterized by high non-tariff barriers with little openness to intra-EC as well as extra-EC trade. Markets are highly fragmented with considerable price dispersion among Members States. Market integration with liberalization of public procurement, in particular, will have a very marked impact on these industries. It is expected that these industries will face important restructurings (mergers, concentrations, closure of non-productive sites in the least competitive countries). As a result, there will be less excess capacity, better exploitation of scale economies, and substantial growth in EC-trade coupled with a substantial narrowing of price dispersion.

Group 3 comprises industries (shipbuilding, electrical and electronic equipment, certain food-processing activities) that are structurally similar to those of group 2, except that price dispersion is much smaller. Intra-EC trade is more developed in these industries, but in some of these industries (shipbuilding, electrical engineering) extra-EC trade plays a more important role. Consequently, much of what will happen here will very much depend on the Community's external trade policy. Restructurings of these industries are happening at a global level. European integration will strengthen the competitive basis of European companies and help to accelerate their adjustment toward global competition.

Group 4 comprises industries characterized by moderate non-tariff barriers, such as different national standards and administrative controls, which cause extra-cost for European suppliers. The industries of this group are already exposed to international competition, but still display a high degree of price dispersion among Member States. Many products in this group are consumer goods (radios, televisions, domestic electrical appliances, clothing, footwear, toys). Further liberalization of trade is expected to improve efficiency in manufacturing, but other changes especially in distribution will decrease price differences between Member States. Improved coordination will stimulate efficiency in the development and marketing of these products. This may be coupled with important intra-firm restructuring of activities.

II. THEORETICAL PERSPECTIVES ON INDUSTRIAL RESTRUCTURING IN EUROPE

A. Within Industries

Within the process of change companies hitherto protected by non-tariff barriers become suddenly confronted with a new competitive environment. The elimination of the different non-tariff barriers and the adjustments that are taking place make the environment very unstable and create a lot of uncertainty, which, by themselves, are important sources of more intense competition. For industries that have previously enjoyed national protection, the relevant arena of competition becomes suddenly enlarged to all possible potential interactions of national and international competitors.

At the same time, the transition from a fragmented to a single market (Figure 2) will entail fewer possibilities for firms to differentiate prices of their products following national differences. The widening of the internal market will also result in a larger scope to differentiate products with more varieties of products or services, aimed at customers segments within the larger EC market. Unwanted product differentiation, based on national market protection, will become less likely. A single market with less "national" adaptations of products will also render R&D investments more effective, and improve the coordination of marketing and distribution efforts across the borders of EC Member States. Improved coordination possibilities and the drive for a better exploitation of scale economies within Europe will change the configuration of activities, such that certain sub-activities will become more concentrated in some Member States. This concentration process goes together with the development of more efficient logistics systems and the deregulation of transportation and telecommunications in Europe.

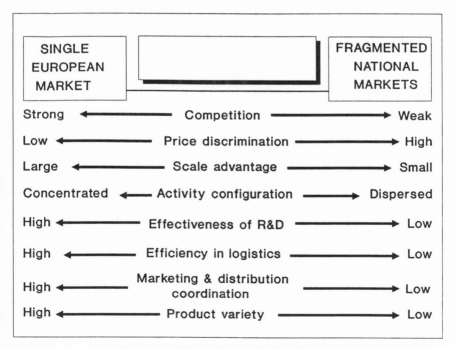

Figure 2. Major Strategic Implications

Efficiency and successful product differentiation will occupy key roles in the newly formulated strategies. In many cases, efficiency gains may result from a better use of scale and scope advantages within an enlarged single market. Scope advantages refer to the economies that come about by operating in several product and/or geographical markets. As an example, R&D programs can be undertaken more effectively when a firm has more direct results and fewer average costs from implementing the innovations in several geographic markets. Scale-economies, on the other hand, lead to lower average cost as a result of larger production volumes per time unit. In a dynamic context, average cost may decline because of learning or experience economies. The more experience a company gains, reflected in cumulative production over time, the more it may improve production or distribution processes, and increase efficiency over time. It follows that when these scale or scope advantages can be coupled with more efficient and less restricted distribution and market penetration possibilities through the removal of the remaining barriers within the EC, larger companies or integrated networks of companies will develop. The advantages will be particularly great for multinational firms or, better, "multiregional" firms that have spread their activities over the different Member States of the EC. Less adaptation to local markets and more efficiency in sourcing and distribution, with less inventory and logistics costs, will help these companies to benefit more from learning, scale and scope economies. This process is expected to substantially improve the global competitive position of those European firms. Typical uni-national firms will find less protected national markets, and can thus no longer differentiate their products according to, for instance, strict natural regulations or preferential treatment from national governments. Instead of focusing on national markets, these companies will have to develop products that find enough customers in a wider European market or a global market.

The arguments can be illustrated in matrix Figure 3 that combines two crucial dimensions or characteristic features of an industrial environment: the existence of S-advantages (scope-scale-network advantages) and the degree of possible product differentiation (quality, advertising, specific production-distribution technologies). These basic features largely determine the structure of the industry.

Within these competitive environments, the combination of the degree of possible product differentiation with varying S-advantages often results in typical competitive strategies (focus, global differentiation, take, volume). This, by no means, implies that every company has to adopt the same strategy in the industry. Successful strategies are to be based on company capacities, which may guide the company in directions opposite to the typically prevailing strategies in the industry. Moreover, in many industries enough room exists for different sustainable strategies, so that strategic groups of companies within the industry emerge (cf. Porter 1980; De Bondt, Sleuwaegen, and Veugelers 1988).

S-advantages (Scale-, Scope, Network-advantages)

typical strategy	weak	strong

high	**_FOCUS_**
	
	- specialised goods and
	  and services (e.g. housing
	  construction, software)
	- sheltered national companies
	  (e.g. telecommunication)
	
	1992 : Drive to exploit scale
	and scope advantages
	after 1992
		GLOBAL DIFFERENTIATION
		
		- multinationals
		  (e.g. car industry, pharmaceut.)
		- scale and scope advantages
		
		1992 : growth and increased efficiency
		due to better distribution, marketing
		opportunities and less national
		adaptation requirements

low	**_TAKE_**
	
	- widely available technology
	- industries dominated by small
	  or medium siezed companies
	  (e.g. wood processing)
	
	1992 : No drastic changes
	to be expected
		VOLUME
		
		- strong scale- and experience advantages.
		- strong price competition
		  (e.g. steel, semi-conductors)
		
		1992 : higher efficiency and export
		opportunities. Much will depend on the
		external trade policy of the EC

	Fragmented	Concentrated

Product-
differentiation
possibilities

Industry-structure
(1988)

Figure 3.   Competitive Strategy Matrix Impact of 1992

The different competitive environments in Figure 3 imply that, even without considering the possible existence of different strategic groups within an industry, there will not be a single dominant or typical strategy after 1992 when all non-tariff barriers are removed. Following the competitive environments for the different industries after 1992, the more typical strategies represented in Figure 3 are:

A. With few differentiation possibilities:
- *volume strategies:* aimed at reaping full benefits from mass-production when scale and experience advantages are present (e.g., steel, electronic components);
- *take strategies:* in many cases, the company is not actively engaged in developing technology, but "takes" the technology from other industries, embodied in specific machinery and equipment. In most cases these technologies are not characterized by significant economies of scale (e.g., wood processing industries).

B.   With strong differentiation possibilities:
   • *global differentiation:*   strategies aimed at developing differentiated
     products or services for global markets. Scale as well as (geographic)
     scope advantages play a very important role in different parts of the
     value-chain: production, distribution, R&D, marketing (e.g., the car
     industry);
   • *focus strategies:*   the developing and marketing of specific products
     or services following differences in customer needs for smaller market
     segments, often regional or national markets (e.g., residual housing
     construction).

Industries with important S-advantages often lead to the development of
large globally oriented companies, and thus, to concentrated industries.
However, some of these S-advantages, especially with respect to R&D
operations, seem to be increasingly realized through partnerships in flexible
networks of independent companies.

Typical focus strategies emerge in regional markets with specific customer
needs and in those industries in which economies of scale are rapidly exhausted,
such as is the case for residential housing construction. However, while the
foregoing industry among others will continue to provide a natural basis for
focus strategies after 1992, many non-tariff barriers in Europe have
"unnaturally" fragmented industries and have given rise to specific competitive
environments in which companies have adopted focus strategies designed to
capture the maximum of returns in the sheltered national market, in spite of
the strong presence of scale economies. Many of those companies act as quasi-
monopolists for products or services in their national market protected through
strong national regulations or discriminating government procurement
policies. Telecommunication equipment can serve as a typical example.
Following market integration, these focus-companies will be forced to expand
or work together with other European or foreign groups and to restructure
and rationalize their operations in order to enjoy scale and scope advantages.
When consumer needs in an integrated single market favor standardized
products or services, the restructured companies will be driven to volume
strategies. If, on the other hand, market integration provides enough room
for successful differentiation, scale and scope advantages will have to be
exploited in an extended geographic network of interrelated activities.
Companies that do not succeed in this adjustment, are doomed to disappear
or to be taken over by more successful foreign groups.

For European multinational corporations with global differentiation
strategies, important gains can be realized in R&D, production, distribution
and logistics. But also in industries where large volume economies are
important, as is the case for electronic components, European companies are
expected to become more competitive vis-à-vis non-EC rivals. For these

industries, much will depend on the external trade policy of the Community. Clearly, a blunt protectionistic attitude leading to a fortress Europe cannot be proposed as a sustainable solution.

For many small and medium-sized companies in regional markets characterized by few differentiation possibilities and little scale economies, the effects of Europe 1992 will be more of an indirect nature. Growing markets and more efficient sourcing will play a significant role in a longer term perspective.

B.   Across Regions

Equally important to analyze is the geographical restructuring following market integration. More intense competition coupled with free trade and free movements of all factors of production necessitate a search for more optimal locations for production and for distribution in Europe. Each company has to investigate to what extent its competitive position is based on, or benefits from, location conditions in the regions where the company operates. Some "specific" competitive advantages are derived from superior technology or product differentiation capabilities of firms that may have little to do with location factors in a region. Therefore, the combination of the post 1992 location-attractiveness score of a region for hosting different activities or industries with the specific competitive advantages that incumbent companies in that region (e.g., technology or product differentiation) have built up, yields an interesting picture of the way activities of a certain industry will develop in the region, and provides an indication of the likely corporate (re-) location-strategies (see Figure 4).

After all non-tariff barriers are eliminated, basic location factors of a region will again play the dominant role. So, if after 1992 incumbent companies in the region remain competitive, they will expand their activity in that region. If, on the other hand, these firms do not prove to be competitive in the single market, but the region provides a good basis for the activity or the industry in which the incumbent firms operate, they will have to restructure and regain competitiveness, or (foreign) firms may enter by means of takeover or by setting up new plants in the region. Thus in analyzing Figure 4, it is important to realize that in the present situation various existing non-tariff barriers cause strong market fragmentation and, as a consequence, render some regions or Member States unnaturally attractive for the location of certain industries. If comparative location conditions become unattractive after 1992, the incumbent firms may decide to leave the industry, or move to other regions in the EC if they have built up transferable competitive advantages.

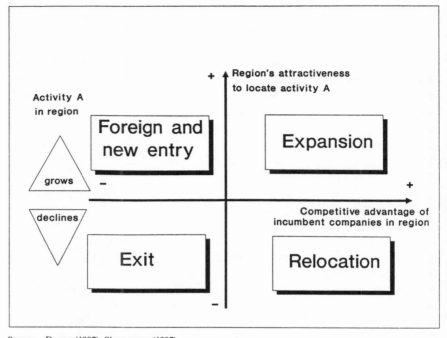

Source: Daems (1987). Sleuwaegen (1987)

Figure 4.   Geographical Restructuring Situation Post-1992

III.   EMPIRICAL PERSPECTIVES ON INDUSTRIAL RESTRUCTURING IN EUROPE

A.   Within Industries

Because companies in the new market environment should be better able to exploit scale and scope advantages, product redesign, production restructuring, specialization and geographical expansion are logical steps towards preparing for a single market. These actions take the form of setting up new units in other Member States, cooperation agreements with foreign companies or mergers and takeovers of national or other European competitors. The last form of strategic action is increasingly being used as is witnessed by the latest recorded figure for the mergers and acquisitions involving one of the thousand largest European companies, shown in Table 2. An analysis of significant mergers and takeovers since 1982 reveals that most mergers take place between companies of the same nationality. These actions can be seen as defensive strategies to avoid easy takeovers by foreign groups, and to effectively prepare for 1992 by rationalizing and increasing the scale

Table 2. Mergers: Nationality of the Partners

Year	National (same EC country)	Intra-EC (different EC countries)	International (EC and non-EC countries)	Total
1982/1983	59 (50.5)	38 (32.5)	20 (17.0)	117 (100)
1983/1984	101 (65.2)	29 (18.7)	25 (16.1)	115 (100)
1984/1985	146 (70.2)	44 (21.2)	18 (8.7)	208 (100)
1985/1986	145 (63.7)	52 (23.0)	30 (13.3)	227 (100)
1986/1987	211 (69.6)	75 (24.8)	17 (5.6)	303 (100)
1987/1988	214 (55.9)	112 (29.2)	57 (14.9)	383 (100)
1988/1989	233 (47.4)	197 (40.0)	62 (12.6)	492 (100)

Source: Reports on competition, EC Comissioner (1982-1989).

of operations. Equally meaningful is the increasing number of cross-border mergers, which often involve larger capitalization values than mergers within the same EC Member State.

The motives for mergers and takeovers are also changing. In line with the expectations about the 1992 impact, production rationalization and restructuring show up as the most important motive, followed by the desire to expand operations. Contrary to earlier merger movements, diversification is no longer a major motive.

Together with the increase in the number of mergers and acquisitions, strategic alliances are gaining importance and seem to be developing into a valuable alternative to mergers. Figure 5 shows for all major European firms the number of strategic alliances reported in the financial press over the period 1986-1989 in combination with the number of mergers and acquisitions. Strategic alliances comprise all sorts of cooperative agreements going from a joint venture to looser contractual arrangements if they involve some sharing of activities in production, research, marketing or distribution. In related work we presented empirical evidence about the prevalence of mergers versus strategic alliances for a sample of representative European industries (Sleuwaegen and Vanden Houte 1990). It was found that mergers or takeovers seem to be preferred in cases where the market position has to be improved and durable scale economies can be realized. Strategic alliances seem to focus on the flexibility of cooperative agreements and the gains from technology sharing in temporary frameworks. Both mergers and strategic alliances were higher in R&D intensive industries and industries for which there existed a large potential EC market, but that were still characterized by high non-tariff barriers. These latter findings suggest the importance of specific 1992-induced effects in the decision to merge

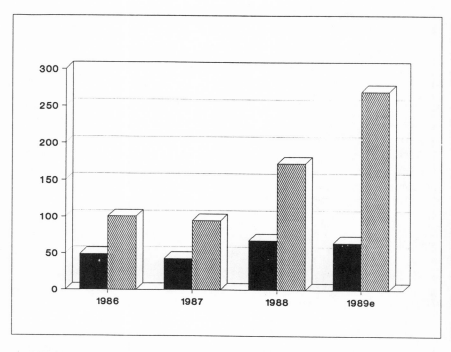

Key: ■ = Strategic alliances; ▨ = mergers and takeovers.

Figure 5.   Company Actions 1986-1989

or cooperate with other firms. The unimportance of scale economies in production with respect to the prevalence of strategic alliances conforms with Van der Zwan's hypothesis that the premiums paid in takeover bids assume that durable synergetic effects can be realized, which need not be the case for the different forms of cooperative agreements that are of a partial and flexible nature and not subject to the public bidding process (Van der Zwan 1989).

B.   Across Regions

In Section II it was argued that if after 1992, when all market protection has disappeared and it appears that the region or Member State is no longer location attractive to host certain industries, the incumbent companies in these industries are likely to disappear or move to other more attractive Member States. Following the logic developed in Figure 4 and in order to trace some of the likely movements in location, it appears instructive to combine Revealed Comparative Advantage (RCA) prior to 1992 with the relative presence of foreign companies for all the different industries in each Member State. The

RCA index is a measure of relative trade performance by industry expressed as the net exports from the Member State divided by the total of exports plus imports. By multiplying with 100, the ratio is rescaled to vary between −100 and +100. Comparable to the RCA index, we introduce a new index, MCA, Multinational Competitive Advantage, which is measured as the output produced by domestically based multinationals minus the output produced by subsidiaries from foreign-based multinationals relative to total output of the industry in the particular country. Using the premise that companies can only go abroad if they have specific competitive advantages that can be transferred and exploited in other countries, a high MCA index means that companies based in that Member State have built up strong competitive advantages (technology, product differentiation) that enabled them to go abroad, and at the same time, prevented other foreign-based multinationals from entering their domestic industry. Companies may use these specific advantages in conjunction with favorable location conditions in their home country, which would explain a very high RCA-index. If, on the other hand, the competitive advantages of these companies are transferable across national borders and can better be used in conjunction with location conditions in other countries, a high MCA index is coupled with a low RCA index and indicate that most companies originating from the particular country have already moved most of their operations to other countries.

If we accept that 1992 will lead to a better exploitation of comparative advantages by Member States, the left quadrant below in Figures 6 and 7, for the Netherlands and Belgium, respectively, contains interesting information for studying economic restructuring across EC borders. This quadrant contains those industries for which the Member States do not seem to possess comparative advantages, but that are dominated by foreign companies. This combination, relatively low export and strong presence of foreign companies, suggests that these industries involve either activities necessarily located close to the market, or, and more importantly in our context, industries that are highly protected by import impeding non-tariff barriers in the particular Member State. The non-tariff barriers would then explain the high rate of import-substituting foreign investments in the particular Member State's industries. Of course, these industries become highly vulnerable in the Member State, once non-tariff barriers are lifted. From a comparison of Figure 6 for the Netherlands with Figure 7 for Belgium, Belgium shows up as an important host country for foreign investment with few industries in which Belgian multinational companies play an important role. As illustrated in Vanden Houte and Veugelers (1989) foreign subsidiaries accounted for about 44 percent of all industrial output in Belgium anno 1985. The strong presence of foreign companies in electro-technical industries, machinery and paper and board industries in Belgium, without that these industries show a positive trade balance, are an important source of concern. Many of the industries belonging

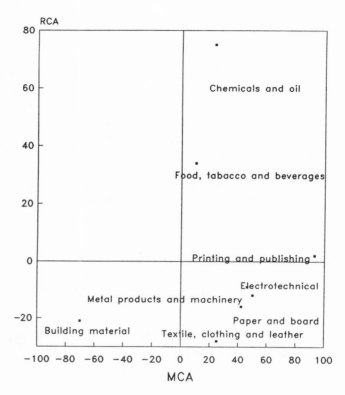

Source: Belderbos (1988), Data For Constructing MCA; Eurostat (1988), Data for Constructing RCA.

Figure 6.   Trade Performance and Multinational Enterprises
in the Netherlands, 1987

to these meso-sectors are indeed characterized by high non-tariff barriers (public procurement, technical norms, . . .) and are rather of the footloose type from the locational point of view, as illustrated in Sleuwaegen and Vanden Houte (1990). The problem arises whether these sensitive industries will disappear in Belgium after all protection disappears or whether these industries may finally find a good export-basis in Belgium when other EC Member States remove their non-tariff barriers and become less protective. In the latter case, the RCA-index prior 1992 was too much biased to be a good indicator of real comparative advantage. Clearly, this issue requires more in depth analysis. At this point the quadrants below in Figure 6 and 7 only serve to identify these industries that are highly sensitive and vulnerable in view of further EC market integration. For the Netherlands we find only one sector in the sensitive left

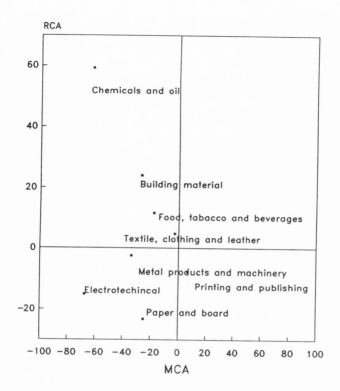

Source: Veugelers and Vanden Houte (1988); Data For Constructing MCA; Eurostat (1988); Data for Constructing RCA.

Figure 7. Trade Performance and Multinational
Enterprises in Belgium, 1985

quadrant below : building materials. Whereas it is clear that this sector is less footloose, it also appears that this sector is highly subject to important technical norms, for which important 1992 effects are expected in the Netherlands (CPB 1989). Another interesting observation for the Netherlands is the dominance of strong multinational companies in the different sectors shown in Figure 6. For these large companies with activities spread across different EC Member States there will be a strong tendency to increase specialization of different intra-firm activities by EC Member State or region. Unfortunately, no data are available to illustrate this intra-firm specialization process.

While the above considerations would predict a strong restructuring across geographical regions, the evidence for the past thirty years does not suggest that radical geographical restructuring processes will take place. The strong regional inequality has not reduced but has tended to increase with further market integration.[1] This seems to suggest that there are strong agglomeration advantages and that location factors can hardly be compressed to some basic variables. Some observers even predict that the integration process will lead to stronger concentration of activities in fewer plants in the center regions of the EC, using the example of industries that have been strongly integrating during the last decades. For activities in soap production, for instance, Unilever closed down several plants in more peripherical regions, with no decline but a strong growth in production and productivity over the period 1974-1989.[2] This restructuring seems to be characteristic for many industries. There seems to be a strong bunching of activities in some center region in the EC. The so-called "banana" which stretches from London to Milan and which is advancing towards Rome, represents the current concentration of population and wealth. Being aware of this concentration phenomenon, the EC Commission has adopted a more radical approach to foster development in the peripherical regions, by drastically augmenting the structural funds directed towards assisting the development of the peripherical regions in Ireland, Spain, Portugal, and Greece and through establishing a close partnership with national, regional and local authorities in selecting and promoting development projects.

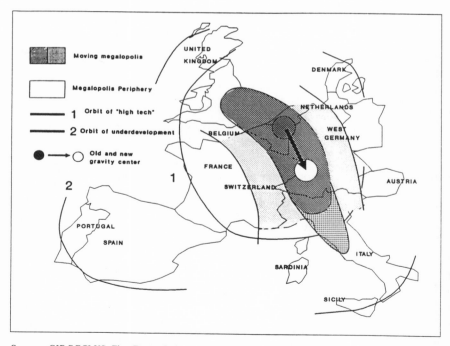

Source: GIP RECLUS, First Europe Ltd.

Figure 8.   Regional Concentration

IV. CONCLUSION

The Europeanization of industrial structure will depend strongly on the success of the new action plan, known as the Europe 1992 program. Although the program concerns many issues, the implemented or implementable measures envisage to increase efficiency and stimulate competition among European firms. The analysis in the paper emphasized the role of different competitive environments on adjustment strategies for the post 1992 era. It was argued that the expected effects of 1992 differ substantially across industries with major effects for these companies in industries currently fragmented by non-tariff barriers to trade. In many cases, the fragmentation made firms adopt focus strategies for their nationally protected markets, in spite of the fact that many of their activities were subject to important scale economies. The empirical evidence about the frequency and motives for mergers and acquisitions in the EC support this view. For a representative sample of industries it was found that mergers occur more often in large high-tech industries where non-tariff barriers were important, technical scale economies existed and concentration was relatively low in the EC market. For strategic alliances, which appear increasingly as an alternative for mergers, scale effects in production seemed to be less important. Finally, it was argued that economic restructuring across the borders of EC Member States will be very marked in those industries where there is currently a lot of foreign investment in an EC Member State although this Member State shows no clear comparative advantage to locate these industries. These arguments were illustrated for the cases of the Netherlands and Belgium.

APPENDIX: LIST OF THE 40 SENSITIVE INDUSTRIES

Category NACE Industry

Group 1 330 Office and data processing machinery
         344 Telecommunications
         372 Medical and surgical equipment
Group 2 257 Pharmaceutical products
         315 Boilermaking
         362 Locomotives, tramways
         425 Champagnes, sparkling wines
         427 Brewing and malting
         428 Soft drinks
Group 3 341 Insulated wires and cables
         342 Electrical machinery

361 Shipbuilding
417 Spaghetti, macaroni, and so forth
421 Cocoa, chocolate and sugar confectionery
Group 3 247 Glass and glassware
248 Ceramic goods
251 Basic industrial chemicals
256 Other chemical products mainly for industrial and agricultural purposes
321 Agricultural machinery
322 Machine-tools for working metal
323 Textile machinery
324 Machinery for food, chemical and related industries
325 Plant for mines, iron and steel industry
326 Transmission equipment for motive power
327 Other machinery for specific branches
345 Radio and television
346 Electric appliances
347 Electric lamps & other electric lighting
351 Motor vehicles
364 Aerospace equipment
431 Wool industry
432 Cotton industry
438 Carpets
451 Footwear
453 Clothing
455 Household textiles
481 Rubber products
491 Jewelry
493 Photographic and cinematographic laboratories
494 Toys and sporting goods

ACKNOWLEDGMENTS

The author would like to thank Peter Van Dijcke and Goedele Akkermans for help in processing the data used in the paper and Pierre Buigues and Jean Bergevin, at the DG II of the Commission of the European Communities, for stimulating comments. The author is also grateful to Herman Daems for suggesting the graphical representation of the arguments in Figure 3 and 4. Financial support from the K.U.Leuven Onderzoeksfonds (05/89/5) is gratefully acknowledged.

NOTES

1. Regional inequalities were of the order 1 to 6, but increased to 1 to 8 in 1988 (Romus 1990, p. 121).
2. See Buigues (1990).

REFERENCES

Balassa, B. 1986. "Comparative Advantage in Manufactured Goods: A Reappraisal." *Review of Economics and Statistics* 68(May): 315-319.

Belderbos, R. 1988. "De Internationalisering van de Nederlandse Economie: een Studie naar Omvang en Determinanten van Directe Buitenlandse Investeringen." Research memorandum 8801, Universiteit van Amsterdam.

Buigues, P. 1990. "Les Rédeploiements Stratégiques en cours dans les Entreprises Européennes." Mimeo. Brussels: Commission of the European Community.

Buigues, P. and A. Jacquemin. 1992. "Quelles Stratégies pour les Entreprises Européennes." *Revue Française de Gestion,* pp. 5-15.

Buigues, P. and F. Ilzkovitz. 1989. "The Sectorial Impact of the Internal Market." *Commission of the European Communities,* mimeo. p. 24.

Buigues, P. and A. Jacquemin. "Strategies of Firms and Structural Environments in the Large Internal Market." *Journal of Common Market Studies* 28(1)(September).

Buigues, P. and F. Ilzkovitz. 1988. "The Single Market Implications for Belgian Industry." *Internal paper of the Commission of the European Communities* Ref. II/420/88-EN, p. 35.

Centraal Plannings Bureau, 'Nederland en Europa '92', Werkdocument no. 28, 's-Gravenhage, 1989, p. 143.

Centrale Raad voor het Bedrijfsleven, Stuurgroep 1992, '1992 : Ondernemingsstrategieën en Nieuwe Samenwerkingsverbanden,' 1990.

Commission of the European Communities, 1988. "The Economies of 1992." *European Economy* 35 (Cecchini Report), Office des Publications de Communautés Européennes, Luxembourg, (March).

Commission of the European Communities. 1989. "Horizontal Mergers and Competition in the European Community." *European Economy,* 40. Office des Publications des Communautés Européennes: Luxembourg, (May).

Daems, H. 'Concurrentievermogen en industriële structuur: Structurele Kenmerken van de Belgische Regio's, Tijdschrift voor Economie en Management, 1987, 22(2), pp. 105-139.

De Bondt, R., L. Sleuwaegen, and R. Veugelers, R. 1988. "Innovative Strategic Groups in Multinational Industries." *European Economic Review* 32(3): 905-925.

De Grauwe, P. 1989. "1992 and Europe's Regions." Mimeo, Katholieke Universiteit Leuven.

De Jong, H.W., ed. 1981. *The Structure of European Industry.* Martinus Nijhoff Publishers.

Dreze, J. 'Quelques Réflections Sereines sur l'Adaptation de l'Industrie Belge au Marché Commun', Comptes Rendus de Travaux de la Société d'Economie Politique de Belgique, no. 275.

Eurostat, Trade Statistics, Statistical Office of the EC, Luxembourg, 1986-1988.

Harrigan, K. 1984. "Joint Ventures and Global Strategies." *Columbia Journal of World Business* 284 (Summer).

Harrigan, K. 1985. *Strategies for Joint Ventures.* Lexington, MA: Lexington Books.

Jacquemin, A. 1987. *The New Industrial Organization.* Oxford: Oxford University Press.

Nerb, G. "The Completion of the Internal Market: a Survey of Europe Industry's Perception of the Likely Effects." *Research on the cost of Non-Europe, Vol. 1.* Série Documents, CCE.

Porter, M.E. 1980. *Competitive Strategy.* New York: The Free Press.

Romus, P. 1990. *L'Europe Régionale.*" Brussels: Editions Labor.

Sleuwaegen, L., with the assistance of M. Nelissen. 1989. "The Impact of Europe 1992 on Manufacturing Industries in the Netherlands." coordinated by D.G. II of the European Commission, 109 p., te verschijnen in European Economy.

Sleuwaegen, L. 1987. "Multinational Enterprises, the European Community and Belgium : Recent Developments." *Journal of Common Market Studies* 26(2).

Sleuwaegen, L. and H. Yamawaki, H. 1988. "The Formation of the European Common Market and Changes in Market Structure and Performance." *European Economic Review* 32 (7): 1451-1475.

Sleuwaegen, L. and P. Vanden Houte. 1990. *Towards 1992: The Role of Mergers and Strategic Alliances in Industrial Restructuring.* Mimeo: K.U.Leuven.

Vanden Houte, P. and R. Veugelers. 1989. "Buitenlandse Ondernemingen in België." *Tijdschrift voor Economie en Management* (1):9-34.

Van der Zwan, A. 1989. "Strategische Samenwerking." *Economische Statistische Berichten* 3735 (Jaargang): 1176-1181.

STRATEGIC CHANGES IN
PERSONAL FINANCIAL SERVICES:
THE IMPACT OF THE SINGLE
EUROPEAN MARKET

Glenn Morgan and Fergus Murray

I. INTRODUCTION

The paper consists of the following sections. In the first section, we summarize the changing regulatory framework for personal financial services constructed within the 1992 framework. We argue that the detailed regulatory changes will take many years to complete in personal financial services. Therefore, 1992 is a symbol of the move toward a Single Market rather than the actual date by which the process will have been completed.

   In the second section, we examine the context within which the Single Market is being developed. In particular, we seek to show the interaction between the internationalization of financial services and the strategic decisions of companies within both their home and their foreign markets. This perspective demonstrates that 1992 does not constitute a once and for all change; rather it is a significant symbolic milestone pointing in a direction embarked on by a number of European financial services groups.

Research in Global Strategic Management, Volume 2, pages 103-123.
ISBN: 1-55938-277-5

In the third section, we develop our argument that 1992 provides a stimulus and clarification regarding the direction of corporate strategy, particularly in relation to two features in the internationalization of financial services. The first of these features is the redefinition of core businesses away from the clear demarcation of banking and insurance and towards what is variously called "bancassurance" in France and "Allfinanz" in West Germany. The second is the role which international links (either through cooperation, merger or acquisition) can play in this process of redefinition.

In the fourth section of the paper, we focus on the emerging integration of banking and insurance. Considering evidence from France, Italy, and West Germany, we examine how far this process has gone and what the impact of 1992 will be. We also consider the issue of cross-border mergers, acquisitions and joint ventures and the role that these play in the emerging corporate strategies of companies operating in the French, Italian, and West German markets for personal financial services.

In the final section, we consider the extent to which artificial (government imposed) entry barriers have been replaced by "natural" entry barriers and how this has affected those firms that were previously sheltered from market forces through government protection.

Our overall argument is that significant differences remain between EC member countries in terms of the formal and informal regulation, ownership and control of financial institutions, the structure of the personal financial services sector, and social structures and cultural attitudes that will have a continuing impact on the consumption of financial services products. National differences will not, therefore, simply be wiped out by the dismantling of artificial government imposed entry barriers as a result of the Single European Market. Instead natural entry barriers will become more significant.

II. THE CREATION OF THE SINGLE EUROPEAN MARKET FOR PERSONAL FINANCIAL SERVICES

Of all the industries considered suitable for the creation of a Single European market, that of financial services has been one of the most important (this section draws from Morgan 1992; see also Cecchini 1988; European Communities Commission 1988a, 1988b, 1988c). The Cecchini report investigated the differences in the price of various types of financial services in Community countries. The wide variation which it found was used as evidence that a single market in personal financial services would benefit consumers by bringing costs down in high price areas through competition from low-price producers. Thus the Commission was charged with preparing proposals that would create a single market for financial services and enable these potential gains to be realized. These proposals consisted of the creation of:

- A single banking market in which a bank can establish branches anywhere in the community and offer its services throughout the Community.
- An insurance market where insurance can be bought on the most competitive terms and provide Community-wide cover.
- A securities and capital market with enough capacity to meet European industry's financing needs and capable of attracting investors from all over the world (European Communities Commission 1989, p. 1).

In order to achieve these goals, the EC emphasised three regulatory features.

1. Harmonization on essential standards for prudential supervision of financial institutions and for the protection of investors, depositors and consumers.
2. Mutual recognition of the competence of the supervisory bodies and standards of each Member state.
3. Financial institutions would be controlled and supervised by their home state though "rules relating to advertising to particular markets should properly belong with the host country supervising" (European Communities Commission 1988b, p. 6).

In the main areas concerning this paper—banking services and life insurance—the Commission presented a series of proposals. In banking, these focused on the creation of a single licence system. This enables a bank licensed in one member country to sell banking services in other member countries without further conditions. This proposal, known as the Second Banking Coordination Directive, is accompanied by directives for harmonized solvency ratios (which lay down common standards for the solvency of banks and other credit institutions) and rules on the annual accounts of banks and harmonizing the concept of a bank's "own funds."

With regard to life insurance, EC representatives have argued that this "sector is much more complex and we believe we are going to need two or three bites at the cherry before we get complete freedom of services" (European Communities Commission 1989, p. 5). The Second Life Insurance Directive (agreed in 1990) gives no single licence for the sale of life insurance. If a company wishes to sell in a country other than its home state, it must apply for a licence in that country. However, customers in one country can, on their own initiative, approach an insurance company located in another country to purchase a life insurance product from it. In this situation, the consumer would be protected by the rules of the country in which the company was located. Following debate and controversy, the Commission has agreed that firms can advertise in other countries to encourage cross-border purchasing and that brokers can advise clients on cross-border purchases.

In summary, whereas the principle of a single license for banking services has been accepted and implemented, in life insurance, only "own initiative" clients are able to purchase insurance products across borders though this may change by the mid-nineties. In the main, customers will be dependent on products purchased from companies established in and licensed by the host country. This situation is little different from that which pertained in life insurance before 1992.

It would, however, be wrong to consider the impact of the Single European Market solely in terms of the details of the Commission directives. In our view, 1992 has a symbolic importance that far outweighs these limited considerations. This is because it is occurring in the middle of a wider series of changes in personal financial services. Seen in the context of these changes, 1992 symbolizes a new future for the industry. In order to understand this, we need to consider the international context of the financial services industry.

III. INTERNATIONAL CHANGE AND PERSONAL FINANCIAL SERVICES

Of all industries, financial services is one of the last to become internationalized (see Morgan 1992). In comparison to manufacturing where European, Japanese, American, and other countries' producers compete directly with each other in most parts of the world, the financial services industry (particularly the personal sector) has remained locked behind national walls. In recent years, these walls have started to come down, a process that 1992 symbolizes.

The only European country that has had a relatively internationalized financial system has been the United Kingdom. While certain major parts have been closed (either informally through control of the retail banking and savings networks or formally through prohibitions on foreign ownership—as in the Stock Exchange) the City of London itself has been the center for a variety of financial dealings designed to lubricate international trading arrangements (see Ingham 1984 for an account on these lines). Even the retail bankers and insurance companies that collected the savings of the mass of the population and recirculated them through the City were international both in investment practices and in their actual operational character (where the existence of the British Empire—both formal and informal—was reflected in branch structures that straddled the globe). This openness in terms of exporting capital and organizational expertise in financial services also meant an openness to inward investment. Particularly from the fifties onwards, American, European, and latterly Japanese banks were willing and able to set up in the City of London as its role as an international financial centre expanded. The regulators of the City, whether in government or the Bank of England, were in the main willing to accept this foreign influx so long as it did not harm their own prospects.

As a result, London retained its position as a center for international finance while the position of the British economy in world trade suffered a considerable decline.

This was reflected in two ways. First, foreign financial institutions set up branch offices in the City of London to take advantage of the markets and skills located there. Second, the high level of trading on the Stock Exchange of the shares of many financial institutions meant that it was possible for foreign companies to make acquisitions.

Other European countries developed a more closed financial system and were less willing to allow foreign entrants. In countries such as France and Germany, a variety of laws, regulations and informal practices were in place which restricted the entry of foreign firms, either to start operations from scratch or to get involved in mergers and acquisitions. Behind these artificial entry barriers, institutions were sheltered from outside competition. This sheltering effect encouraged formal and informal cartels. There was little incentive for innovation or outright competition in this context because consumer choice was constrained within traditional channels of sales and marketing. Thus the large companies tended to grow whilst even small institutions with few economies of scale or marketing skills were able to survive.

Even before the move to the Single Market, however, market stability and regulation was beginning to break down as the provision of *corporate* financial services began to be internationalized. This shift acted as a crucial catalyst for major changes in personal financial services in two ways. First, there was the growing internationalization of trade in manufacturing and commodities in general from the late fifties onwards. Increasingly, corporate customers looked for relations with financial services companies that could serve them on a global basis. Thus, the top tier of insurers and banks in each European country began to develop overseas branches and businesses to serve their newly international clientele (as the British had done much earlier). The range of services required by these clients was simultaneously expanding. As well as normal corporate banking and insurance services, there was a growing need for advice on merger and acquisitions, fund management and treasury operations, loan provisions and currency issues. Thus, European financial institutions had to move out of their home bases if they were not to lose their largest customers to British and American companies.

Secondly, and associated with this, were the more rapid changes in the international financial system from the seventies. Without going into detail here (see, e.g., Strange 1988 for more information), the floating of currencies and the recycling of "petrodollars" in the early seventies created opportunities for institutions capable both of dealing in foreign currencies and setting up loans. It generated a potential for new financial instruments such as currency futures, swaps, and debt paper; at the same time, it led to the emergence of large sums of money capable of speculative investment in currencies and shares. These in turn required institutional channels through which they could flow in order to speculate against particular currencies and companies. Banks and insurance companies became the conduits for, as well as the managers of, these funds (Channon 1988). Failure to act in these markets implied foregoing emerging high profit opportunities that at first seemed to far out-weigh the risks involved (though as the Third World Debt crisis has mounted it can be seen that there is much greater risk than at first perceived). The largest European banks and insurers began to be tempted out of their national enclaves in the search for the opportunities for international corporate business opening up mainly in London, New York, and Tokyo.

Developments at this level had a complex effect on the personal financial services sector. This can be illustrated by examining the British case. In the United Kingdom, the major clearing banks had been accustomed to use the accounts of personal customers both as a source of profit in their own right (through charging for transaction services) and as a source of cheap funds for loan finance and so forth. During the seventies and eighties, however, the growth of alternative methods both of saving and of transacting, meant that this source of profit and funds was increasingly restricted. Building societies offered better interest rates on accounts as well as pioneering "free banking." Insurance companies developed products that offered better rates of return for long-term savings. Banks found themselves having to compete more vigorously for personal customers at the same time as they wanted to expand their international and corporate business. Furthermore, because international and corporate business was becoming so much more risky (as the Third World Debt crisis showed in the eighties), the importance of having a strong profit position in personal financial services grew.

As a result, financial services companies in the United Kingdom became much more strategic about developing their personal customer base. This involved a closer attention to costs, initially pursued through massive investments in Information Technology, but also the development of innovative product ranges that started to undermine the old distinctions between banks, building societies and insurance companies. As a result of these changes United Kingdom companies began to emerge as "financial services" institutions offering a range of savings and loan media for their personal customers.

The dynamism of this market was stimulated by government action both through deregulation and through legislative enactments to encourage different types of personal saving, in particular for personal pensions, which had an important impact on other European countries. First, it provided a model for possible strategic change, both at the level of the organization of the industry (i.e., the integration of banking and insurance) and at the level of the organization of companies (i.e., in terms of cost efficiencies, product design, marketing, and selling and the use of information technology). Second, it provided a possible market for foreign companies to enter. Both of these trends opened the way for the purchase of UK companies by foreign institutions. The purpose of these acquisitions was not simply to make money in the UK markets but also to have access to the skills that were thought to be present within such companies and could therefore be transferred in some way to other markets. Thus, during the eighties, there were an increasing number of acquisitions of UK financial institutions by foreign companies.

Looked at from this perspective, the 1992 EC directives are a further step in the process of internationalizing financial services because what they make more difficult is the ability of companies in conjunction with governments to create regulatory barriers to competition. Thus in theory, the UK financial services industry, which had previously been the most open to foreign competition, would now be able to enter other European Community markets, while the companies of those countries with previously protected financial services markets would now face the prospect of increased international competition. As we shall argue, the actual situation is not as simple as this suggests because natural entry barriers remain significant.

IV.   STRATEGIC CHANGE IN PERSONAL FINANCIAL SERVICES

The complex changes outlined in the previous two sections offer companies a series of strategic challenges. Of overarching importance is the understanding that personal financial services is becoming an increasingly competitive market. Developments in the United Kingdom indicate that it will become increasingly difficult for banks and insurance companies to hang on to their existing markets or to expand into new ones when regulatory barriers come down if they do not start to prepare themselves for that competition. Thus whilst it is clear that 1992 will not see a sudden surge of cross-border selling or new ventures in foreign countries, it is nevertheless the case that artificial entry barriers will have been largely dismantled. Therefore, companies will no longer be able to sit back in the shelter of their home markets, protected by sympathetic domestic governments. Instead they will have to take active steps to ensure that they can overcome and expand across natural entry barriers to other EC member markets. Companies will need to be strong at home to provide a base from which they can attempt to be successful abroad. Thus, the challenge of internationalization (and within that, 1992) is a challenge that affects markets at home *and* abroad.

In the rest of this paper, we focus on two particular responses to this challenge. In this section, we will briefly outline these responses in general terms. In the following section, we will look at how far companies in West Germany, France, and Italy are taking them up. The first response relates to the definition of "core business" in personal financial services. The second concerns the means for securing the core business at home and abroad.

V.   CORE BUSINESS IN PERSONAL FINANCIAL SERVICES

Previously it may have been possible to define the core business of banks and insurance companies in relatively discrete terms. The core business of the retail bank was to provide transaction services to its current account customers. For insurance companies, their core business was the sale of insurance policies. However, as our discussion of the United Kingdom showed, this distinction has been undermined as banks *and* insurance companies have started to compete with each other (and other institutions, such as the building societies in the United Kingdom) for the savings of individual customers. That is, banks and insurance companies are offering savings and loans facilities that in the past may have overlapped with little worry for either party. The extent of that overlap has grown in recent times as companies seek to maximize their earnings from customers and provide them with a comprehensive range of financial services. A corollary of this is that there appears to be a certain logic in integrating insurance and banking services either through merger, takeover or joint ventures. Because banks and insurance companies are bound, at least in the medium term, to retain distinctive strengths, the question of how to create such joint institutions will remain complex. The Single European Market has reduced regulatory barriers to this process as well as providing the possibility of a European-wide market for such integrated institutions.

Linked to the definition of the core business is the question of how it should be secured. Companies can either acquire others or launch joint ventures or set up a new company on their own initiative. These strategies are not mutually exclusive nor need they be confined to foreign or home markets. In the next section, we examine the different patterns of strategies emerging in the three countries under consideration.

VI.   DEFINING AND SECURING CORE BUSINESS

A.   Germany

In both banking and insurance, the German system has been relatively impervious to foreign competition. (We will use the term "Germany," though in the pre-1990 period, we are considering what was then "West Germany.") There have been three main reasons for this:

1.   Insurance and banking regulation has been highly onerous (see Finsinger 1986).

2.   Germany is a heavily banked society. Bundesbank data reported 4,553 banking institutions with 62,289 branches in 1986 giving West Germany a density of 1,020 bank branches per million inhabitants, compared to 900 in France, 800 in the United Kingdom and 400 in the United States. Furthermore, the German consumer still overwhelmingly prefers cash for transactions so banks compete over a more limited range of savings and credit products than in the United Kingdom and the United States. The costs of setting up a banking network in Germany would be huge. The opportunities for new entrants into such an already packed market are, therefore, small.

3.   If the outsider sought a route into Germany through acquisition, this also would be complicated. For one thing there are many co-operative and savings banks that are either state owned or mutually owned and that therefore cannot be bought on the open market. Among those that are quoted on the stock exchange, there is a high level of interlocking share ownership which, although rarely revealed, effectively constitutes a bar to any outsider purchasing a German financial institution. For example, Deutsche Bank (the largest of the commercial retail banks) recently revealed that it held a 10 percent stake in the largest insurance company, Allianz, as well as the largest reinsurer Munich Re (*Financial Times,* October 27, 1989). It appears likely that the insurance companies hold equally large stakes in Deutsche Bank, though there has been no formal announcement.

In the past, this protection from outside competition gave West German financial institutions a reputation for conservatism and complacency. In recent years, however, this has begun to change as the largest institutions have become more active in an attempt to improve their position in the domestic market at the expense of the smaller companies. The unification of Germany and the opening up of potential new markets in the old East Germany has also given a further advantage to the large institutions with capital able to set up branch networks in the eastern part of the country. Thus, whereas previously, both large and small companies co-existed peacefully behind the shelter of government barriers, the Single European Market is making all of them conscious that conditions within the enlarged home market are going to become more competitive.

This can be illustrated through considering the growing importance of what is termed "Allfinanz." This term refers to the attempt to bring together both banking and insurance functions into one unified framework and involves the redefinition of core business to which we have already referred. The particular advantage that Allfinanz offers the consumer is seen in terms of "one-stop shopping" for financial services. From the point of view of the companies concerned, Allfinanz arrangements would allow them to increase their number of distribution outlets and potentially cut costs, enabling them to compete more effectively against the smaller institutions that still play such a large part in Germany's financial life. Thus "Allfinanz" offers an opportunity for the large companies to consolidate and improve their position within the home market while it threatens the future of the medium and small-sized institutions that lack the capital to move into new areas of financial activity.

In order to develop Allfinanz, companies are faced with the choice of the three alternatives suggested in the previous section—acquisition, cooperation, and initiative. Acquisition is largely ruled out for the same reason that foreign predators cannot get into the market. That is, there are few ways in Germany in which a hostile bidder can gain sufficient shares even though theoretically they may be traded on public exchanges. Thus Allfinanz has primarily proceeded through strategies of cooperation.

The major attempt to begin from scratch has been that made by the largest bank, Deutsche Bank, which announced its intention last year to set up its own life insurance company. According to the *Financial Times,*

> While aiming to compete with the country's established life insurance industry on both price and range of services, Deutsche's policies will not represent a radical departure from the industry's norm. Thus the bank has eschewed the idea of flexible fund-linked life products. The aim has been to devise policies which will be sold through the bank's 1300 branches, better attuned to customer demand than those currently available elsewhere (*Financial Times,* August 22, 1989).

In taking this action, Deutsche followed its general strategic direction laid down by its former Chief executive, Alfred Herrhausen. According to the United Kingdom business weekly, *The Economist,* "Deutsche's strategy is to aim for control not just of cooperative deals, wherever it can [but also] to rule out the need for messy compromises with difficult partners" (*The Economist,* December 17, 1988).

Probably only Deutsche Bank would have a chance of pulling off such a new initiative. The two other largest commercial banks have settled for cooperation with insurance companies to achieve Allfinanz. Dresdner Bank, the second largest, announced some three months after Deutsche's decision to set up its own life company, that it would be joining forces with the giant insurer, Allianz, in 5 of the 11 West German states. The bank will sell Allianz life policies through its branches in the first instance, following these with property, casualty and health insurance in the future. Meanwhile, Allianz agents would offer savings and loans facilities from the bank to their customers. The agreement covered only 5 states partly because Dresdner wanted to avoid being swallowed up by Allianz and is hoping to conclude deals with other insurance companies in other states. Furthermore, Allianz itself already had one such agreement with Hypobank in Bavaria.

Other notable Allfinanz agreements concluded in recent years have been that between A&M insurance group and BfG Bank in 1987, Berliner Bank and Gothaer Insurance.

The growth of Allfinanz involves a consolidation of existing large banks and insurers but it also threatens some of the specialist providers of mortgages and home loans as well as the second tier of German banks in which state banks and cooperatives are represented. With regard to the specialist providers of home finance known as the Bausparkassen, they are now increasingly threatened by the large retailers. Commerzbank, the third largest bank, last year bought a 40 percent stake in Leonberger Sparkasse, a leading home financier, while Dresdner and Deutsche Banks set up new operations from scratch.

The growth of the commercial banks within Germany is a potential threat to the old established cooperative and state banks. The DG Bank that represents the local cooperative banks in the wholesale money markets has recently tried to persuade its five regional members to cooperate more closely to meet this threat. It attempted to pursue an Allfinanz option for the cooperative system through purchasing a 75 percent stake in Volksfursorge, one of Germany's biggest life insurers, which is linked to the trade union movement. This fell through however, and DG Bank is finding it difficult to coordinate its five members, two of whom see an independent future for themselves.

Similar tensions exist among the landesbanks that represent the savings banks in the wholesale money markets. The biggest landesbank, WestLB, recently bought the European branches of the troubled banking group, Standard Chartered. It has also set up a new international merchant bank with Standard Chartered to be known as Chartered WestLB that will operate around the world as well as in Europe. In doing so WestLB has signalled its intention to become a major international bank on its own terms and has thus effectively put a stop for the time being to attempts to unify the landesbanks into one coherent body.

In summary, the largest German financial institutions are responding within their own borders to the challenges of the future by following the Allfinanz route. In order to achieve this the most popular option appears to be the cooperative venture while Deutsche Bank provides the best example of a new venture in a mass market-life insurance. Future cooperative endeavors are likely to be increasing at the expense of the smaller local and regional mutual and cooperative institutions. This does lead to the possibility that these institutions will be open to cooperative arrangements with outside companies; if such cooperation fails to materialize, and there is little positive sign of it yet (in spite of various discussions among the European savings banks in particular), a more likely scenario is the gradual decline of these institutions and a growth of the large commercial banks and insurance companies with perhaps one or two landesbank and cooperatives surviving through amalgamation.

From this platform, German financial institutions can use the Single Market to venture forth into new areas of business in other European countries as well as being assured that their home market will remain relatively impervious to outside companies at least for the foreseeable future. In the international arena, however, the move towards Allfinanz is proceeding more slowly. In the main, it appears that German banks seek to combine with foreign banks whereas German insurance companies seek to combine with foreign insurance companies. To this extent, while the conservative characteristic of German institutions is declining within their own borders, it remains typical of their responses *outside* those borders.

Nevertheless, German institutions are certainly positioning themselves strongly in the emerging single market. Of the three methods of entry referred to earlier—acquisition, agreement and initiative—it is the two former that are the most popular, with the latter only occurring in niche markets.

Acquisition as a strategy has not been dependent on the 1992 regulations. In the early eighties Allianz (the largest insurer) demonstrated its ability to acquire large insurers in the United Kingdom in order to give it more market coverage. More recently, WestLB as already stated has taken over Standard Chartered's network in Europe. Perhaps the most spectacular of the recent acquisitions, however, has been Deutsche Bank's takeover of the UK merchant bank, Morgan Grenfell, in November 1989. In making this purchase, Deutsche added to its previous acquisitions of banks in Italy, Spain, the Netherlands, Austria, and Portugal. Thus, within the space of 20 years, Deutsche has gone from having no retail offices outside Germany to having more than 300. Not only does it now have geographical spread but it also possesses a full range of financial services businesses in both the corporate and the personal sector. The only place in Europe where Deutsche does not yet have a significant presence is in France.

Other German banks have preferred to go down the cooperative root when it comes to foreign activity. According to the *Financial Times,* "Commerzbank's strategy is based on taking small stakes in like-minded European institutions" (*Financial Times,* October 30, 1989). After eyeing Credit Lyonnais for some time but finding the French regulators unwilling to cooperate, it recently reached a cooperative agreement with Banco di Roma in Italy. Dresdner Bank has also sought partnership rather than gone for a straightforward acquisition. It has concentrated on expanding from its home-based strengths in treasury management and arbitrage, taking a 33 percent stake in BIP of France, a specialist treasury management operation originally set up by Midland Bank and BNP of France in the early eighties. Dresdner's cooperation with BNP has helped it establish itself in other French financial institutions and it now owns a number of stockbrokers there. BNP and

Dresdner agreed to appoint one director to each other's supervisory board and last year had a joint board meeting. Thus Dresdner is building up a presence in one of Deutsche's few areas of weakness—France.

Whereas all the major institutions in Germany are moving toward integrated product ranges along the lines of Allfinanz within their own borders, they have settled for their traditional line of business in their foreign operations. Within these parameters, however, there is no unified German response to 1992. The actual response depends on a series of factors affecting the managerial decision-makers within the companies. Because they all operate within the same enlarged home market, however, it appears that they hope to be able to exclude foreign competition from the domestic market and use it as a base from which to launch a variety of tactics to expand their operations in the broader European market.

While it is undoubtedly the case that some of these moves could have happened in the pre-1992 environment, it is fairly clear that 1992 has contributed to a speeding up of these processes. The largest German institutions seem well-prepared for the internationalization of financial services. Whereas they may not be as innovative or fleet of foot as some of their British competitors, they possess such wealth and stability that they are clearly going to be as important in this sphere as they already are in manufacturing. Even without the extra impetus to the German economy resulting from changes in Eastern Europe, it would appear that German financial institutions are likely to continue to expand into other countries, while retaining their home market shares. With that extra impetus, their importance will be further increased.

B. France

Much of the French banking and insurance industry has been state controlled in the past and many of the large insurance companies, banks and credit institutions continue to be state owned. In this way, the French government has raised artificial barriers to ensure that the chances of foreign predators gaining a large foothold in France were extremely limited. These barriers were strengthened because French regulators were able to make it difficult for foreign companies to set up and operate in competition with home-based companies.

These conditions began to change from the mid-eighties. In particular, the Chirac government (1986-1988) reprivatized the banks nationalized by the previous Socialist administration, among them the banques d'affaires (mixed merchant banks) Paribas and Suez, and was hoping to begin the privatization of the major insurance groups. Although the Socialist government that followed Chirac stopped further privatizations, the banks have generally awoken from their "bureaucratic slumbers" and under the guidance of a new breed of entrepreneurs have undertaken ambitious merger, acquisition, and joint-venture programs. Even within the state controlled sector there has also been considerable merger activity associated with a lessening of direct state control of individual companies. These activities reflect a realization that the French home market is potentially vulnerable to companies from the United Kingdom and West Germany once regulatory barriers fall. Both the French government and the leaders of the companies have therefore become very concerned to develop a larger and more efficient financial services industry for the future that will constitute a natural (market-based) barrier to foreign entry.

One of the most significant developments in this has been the move towards the establishment of integrated financial services groups consisting largely of banking and insurance interests—the so-called *bancassurance* groups (the French equivalent of Allfinanz). Unlike Germany, however, the virtues of the new definition of core business are hotly debated.

The theological and strategic debate is made up of those for *bancassurance,* Suez, GAN, UAP-BNP and Crédit Agricole and those against it, AXA-Midi, Paribas, AGF, and Crédit Commerciale de France. Spurred by the unwelcome attention of foreign predators, amongst them Generali Assicuarazioni and Allianz, those in favour of *bancassurance* have adopted four different types of strategy.

1. *Insurance buys bank:* France's fifth largest insurance company, Groupes des Assurances Nationales (state owned) took over Crédit Industriel et Commercial (CIC), a group of state-controlled regional banks, with the intention of initially selling accident insurance through CIC's branches and working towards a rationalisation of the two groups' computer operations. Sceptics doubt whether GAN will be able to exert sufficient control over CIC's complex structure.

2. *Bank-Insurance link-ups:* Banque Nationale de Paris and Unione des Assurances de Paris, the largest French commercial bank and insurance company respectively (both state-owned) have exchanged 10 percent share holdings. Given that BNP already sell FFr5bn life insurance through its branches there is reason to suspect that this maneuvre was largely intended to improve BNP's capital adequacy (*Financial Times,* November 2, 1989).

3. *Bank buys insurance:* The large mixed bank, Suez, buys the French insurer, Victoire/Colonia (as discussed in the next section).

4. *Bank sets up insurance subsidiary:* Crédit Agricole set up Predica as its life insurance subsidiary in 1986. In its first three years of operation Predica has been an 11 percent share of the French life insurance market.

Those against the *bancassurance* idea have developed other strategic responses. In particular, the insurers Assurances Generales de France and AXA-Midi have concentrated on acquiring domestic and international insurers. The former, a state-owned company ranked third in the insurance industry, has recently bought 27 percent of the Belgian insurer, Assubel, and gained control of the Italian motor insurer, MAA Assicurazioni. The latter group is the result of a merger between AXA and Midi which had both been acquiring domestic and foreign insurance firms (Midi bought the UK insurer Equity and Law in 1987) before the giant Italian insurer, Generali Assicurazioni, turned its unwelcome attention towards Midi. In 1989-1990, AXA-Midi attempted to acquire the large US insurer, Farmers, from the BAT Group through joining forces with Sir James Goldsmith in the bid to takeover and split up BAT into its constituent parts. The bid, however, failed. At approximately the same time, the company signed a co-operation agreement with Generali.

The above changes have been accompanied by a shake-up of the French insurance league table and the end of the dominance of the state-owned groups. In particular, Suez-Victorie and AXA-Midi are seen to have emerged as industry front-runners.

While the debate about bancassurance is more contested than the idea of Allfinanz in West Germany, it is noteworthy that when it comes to acquisitions abroad, the French show a similar conservatism to their German counterparts. Take for example the activities of Crédit Lyonnais (the second largest state-owned bank) and Crédit Agricole (the largest state owned-bank). The first has acquired the Belgian subsidiary of Chase Manhattan, and has gained effective control of Credito Bergamasco, a large, private North Italian bank. The latter recently pipped illustrious and extremely powerful Italian competitors to gain a 13.3 percent stake of the Italian Nuovo Banco Ambrosiano. In the insurance sector, Axa-Midi is the owner of Equity and Law, a major insurer in the United Kingdom.

However, the French situation is complicated by the existence of the two *banques d'affaires,* Paribas and the Suez group. These two companies, which have complicated histories, have unique structures. They have never been so firmly anchored in either banking or insurance as other institutions. Instead they have operated within complex holding companies whereby particular business opportunities have been taken as they arisen. Paribas, for example, operates (inter alia) a merchant bank (Banque Paribas), a retail bank (Crédit du Nord) and a life insurance company (Cardif). Abroad, Paribas has recently concluded a number of international share swaps and investments in pursuit of its rather loosely defined strategic aims. For example, it has swopped shares with Hafnia (Denmark's second largest insurer) and Banca Commerciale Italiana and taken a 20 percent holding in Banca Commerciale Lombarda, an Italian merchant bank created by Generali and Banca Commerciale Italiana. Without being as focused as those definitely striving to create a bancassurance group, Paribas is both an insurance and a banking group, through it appears to have not yet sought to gain the synergies that are perceived to come from "bancassurance" through closely integrating the two areas.

Like Paribas, Suez was nationalized in 1982 and then reprivatized in October 1987. Since that time the once "sluggish nationalised holding company" has become one of Europe's largest industrial and financial conglomerates (*The Economist*, January 20, 1990). The company's rapid growth is largely due to two fortuitous takeovers. On the first occasion Suez acted as a white knight during Carlo De Benedetti's battle to take over the huge Belgian holding company, Société Générale de Belgique. On the second occasion Suez took over Groupe Victoire which was in turn trying to finance a takeover of West Germany's second largest insurer, Colonia Versicherung. At the time of the takeover battle Suez had 40 percent holding of Victoire and feared this would be diluted by bringing in new shareholders to finance the Colonia bid. Suez bid FFr25.5 billion for Victoire and Colonia and after bitter recriminations succeeded in taking over Victoire. Subsequently Suez sold a 34 percent stake in Victoire to the largest French insurer, the state-owned Union des Assurances de Paris (UAP), and 5 percent stakes to Danish and Japanese insurance groups. Suez has also tried to buy a 80 percent stake in Holland's fifth biggest insurer, Nieuwe Rotterdam, and 23 per cent stake in Denmark's biggest insurer, Baltica.

The Suez group now consists of three arms: the old banking interests centred round Banque Indosuez with strong interests in the Middle East and Asia; industrial and property interests mainly in SGB, and insurance focused on Victoire. Like Paribas, Suez has achieved both banking and insurance interests at home and abroad. Also like Paribas, it has not yet sought to integrate them closely along the lines of the "bancassurance" strategy, though the potential is there.

To summarize the situation in France, then, there remains concern about the impact of 1992 and growing international competition. The fear that the French market would be vulnerable to foreign competition seems to have receded somewhat as the large financial institutions have become more focused and competitive, thus raising natural entry barriers to replace the previous governmental-based barriers. Furthermore, the existence of a significant state sector means that opportunities for foreign acquisitions in France remain limited. Thus French companies have created something of a breathing space for themselves while they debate how far to take "bancassurance" strategy at home and abroad. While *bancassurance* may be the predominant strategic direction in French banking and insurance, particularly with regard to the domestic market, it is still early days and difficult to make an assessment of the relative success of this strategy. Indeed, there are considerable doubts regarding the motives and managerial skills that lie behind a number of *bancassurance* developments and it may be that with the rapid increase of powerful players fighting over the lucrative and buoyant life insurance market the necessary profits to offset the costs of joint ventures and mergers and acquisitions may be hard to come by.

C. Italy

Italy is potentially the most dynamic market of the three that we are considering in this paper. Italians have traditionally been high savers but there have been a number of barriers both to the development of the indigenous financial services industry and the entry of foreign companies. Foreign companies have been particularly put off by the slow and difficult regulatory process, as well as the complex political and social structure of Italy that is still distinctive from the more industrialized and urbanized states of West Germany and France. However, as companies across Europe have searched for more profitable markets, Italy's potential is beginning to outweigh its disadvantages.

Both the Italian state and the Italian companies have begun to recognize the need to adapt to this competitive threat. Two main changes are taking place within Italian banking and insurance. These consist of a wave of domestic bank mergers and a spate of international alliances and joint ventures both in Italian and foreign markets. Moves towards *bancassurance* or *allfinanz* strategies have been weak. This latter weakness is in part explained by the priorities being set by the Bank of Italy in terms of domestic retail bank consolidation and concentration. It may also result from the historical weakness of the life sector compared to its European counterparts. However, above all, *allfinanz* developments have been discouraged by banking legislation that prohibits bank branches from selling life insurance although they can own insurance subsidiaries. In addition, a number of powerful Italian industrial groups (e.g., Fiat, Ferruzzi, Ligresti, Fininvest) have acquired life insurance companies and they may be unwilling to develop bank/insurance links while the state continues to legislate against industrial control of Italian banking groups (Friedman 1988).

In the place of *allfinanz* strategies there has been considerable domestic merger and acquisition activity, taking place between and within the public and private banking sectors. The state has actively encouraged these mergers in an attempt to build up a domestic banking network strong enough to survive foreign competition. This has meant the sacrifice of the sheltered life that some of the smaller companies had in the previous period.

The most significant merger between public and private sector banks occurred when a large public sector bank, the Credito Italiano, took a controlling stake in the country's largest private bank, the Banca Nazionale dell'Agricoltura, in order to rationalize the operations of the latter that were deemed to be inefficient and undercapitalized by the Bank of Italy.

The Istituto Bancario San Paolo di Torino is Italy's leading international bank and has been the first bank to buy into the insurance industry. On the international front it has not been slow in making a number of important alliances with merchant banks. It has an 11 percent stake in Hambros, a 5 percent cross participation with Salomon Brothers, a cross shareholding with the Suez group, a 1 percent holding in Crédit Commerciale de France, a 6 percent interest in the Banque Internationale Arabe de Tunisie, a 10 percent interest in an Hungarian trading bank, Interbank, and it set up a joint venture with the UK's Guardian Royal Exchange in the Italian insurance market.

The biggest Italian-based insurer is Generali Assicuarzioni which in terms of market capitalization is also the second largest insurer in the world. Consolidated group premiums for 1988 rose 11.9 percent to L10,871bn. Only 36 percent of this business was Italian. Profits for the group were expected to be L500bn (St250m) for 1988 while profits from life insurance rose 64 percent in from 1987 to 1988. Along with Fiat, Generali is considered the leading blue chip stock on the Milan exchange. It is a truly international company receiving over half its life insurance premium income from outside Italy. Generali's long-standing international strategy appears to have been based on acquisitions and foreign market start-ups. Generali's primary acquisition in the last few years has been its extended battle to take over the French insurance and industrial group, Compagnie Midi.

Domestically Generali's strategy has been to consolidate its position in the network of cross-shareholding between Italy's northern industrial and financial groups and extend its coverage of different financial service markets through joint-ventures. The former strategy affords it considerable protection against hostile take-over while giving it an important influence in the Italian takeover scene; the latter appears to be a particularly Italian way of moving towards bank/insurance company link ups. With regard to this Generali has recently established a new bank, the Banca Internazionale Lombarda, with the Banca Commerciale Italiana and Paribas to develop innovative financial services in domestic and international markets. Generali has also formed a joint venture with Banca Commerciale Italiana to develop and retail investment trusts and has recently formed a co-operative venture with the Banco di Napoli but it is unclear how this will develop given that it is illegal for bank branches to sell life insurance.

The main focus of Italian banking and insurance in the run up to 1992 was on improving the position and prospects of Italian companies in their own domestic market. Prompted by the Bank of Italy the state- controlled banking sector attempted to rationalize its operations. However, lack of agreement between the political parties of government blocked substantial legislative reform regarding partial bank privatization. This domestic concern has largely forestalled forays into foreign markets in the retail banking area or the development of bank-insurance Allfinanz groups as in France and Germany.

Therefore, we can conclude that Generali and the Istituto di San Paolo di Torino are exceptions to the general rule in Italy. Generali has long had a significant international presence and is firmly established in the major EC markets for life and general insurance and it has been able to use its dominant position in the domestic insurance and equities markets to fund further foreign expansion. The Istituto Bancario San Paolo di Torino is a relative newcomer to domestic and foreign expansion. However, from a strong savings bank base, which gives it privileged access to relatively cheap deposits, it has pursued a dynamic strategy of acquisition and co-operation in Italian and foreign markets.

These companies apart, the major interest of the Italian case is the apparent attractiveness to foreign competitors of its rapidly growing retail financial services markets. Thus there has been considerable foreign movement into the Italian market by foreign firms. This has usually taken place through joint ventures although there have been significant outright acquisitions. Such ventures are particularly concentrated in the insurance sector, where state holdings appear to be less dominant than in retail banking, and in the private and merchant banking sectors. In contrast with Germany the Italian domestic market looks relatively open to foreign competition. However, the very existence of a confused regulatory scene, and a highly politicised banking sector may in the end serve to offer Italian financial institutions considerable shelter from international competition for in this situation it is essential to have extensive local knowledge and the networks of contacts and *racommandazioni* necessary to make the system work for you rather than against you.

VII. CONCLUSIONS

In this paper, we have tried to place the impact of 1992 and the SEM on personal financial services in the context of developments that were already occurring. Our argument has been that as a concrete set of rules, 1992 did not have much of an immediate impact on company strategy. In symbolic terms, however, it awakened companies to threats and opportunities inside and outside their home markets. To a limited degree, the run up to 1992 involves the dismantling of barriers to cross-border activity but these artificial, government-based barriers have in fact been less important in many ways than the informal natural barriers to entry that are left unaffected by the Single Market.

Similarly, the existing structures of national markets will remain significant. Whereas the potential for a redefinition of core business may be similar throughout Europe, we have shown that it is proceeding at a different pace in each country we have looked at. In the United Kingdom, which we dealt with briefly, this trend is most marked. The integration of insurance with banks and building societies is well-advanced. In Germany, the biggest financial institutions are moving strongly down this road with consequent problems for the smaller companies. In France, there is rather less unanimity among the largest companies about the value of this, while in Italy, there remain legal prohibitions against such link-ups, though these are in the process of being dismantled.

It appears that the problems of linking banks and insurance are, however, quite complex. As well as spending to buy into the complementary area or to set up a new organization or even to create a cooperative venture, companies face significant organizational and management problems in linking together two such different areas. Not surprisingly, then, it appears that few are using the relaxation of regulations consequent upon 1992 in order to develop an *international* Allfinanz or bancassurance strategy. Instead, involvement in other countries is usually based on traditional areas of strength, that is, either insurance or banking but seldom both. Whether this will change in the future is uncertain.

In conclusion, we have tried to show how responses to 1992 differ between countries. Whereas all companies in personal financial services face similar issues, the ways they are dealing with them vary. The opening up of the Single Market is one more milestone in the internationalization process. It creates threats and opportunities for the companies but it is only one part of a more complex process of change in the industry. For a variety of reasons, banking and insurance tended to be conservative areas of economic life until the seventies. For the past 20 years, however, change has been coming with ever increasing rapidity. As it has done so, it has challenged old definitions of core business and old strategies of maintaining market position. As a result, the industry has become more competitive and innovative. The Single Market may serve to speed up that process but because of the uneven development of legislative frameworks, market structures and organizational management, it will be a long time before the uniqueness of each country's personal financial services sector disappears. Although artificial government barriers are being dismantled, there will remain natural barriers. In Germany and France, the largest companies have been active in increasing their size and strength in order to make entry to the market even more difficult for outsiders. In doing so, they have undermined the stability within which a range of small and medium-sized companies were able to shelter as specialist, local providers. In Italy, this process has proceeded more slowly, giving foreign companies a better chance of entering the market. In Italy, cultural and political barriers are most important in protecting home industry, though these are slowly declining in significance.

The opening up of the Single European Market in 1992 is part of a long term process of internationalization. National and local differences will remain significant for the foreseeable future. What will have changed, however, will be that these differences will no longer be reinforced by government barriers to foreign entry. Instead, they will depend on the ability of domestic companies to provide an efficient and relevant product to their home consumer. If these conditions are not met, the possibility of foreign competitors entering these markets will increase as a result of the dismantling of governmental barriers.

ACKNOWLEDGMENTS

The authors would like to acknowledge the financial support of TSB plc and the Economic and Social Research Council for the projects from which this research is drawn. We would also like to thank Dr.David Knights, our colleague at the Manchester School of Management, for his comments and support. Finally, thanks go to the editors of this volume for their comments on the original version of this paper that was presented at the Conference on Global Strategic Management which they organized at the European Institute for Advanced Studies in Management, Brussels in May, 1990.

REFERENCES

Cecchini P. 1988. *The European Challenge, 1992, The Benefits of a Single market*. Aldershot: Wildwood House.

Channon D. 1988. *Global Banking Strategy*. New York: John Wiley.

European Communities Commission. 1988a. *Completing the Internal Market*. Luxemburg: Office for Official Publications of the European Communities.

European Communities Commission. 1988b. *Towards a Big Internal Market in Financial Services*. Luxemburg: Office for Official Publications of the European Communities.

European Communities Commission. 1988c. *1992 - Completion of the Single Market*. Luxemburg: Office for Official Publications of the European Communities.

European Communities Commission. 1989. *1992 - Financial Services and Capital Movements*. Luxemburg: Office for Official Publications of the European Communities.

Finsinger J. 1986. "A State Controlled Market: The German Case." In *The Economics of Insurance Regulation,* edited by J. Fensinger and M.V. Pauley. London: Macmillan.

Friedman, A. 1988. *Agnelli and the Network of Italian Power*. London: Harrap.

Ingham, G. 1984. *Capitalism Divided? The City and Industry in British Social Development*. London: Macmillan.

Morgan, G. 1992. "States, Societies and 1992." In *The Internationalization of Financial Services,* edited by D. Knights. Oxford: Blackwell.

Strange, S. 1988. *Casino Capitalism*. Oxford: Blackwell.

Zysman, J. 1983. *Governments, Markets and Growth*. Oxford: Martin Robertson.

EUROPEAN INTEGRATION AND GLOBAL STRATEGY IN THE MEDIA AND ENTERTAINMENT INDUSTRY

Ravi Sarathy

I. INTRODUCTION

Services account for the largest portion of output and employment in the advanced industrialized countries. If we exclude the government sector (which is also considered as a service "industry"), services were 53 percent of GDP (gross domestic product) over the period 1980-1984 in the United States, 47 percent in Japan, 41 percent in West Germany, and 42 percent each in Canada and United Kingdom (Blades 1987). Services typically become more important as an economy becomes more developed. Thus, for the United States, employment in service industries as a percent of total employment was 24 percent in 1870, 31 percent by 1900, 55 percent in 1950 and 72 percent in 1985 (Ott 1987). Similar increases were recorded by Japan with service employment as a percent of total employment increasing from 13 percent in 1890 to 56 percent in 1984, in West Germany from 25 to 53 percent, in France from 27 to 59 percent, and in United Kingdom from 30 to 68 percent. Thus, the service industry as a whole has been increasing in importance for almost a century in the advanced industrialized nations.

Research in Global Strategic Management, Volume 2, pages 125-148.
Copyright © 1991 by JAI Press Inc.
All rights of reproduction in any form reserved.
ISBN: 1-55938-277-5

A major services industry is the global media and entertainment industry. As incomes rise and leisure time increases, people around the world spend more financial resources on, and devote more of their time to media and entertainment industry products. The United States is one of the world's major services exporters (U.S. services exports totalled $56 billion in 1987). Within the services sector, *entertainment was the single largest export, earning $5.5 billion in 1988*. The media and entertainment industry is an area where U.S. companies have long dominated world markets.

As in any industry that is growing rapidly, global competition is intense. There are major changes taking place in the global media industry which may affect the United States' preeminence in this area. Such changes include:

- Deregulation of the media industry overseas in Europe and Japan;
- the impact of new technology such as direct broadcast satellite television;
- growing protectionism in the EC;
- resort to horizontal and vertical diversification in the global media industry; and
- a wave of mergers and acquisitions centering on the United States, with foreign firms buying up U.S. companies.

This paper is concerned with the evolution of international trade and competition in the global entertainment industry with particular reference to the EC. We review the divergent development of the media and entertainment industry in the United States and Europe, indicating why U.S. companies were dominant. We then highlight changes taking place in the European market, and consider how European media firms are responding to the changing competitive environment. In considering the media industry, it is important to note that all services industries have special characteristics that make international trade in services difficult. The Appendix surveys these special features and points out their relevance for international competition.

II. THE GLOBAL MEDIA AND ENTERTAINMENT INDUSTRY

Entertainment has always been a major U.S. industry. The private enterprise ownership system governing U.S. television and the burgeoning of alternative television channels, first pay-TV, then cable television and now satellite television has led to fierce competition between U.S. television stations. Each station seeks larger audiences so as to sell more commercials and charge higher prices for commercial time; this means showing programs that attract the largest audiences. Hence, the United States has an enormous and ever-thirsty market for "software," for programs, films, news, talk shows, variety shows and sporting events, to fill the large number of available hours on a multiplicity of channels.

Table 1.   Strategic Trends Affecting the Entertainment Industry

Deregulation	Proliferation of TV channels overseas, and hence, increased demand for programs to fill air time with.
Technology	Direct Broadcast Systems using satellite (DBS) allow for cross-national TV channels serving many countries and beyond the control of individual governments. They become an alternative to cable TV.
Protection	The European Commission directive suggesting 50 percent European program content on European television implies a greater role for pan-European and co-production agreements involving U.S. interests.
Scale Economies	to be borne; hence, a global trend to acquisitions in the media industry.
Vertical Integration	production, as well as distribution, that is, the TV channels and movie theaters; example: News Corp.'s acquisitions of 20th Century Films and the creation of the Fox network.
Horizontal Integration	Perceived gains from selling ideas through books, record, films and TV programs; example: Bertelsmann or Time Warner's ownership of multiple media.

At the heart of globalization in the media industry are the industry's cost structure and economics. The media industry has some significant characteristics that interact with the environmental changes described above to create the need for new global strategies (see Table 1). Major industry characteristics include:

- A *high fixed cost structure,* with most of the costs incurred in the production of programs and in the establishment of the distribution system that is, establishing the TV network, be it via satellite, on-air, cable or pay channels. The high fixed costs place a premium on obtaining a large subscriber base and create high leverage, with handsome profits occurring once break-even levels are reached.
- The media industry is also *cyclical,* at least in the United States, with sudden jumps in revenue being derived from hit films, TV programs and books and records. Thus, the industry has a high level of risk, and requires abundant capital to survive long periods of negative cash flow. In turn, this creates a bias within the industry to control distribution channels, that is, media outlets, be it book publishers, TV channels or record clubs.
- Another trend is the *maturation of the U.S. market* with lower growth rates and an abundant supply of TV channels as compared to markets in Europe or Japan and the Far East, where fewer channels are available and growth rates are higher since market penetration is low.

- A fourth factor is the *impact of private ownership of television and other media channels*. Such private ownership results in a greater focus on the use of commercials as the basis for profitability. The channel, be it television or magazines or newspapers, seeks to deliver an audience to advertisers, receiving advertising revenue in return. The bait with which to attract a large audience is the program content. The point is, a private ownership channel must be more concerned with the popularity and mass appeal of the program content than a government owned channel, with implications for the nature of programming and its cultural impact.

These industry characteristics result in a bias towards larger sized and diversified media companies, and in a strategic advantage accruing to those companies that are able to produce "software" for the media industry distribution channels while also controlling the distribution channels themselves. That is, companies that own both TV stations and TV film production companies might enjoy higher profits, less risk and faster rates of growth, thus creating substantial natural entry barriers against rivals that are less diversified. Further, because the United States is a relatively mature market as compared to the faster growth presented by the emergence of private media ownership in Europe and Japan, attractive profit opportunities lie in producing programs with global appeal in U.S. studios and facilities (an activity in which the United States has a comparative advantage), and marketing these programs to captive media channels in the United States, Europe, and Japan.

A. The European Media Environment

In contrast to the private ownership pattern prevailing in U.S. film and TV industries, European television was controlled, with television station ownership often a Government monopoly. Basically, government ownership meant non-commercial television. Commercials were rare and restricted as to when they could be shown. Thus, in West Germany, television advertising was restricted to 40 minutes a day, and to 20 minutes a day in Switzerland. In France, only one-fourth of all advertising spending is television advertising, hampered by rules such as those preventing retail chains from advertising their goods on TV, a rule intended to favor the press.

However, this Government ownership of media is giving way to greater private ownership, through deregulation. Deregulation of European television has changed the competitive environment (see for example, Eger 1987; Noam 1987). The use of new technologies (satellite broadcasting, cable and pay TV, all relatively new to Europe and Japan) have all increased the number of channels available in television. For example, in Japan alone, after 1990, 24 hour satellite TV broadcasting will increase the number of channels available from 7 to 12 or 13 channels, depending on how the satellite is used. It is estimated that there will be over 120 TV channels in Europe by 1995, three times the number in 1983 ("Buddy, Can You Spare a Reel" 1989a).

Deregulation and the allowance of private ownership of television media has major market implications.

- First, there are more television stations and more air time to fill, and as in the United States, this will mean greater demand for television programming.
- Second, deregulated TV stations and channels will show more commercials, and there will be more advertising by firms seeking a European market; in turn, more business for advertising agencies and their suppliers.
- Third, more exports for U.S. producers of films and TV shows, as they have the product for a market that needs something to fill the hours with.
- Fourth, pressure to produce and broadcast programs that will allow the media to deliver a large audience, which in turn could justify increasing advertising rates and promise higher total advertising revenues.

These developments have changed and broadened the definition of the media industry. It now encompasses both broadcasting and production of television and motion picture films, while also including books and newspapers, as well as printing services and alternative modes of information delivery including the creation and sale of proprietary databases. The guiding principle is that "software" can be delivered in a variety of ways, on record and cassette, on television and in the movie theater, in book form and as data that can be downloaded from on-line databases.

France is an interesting example of these changes. In 1987, three of France's television channels were privatized. One of the channels, TV6, became 25 percent owned by CLT, a Luxembourg company. La Cinq, another channel, is 25 percent owned by Berlusconi, head of an Italian conglomerate, while TF1 is owned by the Bouygues construction firm. The two remaining publicly-owned channels, Antenne 2 and FR3 are rapidly losing audience share, with a combined viewership percent of 32.6 percent to TF1's 41 percent, La Cinq's 12.5 percent and TV6's 7.4 percent ("French Television" 1989c).

1. Technology's Role in Creating a Pan-European Media Industry

Technology has played a key role in changing the nature of the industry. Europeans are creating new TV channels by using high-power direct-broadcast satellite (DBS) systems that can beam programs from satellites in space directly into the home via a small (18 inch) backyard dish receiver (Koltai 1987). In England, British Satellite Broadcasting received a United Kingdom franchise at a cost of $1.1 billion, and will compete with a similar service from News

Corp., the Sky channel. West Germany and France have similar satellite systems, with 4 channels each. And Luxembourg has launched Astra, a medium-power system with 16 channels, though this will require larger dishes. The obstacle to the spread of this form of TV is that households must buy the small dish receivers. The unwillingness of families to buy such receivers may mean that traditional terrestrial TV stations will take the lion's share of an European TV market estimated to grow to $34 billion a year by the year 2000. The other problem is that satellite TV is an alternative to cable, and if it does not win market share quickly, homes that become wired with cable will be less interested in also buying a satellite TV receiving dish. However, satellite TV has been successful in Japan, with almost half a million dishes being sold within a year of launch of NHK's first two non-commercial TV channels via satellite ("European Satellite TV" 1988).

2. The Importance of a Pan-European Audience

The promise of satellite TV is the possibility of creating a pan-European cross-cultural audience. The satellite channels create overlapping signals. The United Kingdom's satellite channel signals can be picked up in Ireland, Belgium, The Netherlands and large parts of France. France's TDF-1 will reach to Spain, central Europe, and nearly all of Italy and the United Kingdom; while Germany's TV Sat will cover all of central Europe, half of France, nearly all of Italy, eastern United Kingdom and southern Norway and Sweden. Sweden and Ireland also have similar plans. (A hidden benefit of these cross-national TV channels is that they can escape government regulation. Governments can regulate TV and interfere in the content of what goes on TV mainly when the signals emanate from within their borders. TV signals received by a country's citizens from satellites circling overhead are far more difficult to control, though the EC's television directive has sought to address this issue ["All the World's a Dish" 1988a]).

What are the consequences of being able to reach a pan-European audience? First, producers, whether European or American, will have to decide what sorts of programs are likely to appeal to viewers from different European countries. Second, firms who advertise will have to assess whether the possibility of using such pan-European media should change their ways of doing business. For one, they might develop a common brand name to push in their pan-European commercials on media such as the Sky Channel. Thus, Unilever cannot easily advertise its cleaning fluid branded as Vif in Switzerland, Viss in Germany, Jif in United Kingdom and Greece, and Cif in France. Companies must also convince nationalistic country managers to agree to standardized brand names and advertising channels.

It also means deciding to make a big push with advertising. Before the advent of television deregulation in Europe, European companies spent about $5 billion a year (in 1987) on advertising compared to a level of nearly $20 billion in the United States (with a quarter less population). ("Cable and Satellites" 1987). In short, European companies might decide to emphasize advertising more heavily, as have their Japanese and United States counterparts. An example is Philips of Netherlands, which aims to make its name and logo be seen everywhere: Philips ran the same ad in 44 countries reminding listeners and viewers of its sponsorship of the 1986 World Cup soccer tournament. Its sign on the fence surrounding the playing field was seen for 38 minutes of a 90 minute game watched by an estimated 500 million people.

There is little doubt that pan-European advertising is attractive. Large companies such as Unilever Group have become charter advertisers on Sky TV, where they get attractive rates in exchange for a guaranteed level of advertising spending at about £ 4 million (Pounds sterling) over two years. Similarly, Coke sponsors the Coca-Cola Eurochart Top 100 show on the Sky channel, using images and tunes to reach a young audience all over Europe.

3. MTV: The First Pan-European Channel?

Cable TV is not as widespread in Europe as in the United States, and may never become a force because of growing competition from DBS (satellite) television. One of the more successful cable TV stations in Europe is MTV Europe, itself a joint venture of American and European partners. Understanding why MTV has been successful is the key to understanding the potential and pitfalls of a pan-European television network.

MTV President Tom Freston has said, "Music crosses borders very easily, and the lingua franca of rock n'roll is English. Rock is an Anglo-American form; German rock bands sing in English; Swedish rock bands sing in English." Not surprisingly, MTV is now available in 24 countries. It is particularly interested in Europe, with the proliferation of TV channels there. MTV's mission? "We want to be the global rock n' roll village where we can talk to youth worldwide." MTV Europe, in a joint venture with Mirror Newspapers and British Telecom is a 24 hour a day 7 day a week service. In Japan it is restricted to a few hours in the early morning. But its goal is to establish a "brand name" against the day when more TV air time on newer channels will be available in Japan.

The key to cross-national TV networks is language. Will people seeking entertainment deliberately watch a foreign language show? Would they rather watch a dubbed alternative? As the Economist puts it, entertainment in a foreign language is seldom "light." The Germans were glad to watch Sky and Super Channel for a while, until the two German satellite stations RTL Plus and SAT1 were available. Then, Sky and Super Channel lost audiences; however, the Germans watched the same shows, but dubbed into German.

Rock music videos succeed on MTV mainly because language is irrelevant. But even here, cultural preferences are important: teenagers in different countries may prefer different kinds of rock music ("All the World's a Dish" 1988a). In contrast to MTV, SuperChannel, an English-based satellite and cable station lost nearly $100 million in two years. It then changed ownership and its format, choosing to emphasize a mix of sporting events (skiing, rugby, tennis, American and Canadian football, even the World timber championships from Oregon featuring logrolling, tree climbing and log splitting), old Hollywood films and music videos, with a dab of news. Thus, cross-national TV can succeed if the same program can be offered with multiple language tracks; or, cross-national TV channels must focus on special interest programs, such as sports, business news and first-run movies, where the language barrier is not as important.

B.   European Community Directives for the Media Industry

As suggested earlier, deregulation and privatization of European media present a golden opportunity for U.S. media firms. This is because deregulation has stimulated demand for media products in Europe, while domestic (European) capacity to satisfy such demand is limited and high cost. Hence, EC media directives have been passed, to provide a degree of protection for the nascent European media industry. The intent is to stem the onslaught of American companies and their films and variety shows, to create a breathing space and foster the emergence of an "European" film and television program production industry.

In attempting to promulgate directives for the European media industry, the EC had to face several issues. At an *economic* level, the European market for media products was fragmented by national barriers, including language, and small size markets. Scale economies were lacking, and state-owned monopolies that dominated the media industry had little experience or interest in stimulating audience interest. Advertising support was insignificant. However, the central fact was that deregulation and a proliferation of channels would lead to strong demand for media products. (By one estimate, the EC would need about 300,000 hours of programming annually, whereas European supply would only satisfy about one-third of estimated demand.)

At the *technological* level, innovations such as satellite DBS, cable and pay-TV, and video standards for high-definition TV broadcasts were important issues. Governments were concerned about losing control of their media space to broadcasters from outside their national territories, while technical standards had implications for European equipment manufacturers, struggling as always with the threat of lower-priced and technically advanced Japanese equipment in areas such as High-definition Television (HDTV). *Legal* differences also had to be reconciled, including national regulatory differences, and EC member country divergences over controls on advertising, controls over the origin of programming and over the content of programming.

Finally, there is the *political-cultural* dimension. The EC directives are in part an outgrowth of the alarm in Europe over the domination of films, TV channels and air waves (radio) by U.S. product and by extension, U.S. culture. Smaller countries fear that their culture will be overrun by programs from countries with large internal markets such as the United States; the French fear that English will become even more accepted as a world language.

In October 1989, the European Community adopted a directive requiring that a majority of the shows on European television be of European origin, "where practicable" that is, a minimum of 50 percent local content, excluding news, sports events and game shows. The directive also removed restrictions on cross-border transmissions (EC 1989). In addition, the EC has launched the "Media 92" program, to provide subsidies for European film production, distribution, script-writing, cartoon animation, education and training, translation, European video industry and so forth. Also announced was the "audiovisual Eureka" program to provide about $275 million in subsidies (in total) for European film production.

1. Barriers to Entry and the Media Industry

The differential patterns of growth in the European and U.S. media industries has created some interesting barriers to entry that have affected the EC directives issued to help the European media industry. Following Rugman and Verbeke (1990), we can analyze the media industry in terms of (a) the degree of economic and institutional integration; and (b) the degree of natural entry barriers and government-imposed entry barriers. With regard to economic integration, the media industry has been dominated by U.S. interests, with exports from the U.S. to Europe being the major trade flow. With the exception of the U.S. media industry, the rest of the world industry has primarily consisted of a series of national industries with relatively little international trade. Wildman and Siwek note (1988, p. 35), "as a global film exporter, there is no close second to the U.S." Given this structure of international trade, institutional integration has not been an issue, with little pressure or impetus by U.S. firms to seek national treatment, reciprocity and harmonization.

Natural entry barriers benefiting European firms are primarily cultural and language oriented, with economies of scale and managerial and artistic resources being a second type of entry barrier. The language and culture barrier is easy to understand. Films made in one country cater primarily to a regional audience, with the exception of the United States' that possesses the advantage of a large internal market and a homogeneous English language audience. The United States' long experience with film and TV program production, along with the need to please large audiences because of the industries dependence on advertisers are a reason why U.S. programs have been able to cross cultural borders. Equally important as an entry barrier is the existence in the U.S. of capital willing to commit to the risky business of making film and TV programs: the average United States film budget now exceeds $25 million. Such capital pools together with "talent"—the film stars, producers and directors and other experienced personnel—constitute a major entry barrier, because replicating these resources is costly, time-consuming, and risky.

2.   European Community Media Directives as Government Imposed Entry Barriers

Against this background, we can see EC directives as increasing Government imposed entry barriers even as natural entry barriers are decreasing because of the removal of restrictions on cross-border transmission and the emergence of a pan-European audience. The 50 percent local content requirement amounts to a type of infant industry protection, while the subsidies for film and video production serve to bridge the shortages of capital for film and TV program production. Thus, outsiders such as the dominant U.S. firms will find themselves faced with lower natural but increased artificial entry barriers benefiting European companies, again following Rugman and Verbeke (1990). Yet, the experience factor will work in favor of U.S. "outsider" firms, and help them reach an accommodation with European media interests. That is, guaranteeing market share and providing capital cannot alone ensure that the programs consequently produced (by favored European companies) will attract large audiences. At least for the time being, U.S. production companies will be needed as joint venture partners to provide expertise to create mass appeal programs.

The deliberate vagueness of the European Commission directive means that individual countries can interpret the directive as they choose in controlling the quantity of U.S. programs shown. France has decreed that beginning in 1992, programs on the 5 French TV stations (excluding pay TV, cable and satellite TV) must broadcast 60 percent Eurocontent during prime time, and 50 percent French content. The French consider television to be Europe's cultural cement and see the issue as one of cultural imperialism ("The Battle for Europe's TV" 1989b). Of course, when the EC insists on European origin programs, it is not clear why a German program is preferable in Spain to a program originating from the United States.

Generally, the most popular show in any European country is a local show. Thus, in Germany, "Schwartzwaldklinik," a German sort of St. Elsewhere set in a health spa; in Italy, "La Piovra (The Octopus)," about an investigator against the Mafia set in Palermo; in Spain, "Juncal," about an aging bullfighter. American shows are generally the second most popular shows. The remainder of local programming is generally cheap-to-produce talk and variety shows. Given the sudden increase in the number of hours to fill on the new channels, it is not surprising that U.S. programs are being purchased ("The Battle for Europe's TV" 1989b). Many of the U.S. shows being purchased are older recycled programs such as the Lucy Show, and General Hospital. In Fall 1989, the most popular U.S. shows in the international market were Dallas, L.A. Law, Midnight Caller, Tour of Duty, and Dynasty.

The proliferation of channels implies that Europe will require many more hours of new programming per year. But in 1987, an hour of Dallas, the popular American TV show could be licensed for a fee of $32,000, as compared to the $400,000 cost of producing one episode of the Chateuvallon series on France's A2 station. By 1989, the rights to an American television movie could be purchased for about $70,000 as against an estimate of $1 million to produce an original French production ("The Media Barons" 1987; "Keeping up with the Murdochs" 1989a). As the number of TV channels proliferates in Japan and Europe, the competition for American films and TV programs pushes their price up.

The other reason that U.S. shows are attractive is their ability to attract and hold audiences. American TV stations have always lived in an environment where commercials must be sold, and profitability depends on high audience ratings which will attract more commercials and at higher rates. Hence, U.S. producers are constantly aware of the need to keep viewers who would otherwise zap their way past boring programs. For this reason alone, U.S. film and TV producers have learnt how to hold the viewer's attention better than anyone else.

An interesting response to the need for home-grown "European" programs is the decision to produce a pan-European soap opera, "Monte Carlo," by the New York-based EC Television subsidiary of the Interpub advertising agency. The plan is to produce 260 episodes a year in English, to be dubbed later in French, German, Italian and Spanish. The estimated cost of production of $40 million is almost completely bankrolled by TV stations in the four largest European markets: Granada in The United Kingdom, TDF1 in France, Berlusconi in Italy, and Studio Hamburg in West Germany. The program will meet Eurocontent requirements because it is controlled by EC companies. Furthermore, many of the TV stations will pay for the show by bartering airtime, which the agency will then sell to clients desiring commercial time on these stations. The growing demand in Europe for programs is not only fostering a European TV production industry, but is also providing a diversification opportunity for advertising agencies who presumably bring some people-pleasing skills to be combined with their experience in producing attention-getting commercials ("Monte Carlo or Bust" 1989b).

C.   Strategic Response by European Media Firms

Perhaps even more important than EC level measures aimed at the media industry, is the growing move by European and Japanese media firms to acquire major U.S. media companies. Table 2 summarizes some of the major acquisitions taking place since 1988 in the media industry.

Table 2.   Global Media Empire Building: Acquisitions Since 1988

Acquirer	Acquisitions Made
Sony Corp	CBS Records, Columbia Pictures, and Gubers-Peters Productions.
Time-Warner	Merger: combining books and magazines, pay and cable TV, film production, records and movies.
Bertelsmann	RCA Records, Bantam books, and Doubleday books.
News Corp	20th Century Fox films and several TV stations: the Fox network, Sky TV in Europe, TV Guide (Triangle Publications) and Premiere magazine; and Harper/Collins books.
Hachette	Diamandis (magazines), and Grolier (encyclopedias).
Maxwell	McMillan Publishing, Official Airline Guide
Cap Cities	Through ESPN, 40 percent ownership of Japan Sports Channel, and 25 percent of the British-based pan-European cable network Screensport.
U.S. West	A joint venture cable TV franchise for all of Hong Kong (1.5 million homes), and cable TV properties in United Kingdom and France.
Fujisankei	Virgin Records, David Puttnam's Enigma Productions
Television South Pic	MTM (Mary Tyler Moore) Productions.

As Table 2 shows, the bulk of activity has been concentrated in the United States. There are several reasons for this U.S. focus.

1.   The United States has had long experience in developing films and TV programs, and Hollywood and U.S. productions have enjoyed worldwide success. Owning these facilities would deliver a stream of films and TV programs, books, records and magazines to be then marketed around the world.

2.   A second reason is the size of the U.S. market and the profits to be derived from having a market share of the world's premier entertainment market. It is also a lead market, with a good chance that programs successful in the United States can then be sold to Europe successfully.

3.   A third reason might be to gain "technology," in the shape of film and TV production technology, as well as the talent and experience of U.S. based film and TV production crews; this is primarily a people issue, and rather than try to transport talent to European markets, companies may want

to acquire this talent in the United States through acquiring the U.S. company.

1. News Corporation

The best example of this globalization phenomenon is News Corp. controlled by Australian entrepreneur Rupert Murdoch. He first expanded from Australia to the United Kingdom, primarily in TV and newspapers. He built up Sky Channel as a pan-European service using both cable and satellite delivery; next, he developed a United States base, buying several independent TV stations and the 20th Century Fox film production company, along with its library of films, as the nucleus for creating a fourth U.S.-wide on-air TV network. The network would distribute that is, show films produced by 20th Century Fox, and the same material could appear in the United Kingdom and Europe on Sky Channel. Then, he acquired TV Guide and created Premiere magazine, both vehicles to appeal to the United States national TV audience and further publicize his network.

News Corp. has been similarly active in the book business. It began with purchasing Harper & Row in 1987, a mid-sized U.S. publisher with sales of $244 million. It subsequently acquired Zondervan, a United States religious publisher, the book publisher William Collins and Sons in the United Kingdom, and most recently, the United States Scott Foresman textbook publishers. By 1990, its Harper/Collins and other book units revenues exceeded $1.5 billion. Book acquisitions at News Corp. have been fueled in part by plans to use books as raw material for film and TV programs. Murdoch's News Corp. is an example of the implementation of a globalization strategy in a global services industry. The principal points of his strategy include a physical presence in two major markets, Europe and the United States, and combining of both distribution channels, the TV stations and channels themselves, together with production facilities and software, including books and a back-list of films and TV programs to be continually resold.

The *music industry* is also rapidly becoming global; the worldwide popularity of rock and roll owes much to MTV. Here, one can see how culture can influence the international marketing of services, in this case, an entertainment product. Bertelsmann, a music conglomerate, has consciously tried to sell pop music around the world. They acquired RCA records, because they saw the U.S. music industry as the primary source of innovation and creativity in the international music business. Upon acquiring RCA, Bertelsmann, which is a German company, moved its music division headquarters to New York. Michael Dornemann, the CEO of Bertelsmann Music Group (BMG) follows a policy of "breaking" an artist into a country's market by launching the act on TV and on stage, and through publicity in newspapers and magazines. Only then will he begin to bring in records and tapes. That is, he designs a separate marketing program for each artist for each country.

The same trend to global expansion and diversification affects other segments of the media industry such as the news segment and cable television. For example, Cable News Network (CNN) which is an all-news format now sells condensed versions of its news production, being shown in 83 countries in 1989 ("Keeping up with the Murdochs" 1989). The news is somewhat customized, to include local weather and some local news. It is available in hotel rooms around the world through cable feed by satellites. As CNN goes global, it needs to internationalize its product by supplying more international news, and is therefore opening more international news bureaus, 18 in total by the end of 1989.

In cable TV, major U.S. companies are looking for growth overseas. Growth in the number of U.S. homes receiving cable is slowing down, as much of the potential market already receives cable hookups. But cable TV is in its infancy in the rest of the world. The U.S. telephone deregulation laws preventing U.S. phone companies from entering the cable industry is one reason for their interest in overseas markets. Of course, overseas government regulations similarly limit the participation of U.S. firms. In many countries, cable TV is viewed as a public utility and controlled by a utility company. Cable fees are set by governments and thus limit the potential profitability of overseas cable operations. Still, the U.S. cable companies greater experience with developing the cable network infrastructure and then running the business means that they have an edge in countries where regulation has not reduced cable's attractiveness. The real issue for cable is competition in the form of satellite DBS systems that can be picked up with dish antennas. Yet, as Table 2 shows, U.S. West, one of the Baby Bell companies, is willing to invest $500 million in building an advanced cable network in Hong Kong which would handle fax, videotext and TV. (Recently, Hong Kong also approved HutchVision, a satellite TV network, and Government regulation will decide the relative penetration of cable vs. satellite TV in Hong Kong).

Sports represents another segment of the entertainment industry which is rapidly becoming globalized, principally because of the media industry itself. C. Itoh corporation, the giant Japanese trading company, has entered into a joint venture with ESPN, for example, giving it a 40 percent share in the newly formed Japan Sports Channel. For ESPN, this alliance is part of its plans to derive incremental overseas revenues by broadcasting American sports events for which it has already obtained rights, such as National Football League games. At the same time, ESPN hopes to get rights to foreign sporting events and show them to U.S. viewers as well as worldwide.

D.   Sony: A Case Study

Sony is an example of the impact of entertainment industry changes on basic global strategy. Sony is interesting despite the fact that most of its media strategies are focused on the U.S. market with the EC only tangentially involved. Sony is particularly interesting because it is a manufacturing firm that has been gradually changing itself into a firm with a strong service industry and media orientation. As such, it is a precursor of the directions from which new competition can be expected. We briefly consider Sony as a case study to better appreciate the magnitude of entertainment industry changes and their impact.

Sony has long been known for its innovative consumer electronics products, such as the pioneering Walkman. It is an international corporation, with 70 percent of its sales coming from outside Japan, and non-Japanese owners owning about 23 percent of Sony stock (situation in 1989). Sony also manufactures about 20 percent of its output outside Japan. However, it was primarily a consumer electronics company getting the bulk of its sales from manufactured products. Sony's products could be divided into four distinct product groups: video equipment (VCRs), audio equipment (compact disc players), televisions (the Trinitron), and other products (records, floppy disk drives and semiconductors). As of 1986, its sales mix was: video equipment = 33 percent, audio equipment = 22 percent, televisions = 22 percent and other products = 17 percent. Sony has always emphasized research and development, spending about 9 percent of sales on R&D.

1.   The Betamax Experience

Sony however has been facing increasing competition from other Japanese companies and from countries with lower labor costs such as Taiwan and South Korea. Its strategy of inventing new advanced technology products and then waiting for the market to buy its products seemed to be faltering in the market. Sony's biggest failure was the Betamax. Sony had invented the Betamax format for VCRs and refused to license the technology to other manufacturers. It was higher-priced and recording times were somewhat shorter than the competing VHS format, even though quality of the images recorded with Betamax was higher.

Sony's competitors, such as Matsushita (Panasonic), Hitachi and Toshiba all banded together around the VHS format. They licensed the format to any manufacturer who wanted it, which had two results. The total number of VHS sets produced and sold was far higher than the Betamax format VCRs, which meant lower retail prices because of accumulated volume and resulting economies of scale. Secondly, far more "software" was available for the VHS format; that is, movie producers were more likely to make home video copies of their films available for purchase and rental on VHS tapes. This further increased demand for VHS format VCRs. The net result was that Betamax gradually faded and Sony stopped production of Betamax format VCRs in 1988.

2. Rethinking Basic Strategy

The difficulty of selling advanced technology coupled with the speed of imitation and the impact of low-wage country competitors led Sony to change its basic corporate strategy. The CBS/Sony Group Inc., a 50-50 joint venture between Sony and CBS, Inc. has grown dramatically over a twenty year period to become an industry leader in the multibillion-yen Japanese music industry. It releases recordings in Japan, Hong Kong and Macau, on compact disc and other formats, by popular Japanese artists, such as Seiko Matsuda and Rebecca, as well as foreign artists.

3. Sony's Diversification into the Entertainment Industry

Therefore, Sony's diversification into the global music industry is not unexpected. In January 1988, Sony agreed to buy CBS Records worldwide for $2 billion. But subsequent moves have dramatically transformed Sony, as it moves to become more of a service company. Table 3 summarizes the major entertainment industry acquisitions made by Sony since 1988.

Table 3.   From Electronics to Entertainment:
Sony's Acquisitions Since 1988

Date	Company Acquired	Price
October 1989	Guber-Peters Productions	$200 million
September 1989	Columbia Pictures	$3.4 billion
January 1989	Tree International country music publishers	$30 million
January 1988	CBS records	$2 billion

The acquisitions themselves are large, totalling over $5 billion, or about half of Sony's total assets. More interesting is the reasoning behind Sony's decision to acquire a slew of entertainment companies. The motives for the several acquisitions are summarized next.

1. *CBS Records*—For $2 billion, Sony was able to acquire control of the world's largest record company. Sony had traditionally sold music hardware, being one of the world's largest producers of compact disk players, tape recorders including the phenomenally successful Walkman, and stereo television. But all of these products were subject to competition, as innovative ideas could be imitated and prices cut. Sony realized that being in the music business allowed it to take advantage of the entire installed base of compact disk players around the world, not just those manufactured by Sony. Imitation was impossible as each music act was unique; however, the music business was a creative one, consisting of managing personal relations with relatively young pop stars with large egos. Managing such a creative business required far greater cultural sensitivity and required the use of local managers rather than predominantly Japanese management.

The music industry is also a fast growing business. In 1988, over 150 million CDs were sold in the United States alone, and there were over 11 million CD players in households. CBS Records, Inc. consists of CBS Records (Domestic), CBS Masterworks, CBS Records International, CBS/Sony, Columbia House, and CBS Musicvideo. The acquisition gave Sony an immediate international presence in the music industry.

2. *Columbia Pictures*—The major attraction here is a large library of movies that continue to earn revenues every time they are shown at cinemas and on video around the world. Columbia also has a profitable TV production and syndication business. Thus, the acquisition gives Sony products to sell to owners of TV sets and VCRs, in a manner analogous to providing music on record and tape for owners of CD players and tape recorders.

There are two other reasons why Sony might have found Columbia Pictures attractive. One, TV in Japan is being liberalized, with a doubling in the number of TV stations and on-air time because of the launch of satellite television. There will be a sudden increase in demand for product, such as films and TV shows, to fill air time on Japan's satellite stations. Sony will be in a position to supply such product at a time when demand will be increasing, thus being able to charge premium prices in yen.

The other reason is hardware related. Sony has been trying to establish its 8 mm. camcorder format, again in competition with a VHS-C based format from competing Japanese producers. This standards battle brings to mind Sony's previous experience with Betamax. Except that, Sony realizes the need to build up the installed base. Hence, it has licensed the 8 mm. technology to other producers and is willing to manufacture 8 mm. camcorders for sale by others under their own brand names. Thus, Sony is taking care of one side of the equation: making sure that volume sales of the 8 mm. camcorder will be achieved, resulting in economies of scale and lower prices. The next step is stimulating demand for the 8 mm. format, by making available a variety of movies in this format. Sony can do this by putting the entire Columbia Pictures catalog on 8 mm. video, thus giving consumers a reason to buy the 8 mm. camcorder, as a way of being able to watch the 8 mm. videotapes. This availability will be crucial to the success of Sony's newly introduced 8 mm. video Walkman, a pocket-sized portable color television set, which will become appealing to the extent that videos are available for use with the video Walkman.

Thus, with the CBS Records and Columbia Pictures acquisition, Sony becomes one of the world's major producer of entertainment hardware and software: record producer and CD player producer; a leading manufacturer of TV sets and an owner of a library of classic films.

3.   *Guber-Peters Productions*—When Sony purchased Columbia pictures, it obtained a film library as well as film production facilities such as a film studio. Columbia had gone through four producers in five years, and needed more capable film production management. The logical step was to take over one of Hollywood's most successful film production companies, Guber-Peters (formerly Barris Productions). Guber-Peters had been responsible for Batman, one of Warner Communications all-time best selling films. In fact, G-P had signed a five year exclusive agreement with Warner, to produce movies on their behalf. G-P's expertise lay in spotting hot properties, signing them up, and then convincing major studios to bankroll and distribute the resulting films. What G-P had was a unique culture-specific talent, for working in and with Hollywood, and producing successful films for the huge U.S. TV and film audience. Sony acquired G-P for over $200 million, or about 5 times G-P's latest year revenues. The two key producers, Peter Guber and Jon Peters received about $50 million for their stock in G-P, a 10 percent stake in future profits at Columbia Pictures, 8 percent of the future appreciation of Columbia Pictures' market value and about $50 million in total deferred compensation.

Warner immediately sued Sony, for acquiring G-P Warner refused to release Peter Guber from the long-term contract. Of course, Sony and Warner ultimately settled out of court, exchanging valuable assets such as a share of the movie studio, video rights and so on. Clearly, Sony wanted the management talent, Americans who knew Hollywood and could hire the right people, had the appropriate financial and creative contacts, and, most important, knew how to make hit films.

4.   *Tree International*–Sony also acquired, through CBS Records, the ownership of Tree, the premier country music publishing company. Once again, the ownership of rights to several generations of hit country songs guarantees

a steady stream of revenues, specially as the catalog is further popularized around the world and in Japan through Sony's music and video production divisions. Whereas this is a minor acquisition, it may point to a trend towards acquiring other music publishing companies, as a means to further controlling the software end of the entertainment business.

Looking to the future, Sony is heavily involved in new hardware technologies such as advanced high-definition television, computer workstations and compact disk interactive technology. These hardware advances will require further research and development; but their acceptance by consumers will depend equally on the availability of software products that showcase the new hardware products. Long-term, Sony is becoming more of a services and entertainment company; and paradoxically, this will also help it become a stronger hardware company, while reducing risk by smoothing revenue fluctuations and providing the stability of recurring earnings from sales of music, film, and videotapes.

E.   Outsiders: How Should They Respond?

The major outsiders in the European media industry are the Americans. The effect of possible quotas, and possible subsidies for film and TV program production in Europe, is that *U.S. production companies will attempt to become insiders*. They will have to set up shop in Europe. An example is Paramount Pictures' decision to open a European development and production unit. Paramount's goal is to begin with two to four movies a year; in preparation, it acquired a 49 percent interest in Zenith Productions, the United Kingdom's leading television producer. It has also indicated that it will use European themes and properties as the basis for films and TV programs (a recent example would be the film based on the French novel, "Dangerous Liaisons"). Another such attempt is MTV Europe producing a non-MTV series youth program in London called "Buzz." The important principle is to ensure that programs be judged of European origin; in practice, this will encourage U.S. joint ventures with European production organizations.

A second possible consequence is the attempt to *own and control European media channels*. Regulations preventing majority foreign ownership and reciprocity considerations in light of European ownership of U.S. media properties mean that significant U.S. ownership of European media (though less than a majority stake) will increase over the next few years.

Another, more defensive move would be to *block the continuing acquisition of U.S. media production companies by foreign interests*. In March 1990, MCA Inc, a U.S. entertainment company was able to purchase Geffen Records, the last independent record company, beating out United Kingdom-based Thorn EMI Plc in the bidding process. Geffen had an 8 percent share worldwide, and it would have been a critical acquisition for any one of the three market share laggards, namely MCA, EMI and Bertelsmann.

A fourth consequence that is possible is *shelter-seeking behavior by European media interests*. That is, as outsiders seek to establish themselves within the EC so as to qualify for local treatment and have their programs and films considered as being of European origin, it is likely that European interests will attempt to delay or block such moves. There is considerable ambiguity in what constitutes a program of European origin, and there is scope for selective interpretation of such laws so as to provide a non-tariff barrier. Such postulated behavior is in line with Rugman and Verbeke's (1990) pronouncements on the impact of 1992 on outsiders: that is, less efficient insiders will attempt to use trade laws to keep out outsiders as well as new insiders, such as U.S. media companies striking up production and distribution partnerships with European interests. At present, the EC directive concerns TV program content. About 85 percent of the top grossing films in Europe are American in origin, and an extension of Eurocontent rules to films could be sought as European film production capability increases. This would have immense consequences because the U.S. film industry earned about $3.4 billion in 1989 from overseas sales.

Lastly, there is the issue of *elitism*. European television, dominated by Government-owned channels, had assumed the mantle of "quality" programming, of broadcasting programs in the public interest, programs that were intended to be educational and uplifting. Mr. Rupert Murdoch in his McTaggart lecture at the Edinburgh television festival in September 1989, noted "For 50 years British television has operated on the assumption that the people could not be trusted to watch what they wanted to watch, so it had to be controlled by like-minded people who knew what was good for us . . ." With deregulation and privatization, Europe has opened itself to commercial television, with all the crassness that it is capable of. In legislating 50 percent Euro-content, there may have also been the notion of preserving high-minded television. Inevitably, commercial television will offend the elitists in their quest for larger audiences. It remains to be seen whether Euro rubbish will be deemed superior to imported rubbish, a novel implementation of a non-tariff barrier.

III. CONCLUSIONS

In sum, the globalization of the media industry has enormous implications. The proliferation of TV channels and other media offer a profit opportunity in themselves. The EC has attempted to ensure that the fruits of such deregulation go in part to European firms. At the same time, European and Japanese media firms have adopted a global approach, by seeking dominant positions in the large and paramount U.S. market. By their actions, they indicate that European market success will follow and is at present secondary to establishing competitive parity in the U.S. market.

Whereas foreign companies have been aggressive in obtaining ownership interests in U.S. media properties, U.S. firms have been more lackadaisical about overseas opportunities. But the globalization of the media industry presents enormous and rapidly growing markets for U.S.-made entertainment, sports and news programming. The opportunities are there and U.S. firms, after a slow start, are likely to carry out the competitive responses necessary to successfully reap profits from their comparative advantage in this industry.

APPENDIX

Services—How Are They Different From Products?

Services have been defined as "those fruits of economic activity which you cannot drop on your toe: banking to butchery, acting to accountancy" ("Service Area in a Fog" 1987a). Indeed, services are mostly intangible. Table A.1 summarizes the major characteristics of services and points out their relevance to the entertainment industry. The distinguishing characteristics of services (Zeithaml et al. 1985) include:

1. *Intangibility;* services are often performances, such as performing an audit, designing a building, fixing a car; a more complete classification consists of asking whether tangible or intangible actions are being performed on people or things. Examples of each of these classes of services are air transportation, air freight, insurance and education (Lovelock 1983). Questions pertinent to the international marketing of services would include deciding whether the customer needed to be physically present during the service, or only at initiation and termination of the service. Is it enough that the customer be mentally present? Can the service be performed at a distance?
2. *Services are heterogeneous;* that is, different people within a company will all perform the same service; it is difficult to make sure that the service is performed in exactly the same way each time, particularly when different people are involved. Thus, one sales clerk may be more rude than another, resulting in greater consumer dissatisfaction. The major implication of heterogeneity is that *quality is difficult to control.*
3. *Services are perishable and are difficult to save or store;* thus, a plane seat that is not sold when the flight takes off is lost for ever. This makes it harder to adjust the supply of a service to fluctuating demand, especially at times

Table A.1.   Characteristics of the Entertainment Industry

Characteristic	Decision	Example
Intangibility	How to capture a performance and offer service at a distance?	Recorded films and music, delivered through satellite.
Heterogeneity	Different people deliver the service in different ways.	Quality difficult to control; so, bet on people: the talent.
Perishability	How to inventory the service?	Record performance; then, multiple channels of delivery: first film, then video, then TV, both cable and "free TV," and syndication.
Simultaneous production and sales	How to export and tap foreign markets?	Foreign direct investment, licensing, and mergers.
Pricing	High fixed costs.	Recover costs in domestic markets, foreign income streams as annuities.
Quality	Difficult to measure. What does the customer expect?	Sell American images to a global audience: the "Dallasization" of France.
Generating repeat business	How to ensure loyalty?	Serial soap operas, "brand-name stars."
Product development	How to consistently develop hits?	"Nobody knows anything." Diversify and if you produce enough shows, one will be a hit. Hence, importance of deep pockets.

of peak demand. The growth of the entertainment industry can be traced to innovations allowing recording and subsequent broadcast of live performances, and further innovations such as time-shifting with the help of the VCR.

4.   *In services, production, and consumption of the service often takes place at the same time;* that is, the producer and the seller of the service is often the same person. Moreover, the customer must often be present for the service to take place. International marketing of a service often means that the service

cannot be exported, but instead must be performed by the firm itself. The entertainment industry has chosen to establish itself in overseas markets, through franchising or licensing, through a direct investment, and sometimes through acquisition. The fundamental question is, can the service be performed at a distance? An if not, how should the firm position itself in a distant market in order to offer the service?

5. *Services are difficult to price, because it is difficult to calculate the cost of producing a service* (Huiltinan 1987). Service businesses have a high fixed cost ratio. Hence, if the service can be offered without much modification in many national markets, prices can be lower since the fixed costs have presumably been recovered in the home market. Thus, there are some advantages of scale to U.S. entertainment companies that have recovered their film and TV program development costs in the large U.S. market. Generalizing, a large linguistic market becomes a comparative advantage for English language producers in the United States (Wildman and Siwek 1988).

6. *Service quality is difficult to measure.* It is unclear what the consumer expects, and quality is a matter of consumer perception. In the entertainment industry, since customer perceptions are so difficult to predict, the industry relies on a scattershot approach, assuming that if enough entertainments are provided to the customer, some of them will be found acceptable.

7. *Because services cannot be stored, a basic strategy is to ensure repeat business and thus generate a recurring revenue stream from existing customers.* How does a firm maintain relations with its existing customers, and what methods are used to promote loyalty? Thus, firms can use devices such as frequent flyer plans to reward customer loyalty. In entertainment, this is done through reliance on shows delivered in serial sequence, through the use of "brand-name" stars, and by blanketing the distribution channels: that is, simultaneous release of a film in several theaters in a city and all over the country. A complication is deciding how such plans should be modified to accommodate consumers having different cultural characteristics in different countries. Loyalty can also be maintained and rewarded through pricing, and the question that must be ascertained for each national market is whether volume discounts and membership strategies (i.e., on pay-TV and on cable TV) work equally well in all markets.

ACKNOWLEDGMENT

The author gratefully acknowledges the support of the College of Business Adminstration, Northeastern University, for research and travel funding through the grant of the Walsh Research Professorship for 1990-1992.

148   RAVI SARATHY

REFERENCES

"A Changing Sony Aims to Own the Software That its Product Need." 1988. *Wall Street Journal* (December 30).
"All the Worlds a Dish." 1988a. *The Economist* (August 27).
"Beaming Soap to Babel." 1988b. *The Economist* (October 26).
Blades, D. 1987. "Goods and Services in OECD economies," *OECD Economic Studies* (Spring).
"Buddy, Can You Spare a Reel." 1989a. *The Economist* (August 19).
"Cable and Satelites are Opening Europe to TV Commercials." 1987. *Wall Street Journal* (December 22).
"Dynamic Duo: Producers of 'Batman' Stir Whammo Battle Over Future Services." 1989d. *Wall Street Journal* (October 20).
Eger, J.M. 1987. "Global Television: An Executive Overview. *Columbia Journal of World Business* 22(3).
"Europe May Slap a Quota on General Hospital." 1989b. *Business Week* (March 27).
European Community. 1989. Council Directive, 3rd October. *Official Journal of the European Communities.*
"European Satellite TV: Just so Much Pie in the Sky?" 1988. *Business Week* (October 24).
"Fancy Free: A Survey of the Entertainment Industry." 1989d. *The Economist* (December 23).
"French Television: A Disgrace." 1989c. *The Economist* (October 14).
Huiltinan, J.P. 1987. "The Price Bundling of Services: A Normative Framework." *Journal of Marketing* 51 (April).
"Keeping Up with the Murdochs." 1989a. *Business Week* (March 20).
Koltai, S.R. 1987. "Coming Attractions on European TV: Problems and Prospects for Cable and Satellite Television." *Columbia Journal of World Business* 22 (3) (Fall).
"A Boob Tube: Europe Complains About U.S. Shows." 1989c. *Wall Street Journal* (October 16).
Lovelock, C. 1983. "Classifying Services to Gain Strategic Marketing Insights." *Journal of Marketing* 47 (Summer).
"Monte Carlo or Bust." 1989b. *The Economist* (September 2).
Noam, E.M. 1987. "Broadcasting in Italy." *Columbia Journal of World Business* 22 (3) (Fall).
Ott, M. 1987. "The Growing Share of Services in the U.S. Economy—Degeneration or Evolution?" *Federal Reserve Bank of St. Louis Review* (June/July).
"Playing the Global Game." 1989. *Forbes* (January 23).
"Service Area in a Fog." 1987a. *The Economist* (May 23).
"Sony Sees More than Michael Jackson in CBS." 1987b. *The Economist* (November 28).
"Sony Sets Pact with Coca-Cola for Columbia." 1989a. *Wall Street Journal* (September 28).
"The Battle for Europe's TV Future." 1989b. *Wall Street Journal* (October 6).
"The Media Barons Battle to Dominate Europe." 1987. *Business Week* (May 25).
Wildman, S.S. and Siwek, S.E. 1988. *International Trade in Films and Television Programs.* Cambridge, MA: Ballinger Publishing.
Zeithaml, V., Parasuraman, A. and Berry, L.L. 1985. "Problems and Strategies in Services Marketing." *Journal of Marketing* 49 (Spring).

PART III

JOINT VENTURES AND
EUROPEAN ECONOMIC INTEGRATION

STRATEGIC ALLIANCES AND PUBLIC POLICY IN THE EUROPEAN COMMUNITY:
THE CASE OF INFORMATION TECHNOLOGY

Arthur F.P. Wassenberg

I. INTRODUCTION

Europe is experimenting with new forms of industrial cohabitation. One of them is the European Strategic Program for Research in Information Technology (ESPRIT). The internal dynamics of ESPRIT can only be understood if we take into account two external realities. First, the reality that justifies the basic philosophy of ESPRIT: the international conditions of competition between Japan, the United States and Western Europe as these changed since the beginning of the seventies. This is the global setting of ESPRIT or, in Ohmae's terminology, Triad Power (Ohmae 1985). The global setting sets the *drive* for ESPRIT.

Second, there is the reality that will determine the operational outcomes of ESPRIT: a loose-knit assembly of intra-european but non-Community framed

Research in Global Strategic Management, Volume 2, pages 151-201.

agreements and programs such as EUREKA (European Research Coordination Agency). Geo-politically, EUREKA is the european reaction to the U.S. Strategic Defense Initiative program; regiopolitically, EUREKA is the nationalistic and national champions' device to escape from the supranational discipline associated with programs emanating from the Community's headquarters; industry-politically, EUREKA is reported to be inspired by a "market pull" orientation competing with the "technology push" orientation of the Community programs. Programs like EUREKA, sponsoring projects such as HDTV (high definition television) by Thompson, Siemens and, in this case, Philips as the major go-between, are at first sight based on a bilateral philosophy: negotiations are primarily governed by the partially cooperative, partially competitive dyad Paris-Bonn but other nationalities—tipping the balance from case to case—serve as a third party, thus constituting a sort of "Triad Power" on the regional level. It is this regional dyad-plus-one setting that defines the effective limits or the *scope* for ESPRIT.

While strategically escorted by these two realities, ESPRIT itself can be seen as the product of again another kind of "Triad Power," namely as the outcome of ongoing negotiations between European multinational companies, national politicians from the member-states, and supranational EC officials. Embedded in the twisting of the global and the regional triad power games, the communautarian triad power game is left to define the elan or the *spirit* of ESPRIT.

The overview presented in Section II depicts the formally stated essentials, to be found in policy documents, statements by EC-officials and spokesmen of the firms involved. This picture may be called the "normative" arena and agenda, where "normative" alludes to the idealized features of the network of official relationships between the participants. This idealized representation will be confronted by the "empirical" network in Section III of the chapter.

Section IV offers a conceptual framework for explaining the moves and movements documented in Section III. The chapter concludes with Section V by formulating some theoretical and practical implications from the preceeding analysis.

II.   A MOSAIC OF POWER

The three Triad power settings identified in the Introduction (see Figure 1 for a graphical summary of the "Embeddedness" of ESPRIT) differ sharply in terms of the stakes and the resources as well as in the pattern of participation and the types of commitments prevailing in each of them. Despite these substantive differences, the *formal* logic of the "game of shifting alliances" within the

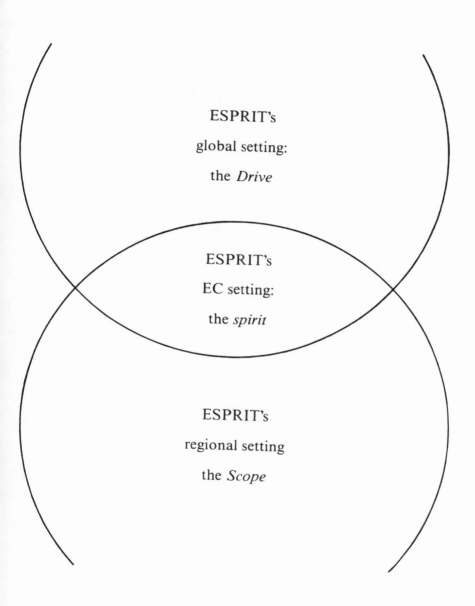

Figure 1. The Dynamics of ESPRIT as a Function of
Three Triad Power Settings: The Global, the Regional and the EC-Setting

communautarian setting is analogous to the type of coalitional dynamics which
we find within the regional and global setting. The coexistence of the global, the
regional and the communautarian setting—in fact a *mosaic* of triad powers—
determines the discretionary power of the participants in ESPRIT. The actors
differ in their relative capabilities to influence the returns from participation—
in fact: the returns from investment—in the respective power-settings. Three
questions, then, are of special interest in this perspective: how *rational,* in the sense
of purposeful, calculated and controlled, are the decisions of the respective actors
(multinational companies, national governments, supranational institutions) to
invest in the different settings? Second, what about the coordination of strategic
choices *across* the different settings? Last but not least: given the necessity for each
of the actors to find a manageable balance of level-specific commitments, what
about the relative *freedom* to choose for each of them?

The ESPRIT case, though still too young to offer firm conclusions, suggests
some tentative answers. Intuitively it seems safe to assume that the rationality
of investment in this mosaic of triad powers must be somehow a combined
function of the need versus the expected returns versus the potential for
interorganizational coordination. Let us first look at the basic mechanics.

A. The Antecedents

The official narrative states that Europe has been in serious trouble since the
mid-seventies. As the saying goes: the old continent launched the first two
industrial revolutions but seems to miss the benefits of the third. That insight
is not new. In 1967 a French journalist, Jean-Jacques Servan Schreiber, published
his widely read *Le Défi Américain* (including, beyond the limits of the title, the
rapidly emerging *Défi Japonais*), warning against issues that became fully
manifest around the mid-seventies. Since that time one may speak of conventional
wisdom. Conventional wisdom relates Europe's backward position vis-à-vis
Japan and the United States to the following facts and circumstances:

- The amount of R&D as such is not a problem but compared to their
  competitors, European firms are too diversified, leading to fragmentation
  of research, cutting up of development expenses and an uncontrolled
  duplication and overlap of R&D activities;
- There is a disproportional attention to process innovation oriented R&D,
  neglecting marketing and product innovations; the continental bias
  towards process rather than product innovations means that time and
  again Japan and U.S.-producers appear to be far ahead in marketing
  terms—in spite of Europe's qualities in terms of research;
- domestic markets are relatively small (the German market, for instance,
  amounts to half of Japan's or one quarter of U.S.' domestic market); and
- new technologies do not stop at national boundaries; defensive reactions
  such as protectionism ("Europe's problem is that it is attached to stability

in an age when stability is a comparative disadvantage," [*The Economist*, 24-11-1984]) do not stimulate adaptation to new international standards and conditions. (This is not to say that Europe's rivals are less excelling in protectionism or less interested in the enactment of non-tariff barriers, but what they tend to protect is a comparative advantage.)
- Lack of standardization and harmonization—the "administrative" core of the Community's integration deficit—is standing in the way of reaping the fruits of large scale production.

Contributing to the integration deficit is the absence of government-induced incentives for policy coordination, like defense-related programs in the United States or MITI-inspired concerted action in Japan. In addition, Europe does not have a homogeneous or uniform structure and culture of labor relations at its disposal. As a result of these conditions first American and then Japanese companies surpassed the European firms as major suppliers of electronics and computer related products. Table 1 summarizes the international stratification in the industry around the mid-sixties.

In 1975 Europe still enjoyed a trade surplus in information technology, four years later this situation was reversed into a trade deficit of $5 bln, while officials expected a $10 bln deficit for 1982. In spite of an increase in the marketshare of European firms on this market, from 20.4 percent in 1977 to 26.7 percent in 1982 (U.S. Department of Commerce 1983, p. 19), the EC balance of trade deficit for electronic products was expected to deteriorate further to $16 bln by 1990 (Caty 1984, p. 28; medio 1991, the moment of finishing this chapter, newspapers report an European trade-deficit in electronics of more than $*35bln* as against a Japanese surplus of some $165 bln). In view of these discomforting outlooks the European Commission decided to act.

The driving force behind the Commission's answer to the dramatic deterioration of Europe's international IT position was Viscount Etienne Davignon, the then commissioner for Industry in the European Commission. Around 1977 Davignon invited the 12 leading IT companies in Europe (3 from Germany, 3 from United Kingdom, 3 from France, 2 from Italy, and 1 from the Netherlands) to discuss possible remedies for Europe's position. Against the background of earlier failures of communautarian interfirm cooperation (UNIDATA: Philips/Siemens/CII, started in 1972, dissolved in 1975 when CII opted for a merger with the U.S.-firm Honeywell-Bull), the participants of the 1977 Round Table decided to restrict discussions to cooperation in the area of "pre-competitive research." (The restriction to "pre-competitive" efforts had to do, apart from negative UNIDATA-reminiscences and other sentiments, with the strictness of the Treaty of Rome regulations on cartels and other collusive practices. Nevertheless, the *pre*-competition label is rather elastic because as long as the interested firms will argue that they need additional or continued research, the collaboration is supposed to be of a "pre-competitive" nature.)

Table 1.   Largest Firms in Electronics and Computer-Industries Around 1965*

Name	Country	Rank	Sales ($ mln)
IBM	US	1	3.573
Western Electric	US	2	3.362
Westinghouse Elect	US	3	2.390
Philips	**NL**	**4**	**2.084**
RCA	US	5	2.042
GTE	US	6	2.036
Siemens	**BRD**	**7**	**1.795**
ITT	US	8	1.783
Hitachi	Jap	9	1.149
AEG Telefunken	**BRD**	**10**	**1.034**
Tokyo Shibaura Elec	Jap	11	823
Matsushita	Jap	12	772
Bosch	**BRD**	**13**	**741**
National Cash Reg.	US	14	737
Associated Electronic Ind.	**UK**	**15**	**712**
English Electric	**UK**	**16**	**685**
Brown, Boveri	CH	17	685
TRW	US	18	665
Whirpool	US	19	631
CGE	**F**	**20**	**578**
Mitsubishi Electric	Jap	21	535
Motorola	US	22	517
Raytheon	US	23	488
General Electric	**UK**	**24**	**472**
Zenith Radio	US	25	471
Olivetti	**It**	**26**	**450**
ASEA	Sw	27	449
Texas Instruments	US	28	436
Xerox	US	29	393
Ericsson	Sw	30	385
Thomson	**F**	**31**	**381**
Magnavox	US	32	333
Northern Electric	Can	33	331
Plessey	**UK**	**34**	**293**
Nippon Electric	Jap	35	287
Collins Radio	US	36	282
EMI	**UK**	**37**	**281**
CSF	**F**	**38**	**261**
Cons. Elect. Ind.	US	39	275
Thorn	**UK**	**40**	**238**
Furukawa Electric	Jap	41	237

Note: *In order to stress the relative position of the European multinationals, their names, nationalities and rank order according to sales are emphasized in the table.

Source: Compiled and computed on the basis of the two rankings of the 500 largest U.S. firms and of the 200 largest non-US firms, in *Fortune* (July 1966, August 1966).

After roughly four years the European Commission formulated the ESPRIT program. Following a 1-year pilot stage, the European Council of Ministers gave its official fiat: February 28, 1984 ESPRIT started with a threefold official mission:

- promotion of intra-European cooperation in pre-competitive R&D in the area of IT;
- procurement of basic technologies to improve Europe's midterm and longterm competitive capacity on the world market; and
- promotion of European standardization.

The ESPRIT program is divided into two stages (ESPRIT 1: 1984-1988, ESPRIT 2: 1989-1993), "to accommodate goals and means to changing conditions in the (global) IT sector." Half the funding of approved R&D programs had to be provided for by the European Community. The initial budget was fixed on ECU 750 mln for the first five years. The rules for selecting proposals had to be "competitive on terms of merit and stringent about both commercial exploitation and the dissemination of results." Submitted projects should fulfil the following criteria:

- show significant industrial impact and conform to the ESPRIT work program;
- show the potential for exploitation of the results;
- specify as far as possible in quantitative terms what improvements over existing technology will be achieved;
- preferably lead to demonstrable results or prototypes; and
- contain clear review points and preferably quantitative specifications for assessment of progress.

Participants had to be "established" in the EC (with the ironical consequence that no formal entry-objection could be raised, for instance, against Europe-based *IBM* subsidiaries or, more recently, against an increasing number of *Japanese* IT-champions establishing new plants or joint ventures inside fortress Europe). Candidates must be involved in IT research and development and each project has to be backed by industrial partners from at least two different member states.

We have discussed the background and the philosophy underlying Europe's answer to the international challenges in information technology. However, who were supposed to execute the scenario and decide the division of roles? This will be discussed in the next section.

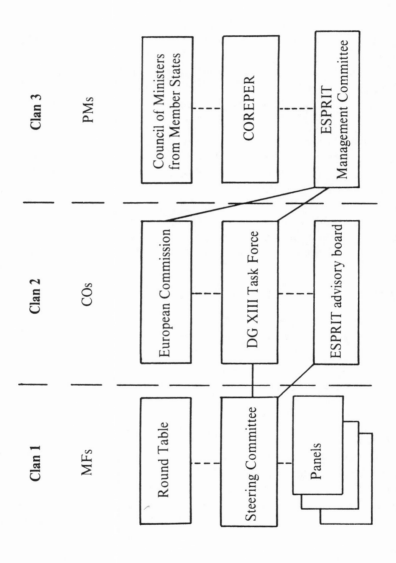

Figure 2. The Architecture of ESPRIT

158

B. The Cast

The public/private structure of the management of ESPRIT has to be subdivided into three circuits, corresponding with the earlier mentioned triad on the community level: multinational firms (MFs), supranational or communautarian officials (COs), and politicians from the member states (PMs).

The architecture of ESPRIT is held together by an intricate web of vertical, horizontal and diagonal relationships, each governed by different principles of integration:

- *Within* the clans, the logic of *as*sociation prevails: the purpose is "vertical" integration (LHT: "living hierarchically together").
- *Between* the clans, the logic of *dis*sociation rules: a formal logic of armlength relationships, permitting "horizontal" coordination but precluding hierarchization or incorporation (LAT: "living apart together").
- *Among* the clans, the logic of *con*sociation reigns: an informal structure of "diagonal" relationships mediating between the opposing principles of association and dissociation (LOT: "living organically together").

The clans—the respective *foci* of associational power—are composed of the following actors:

Clan 1: The Multinational Corporations

Round tables. The round tables are the meeting places of the highest representatives of the 'big 12' of Europe's IT-industry (as of 1984: Siemens, AEG, Nixdorf, GEC, ICL, Plessey, Thomson/EFCIS, Bull, CGE/CIT Alcatel, Olivetti, STET [SGS/ ITALTEL/CSELT], Philips). The round tables constitute the apex of the private circuit which defines the overall strategy or the "mission" of the ESPRIT-program.

Steering committee. The steering committee consists of representatives of the "big 12" interlocked with the director of the Task Force (see Clan 2). It takes care of the operationalization of the plans emanating from the Round Table and issues guidelines for the "panels" representing the main areas of ESPRIT. The steering committee serves as the linking pin between these panels and the ESPRIT-advisory board (see Clan 2).

Panels. The panels, covering each of the five main areas of ESPRIT (Micro electronics; Software technology; Advanced information processing; Office systems; Computer aided production systems) are composed of technical experts from the "big 12." The activities of the panels are sifted and combined into a Work Plan. On the basis of the Work Plan, European companies, research institutes and universities are invited to formulate their research proposals.

Clan 2: The Communautarian Officials

European Commission/Task Force. The Euro-Commission carries the chief executive responsibility for the implementation of the ESPRIT-program. For this purpose the European Commission is supported by a Task Force. The Task Force is a management group of "public" experts, although they are recruited de facto from European industry (for a five year term). Recently the Task Force merged with the Directorate General "Information and Market Innovation" into a new DG XIII, relabelled "Information Industry, Telecommunication and Innovation."

ESPRIT Advisory Board (EAB). Like the Task Force, the EAB has a hybrid composition (16 members, à titre personnel, but originating from the European IT industry)—serving as the linking pin between the European Commission (in particular the Task Force) and private industry, research institutes and universities.

Clan 3: The Politicians of Member States

Council of ministers (member states). The Council formulates the grand design and the direction of technology policies in general, but refrains from interfering in ESPRIT management affairs.

COREPER. The abbreviation stands for a committee of "permanent representatives" (national government officials of member governments) which play an essential role in filtering, combining and forwarding proposals from the ESPRIT Management Committee (EMC) to the Council of Ministers.

ESPRIT Management Committee. The EMC is a general assembly of representatives from national governments (10 votes for Germany, France, United Kingdom and Italy each; 5 votes for the Netherlands, Belgium, and Greece each; 3 votes for Denmark and Ireland each; 2 votes for Luxembourg), taking care of the coordination between the ESPRITprogram and the national technology programs of the respective member states. EMC's task is to advise the European Commission/Task Force/DG XIII. It plays a crucial role in approving project proposals (worth 5 mln ECU or more). EMC—voting by majority rule—is entitled to decide on *exemptions* or *deviations* from the official rules of the ESPRIT charter (see the "eligibility" criteria listed at the end of Section II. A). EMC has a final say in the (formal) approval of all project proposals. Project proposals are accepted if gathering 45 votes or more.

So far we have discussed the formal rules and roles of ESPRIT. At the closure of Section 1, two things will be clear. First, it will be clear that the "nervous system" of ESPRIT is formed by a web of *diagonal* interlocks— governed by the logic of LOT: living organically together—between Steering committee and ESPRIT advisory board at the one and the ESPRIT management committee at the other side and DG XIII/Task Force at the discretionary center of gravity. This formula reduces the administrative complexity of ESPRIT, by mediating between the opposing logics of distance between ("dissociation") and hierarchization within ("association") the respective clans. However, the formula is not necessarily sufficient for solving the dilemmas of interest *intra*mediation within the respective clans; the logic of association produces "vertical" integration between Round Table, steering committee and panels, but it definitely does not eliminate "horizontal" conflicts of interest and competitive passions among the "big 12" sitting around that European table. This is my second point: it will be clear that within the web of diagonal interlocks the *partner/project/timing*-choice will be a delicate one. The section that follows documents the delicacy by presenting some facts and figures about strategic partnerships in the European IT-industry. The management of complexity (Section I) appears to be something else than the management of contradictions (Section II).

III. NETWORK ANALYSIS

The "empirical" network of ESPRIT, the *back*stage, has to be distinguished from its *front*stage or "normative" counterpart as described in Section 1. Whereas the formal division of authority can be seen as the cornerstone of the normative network, the core concepts in the representation of the empirical network are *flexibility* and *power*. Flexibility is defined as a cultural and structural regime in which actors try to optimize the predictability of other actors while maintaining their own range of alternatives as much as possible. As Schattschneider (1957, p. 937) argues: "The definition of alternatives is the supreme instrument of power [..]. He who determines what politics is about runs the country because the definition of alternatives is the choice of conflicts, and the choice of conflict allocates power."

The empirical or backstage network is characterized by two dimensions: the economics and the politics of flexibility. The *economics* point to the degree of concentration and the entry and exit options of individual firms, member states and public officials in a specific policy domain. The *politics* refer to the degree of coordination of regulative and (re)distributive decisions among organizations like MFs, COs and PMs. The politics of flexibility refer to the *uses* of (public and private) power (e.g., the centralisation of decision- and of nondecision making) whereas the economics of flexibility relate to the *bases* of (public and private) power (e.g., the concentration of critical resources: cash, competences and connections). The uses of power have to be seen as the strategic or tactical response to the opportunities and constraints implied by the bases of power.

A. Economics of Flexibility: The Concentration of Cash, Competences, and Connections

The economic background of ESPRIT is given by the historical evolution of the IT industry and its direct economic environment. The IT industry has developed into a separate industry from two mother-industries, the (heavy) electromechanical industry and the (light) electronics industry. The former contributed the know-how of systems-building whereas the latter was the source of technological innovations such as chips and lasers. Their offspring, culminating in such products as digital switching telephone exchanges, constitutes the IT industry. The IT industry enjoyed the growing post-war markets and a heavily equipped manufacturing base which allowed economies of scale. Furthermore R&D activities were primarily oriented toward product differentiation, which means that new technology was developed to service well established markets.

The basis for these industry-wide, "more of the same" policies eroded in the sixties when the IT-industry was confronted by a declining rate of productivity growth, which was followed in the seventies by slow economic growth and high unemployment. This meant a change in the competitive position of the major firms in the IT-industry. The slow pace of productivity growth resulted in a direct loss of competitiveness and the slow growth of the economy resulted in saturated markets. "With markets under pressure [. . .] flexible response increasingly came to play a central role in the strategy of knowledge-intensive firms." (Mytelka and De la Pierre 1987, p. 231)

The ensuing essential change in strategy was an intensification of the quest for external control: a switch from controlling market*shares* to controlling market *transformations*. Technology development in this changing context meant outflanking competitors on capabilities rather than on markets. The essence of that strategy is the development of knowledge out of which products can be generated for multiple (not yet precisely defined) markets.

1. Industry Structure

One of the aspects mentioned in Section II.A reporting on Europe's backward position vis-à-vis Japan and the United States, is its specific industry structure: European firms tend to be more diversified than their overseas rivals. Furthermore

Table 2. Largest Firms in Electronics and Computer-Industries Around 1988*

Name	Country	Rank	Sales ($ mln)
IBM	US	1	59.681
General Electric	US	2	49.414
Hitachi	Jap	3	41.331
Siemens	**BRD**	**4**	**27.463**
Matsushita	Jap	5	33.923
Philips	**NL**	**6**	**28.371**
Samsung	Kor	7	27.386
Toshiba	Jap	8	25.441
CGE	**F**	**9**	**21.488**
NEC	Jap	10	19.626
ASEA Brown Boveri	CH	11	17.562
Daewoo	Kor	12	17.251
Mitsubishi Electric	Jap	13	16.857
Xerox	US	14	16.441
Fujitsu	Jap	15	14.797
Thomson	**F**	**16**	**12.567**
Westinghouse Elect.	US	17	12.500
Electrolux	Sw	18	12.055
Digital Equipment	US	19	11.475
Sony	Jap	20	10.134
Unisys	US	21	9.902
Hewlett Packard	US	22	9.831
General Electric Co.	**UK**	**23**	**9.457**
Sanyo	Jap	24	9..375
IBM Japan	Jap	25	9.269
Canon	Jap	26	8.631
Sharp	Jap	27	8.608
Motorola	US	28	8.250
Raytheon	US	29	8.192
Honeywell	US	30	7.148
TRW	US	31	6.982
IBM Great Britain	**UK**	**32**	**6.901**
Emerson Electric	US	33	6.652
IBM Germany	**BRD**	**34**	**6.471**
Olivetti	**It**	**35**	**6.459**
IBM France	**F**	**36**	**6.409**
Texas Instruments	US	37	6.295
NCR	US	38	5.990
North American Philips	US	39	5.424
Northern Telecom	Can	40	5.408
Bull	**F**	**41**	**5.298**
Noika	Fin	42	5.204
Thorn EMI	**UK**	**43**	**5.201**
Ericsson	Sw	44	5.101
Ricoh	Jap	45	4.869
Whirlpool	US	46	4.421
Teledyne	US	47	4.401
Cooper Industries	US	48	4.258
Warner Communications	US	49	4.206
STC	**UK**	**50**	**4.198**
Rank Xerox	**UK**	**51**	**4.098**
Apple	US	52	4.071
Fuji Electric	Jap	53	4.029

Note: *In order to stress the change in the relative position of the European multinationals vis-à-vis Table 1, their names, nationalities, and rank order according to sales are again emphasized.

Source: Compiled on the basis of the two rankings of the 500 largest U.S. firms and of the 500 largest non-U.S. firms in *Fortune* (April 1989, July 1989).

they have to put up with smaller "home-markets." Van Tulder and Junne (1988, p. 126), on the other hand, find that European firms are no longer smaller than their American and Japanese counterparts. Compared with the sixties (see Table 1), then, it is not their size as such (see Table 2) but the *way* they have won their size, that is, by choosing a diversification strategy, that marks the difference in the international arena.

Diversification has consequences the way the R&D budget, which is an important indicator of competitiveness, is employed. First, the R&D budget has to be distributed among (too) many divisions, hardly compensated for by assumed or prophesied synergies. Second, the historical alternative for companies with relatively small or dispersed R&D budgets, namely adopting a "followers strategy" (which is reported to require only 40 percent of the R&D expenditures of a "forerunner": Van Tulder and Junne, 1988, p. 127) has become more risky due to shortened lifecycles. So the diversified European companies face the problem of matching their R&D efforts to those of their— more concentrated—Japanese and American rivals. Yet, comparing the Fortune rankings of 1965 and 1988, the available data do not permit an unambiguous conclusion. Part of Servan Schreiber's early warning seems to have materialized: in quantitative terms Europe's position deteriorated dramatically, but so did America's position. Simple arithmetic shows that the share of U.S. companies among the combined "500" has decreased from 41 percent in 1965 to 37 percent in 1988, the share of EC companies has decreased from 34 percent in 1965 to 25 percent in 1988, whereas the share of Japanese companies has increased from 15 percent to 25 percent in 1988.

It would be unjustified, by whatever standard, to conclude that the American *Défi* is replaced by an American *Defeat*. However, one has to wonder how far quantitative rankings based on size distributions provide a genuine insight in real strengths and weaknesses—from individual firms to economic blocks— as long as firms rather than *clusters* of firms are taken as the unit of analysis.

2. Industry Strategy

One of the methods to augment a firm's knowledge base and simultaneously increase its flexibility—"without adding to the inertia of the firm," as Mytelka and De la Pierre (1987, p. 235) formulate it—is by establishing linkages between universities and commercial research institutes within a context of inter-firm cooperative agreements in R&D. Cooperation does not stop here. At variance with official rethorics about the preeminence of "pre-competitive" partnerships, Table 3, summarizing the growth of inter-firm agreements from 1980 to 1985 between at least one European partner and others (European as well as non-European) demonstrates that the growth of inter-firm agreements in "pre-competitive" R&D is matched by a comparable intensification of cooperative agreements in production and market operations as well.

Table 3. Distribution of Inter-firm Agreements by Function 1980-1985

Year	Knowledge	Production	Commercialization
1980	11	12	6
1981	15	13	10
1982	17	16	15
1983	24	25	31
1984	36	37	36
1985	47	39	51
Total	150	142	149
(%)	(31.2)	(29.5)	(31.0)

Source: LAREA/CEREM (1986, p. 8).

The more salient the switch from "classic" market share towards "modern" market transformation strategies, the more obsolete our familiar concepts of competition: *competitiveness,* paradoxically, becomes to rely on the choice of the right *cooperation* agreements (van Tulder and Junne 1988, p. 220). In addition, the choice of the right cooperation partner appears to be more decisive than the decision of which technology to pursue. Both considerations are bound to lead to changing conceptualizations of competitiveness: they represent a shift from atomistic "market competition" to organized "network competition." Van Tulder and Junne present the Olivetti experience as a case in point: the company—thirty-fifth in the international and only eighth in the European ranking (see Table 2)—does not have a reputation as a technological high-flyer and does not spend as much on research and development as competing companies. Under the chairmanship of De Benedetti, however, the company embarked on a comprehensive strategy to enter into a great number of alliances with well established firms. Most notable among these was Olivetti's deal with the number three of the international ranking, the *American* giant AT&T.

3. Alliance Behavior

The phenomenon of network competition has spread quickly throughout the European IT-industry since the beginning of the eighties. The phenomenon manifests itself in two contrasting shapes. The first manifestation is the creation of a network of linkages between previously competing European firms: we witness the birth of the European IT-clan. Figure 3 charts the clan, where the numbers on the connecting lines correspond to the number of inter-firm agreements. It is important to note that these links emerged *prior to* or *apart from* the development of the ESPRIT program.

In spite of the unmistakeably European foundations of the clan, the dualistic nature of network competition manifests itself in the inter-firm agreements concluded by each of the members of the clan when we look at them separately. Van Tulder and Junne (1988, p. 233), listing the major international cooperation agreements in the core technologies during the period of January 1980 to July 1986—among them the IT industry—counted 193 alliances: 47 alliances in telecommunications, 38 in semiconductors, 31 in computers and software, 29 in robotics and automation systems (and furthermore 21 in new materials and 27 in biotechnology). Their remarkable conclusion: in no less than 59 percent of the observed international alliances European multinationals are involved with *American* MF's; another 23 percent of the alliances are between European firms and a *Japanese* partner. Conclusion: in only 18 percent of the cases did European firms start strategic alliances with other *European* firms.

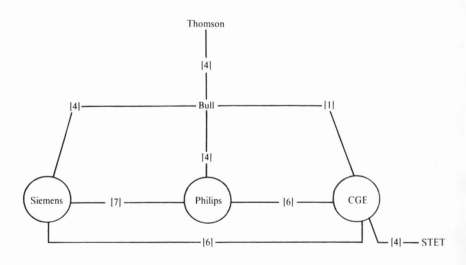

Source: Mytelka and De la Pierre (1987, p. 242).

Figure 3.   Intra-EC Cooperation Agreements:
The Emergence of the European IT-Clan 1980-1985

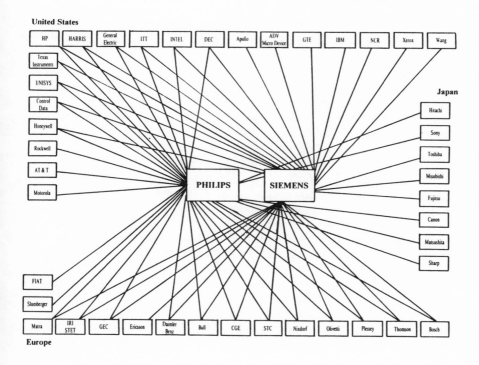

Note: *The threads represent different degrees of interfirm integration: consortia, unilateral participations as well as bilateral ventures.

Source: Van Tulder (1990), borrowing from G. C. Carnarca, M. G. Colombo, and S. Marriotti. (1988).

Figure 4.   The Global Triad Power Repercussions of a
Regional/Communautarian Deal: The Philips-Siemens Web.*

However, even when EC-based firms do decide to intensify their cooperation, such a decision tends to interfere with the loyalties and conflicting domain-interests induced by preexisting *non*-European alliances concluded at an earlier stage (and possibly with divergent motivations) by each of them. The example of the Siemens-Philips alliance illustrates the complexities of the phenomenon (see Figure 4).

The 47 alliances in telecommunications offer a good cross- section of the particular nature of European network competition in this area. In the Netherlands, Philips concluded a joint venture with AT&T (U.S.) in 1984 to develop and market switching exchanges outside the United States and South East Asia. In the United Kingdom most of the alliances are between a national and an international partner but there are also United Kingdom combinations who team up with large international partners. The joint manufacturing agreement of the TELECOM cashless shopping system between IBM (U.S.) on the one and British Telecom and British Aerospace on the other hand is such an example. Though the French can be said to be more inner-directed as a result of state induced mergers and takeovers (CIT-Alcatel and Thomson-CSF combined their telecommunications activities, wiping out free competition in the national market), international alliances have emerged after a consolidation phase; for instance, Alcatel-Thomson and Fairchild Industries (U.S.) joined their activities in networks and services on each other's markets in 1985. In Germany, Siemens took an 80 percent interest in GTE's (U.S.) European transmission activities and public switching in 1986. In Italy, Olivetti and Toshiba (Japan) started a joint venture for office automation and Japanese marketing of Olivetti equipment.

B.   Politics of Flexibility: The Centralization of Decision and Non-Decision Making

Why do firms cooperate? The following reasons are normally given by industry and academic orthodoxy. First, rising R&D costs and shortening lifecycles are said to inspire companies to combine their pre-marketing efforts. Second, national monopolies have reason to doubt their future viability due to the declining importance of the relatively small home markets and a gradual eclipse of national barriers. Third, companies make deals for the joint marketing of products enabling them to enter each other's markets. Finally, and more recently, economies of scale promised by the "unified 1992 market" may have triggered a fourth wave of cooperative agreements.

These arguments, however, do not cover a more intriguing trait in the above-sketched portrait of European cooperation: a persistent non-European orientation in the selection of strategic partners by European firms *coexisting* with an equally outspoken belief in the urgency of European integration and the indispensable role of ESPRIT in that context.

Theories of economic integration focus narrowly on the determinants of inter-state trade and the welfare effects resulting from that trade. They facilitate the analysis of foreign investment and its impact on the Common Market or the effect of trade liberalization on intra-community capital flows. Where these theories give an explanation of inter-firm agreements involving the gross exchange of assets or equity, as in the case of mergers and acquisitions or take-overs, they do not explain inter-firm agreements involving the exchange of more specific or specialized functions such as R&D, production or commercialization. At first sight, the industrial organization literature seems to offer a more informative approach to the latter phenomenon by starting from microstrategical considerations. Inspired by Coase's seminal essay on the firm and the market as alternative modes of organizing exchange (Coase 1937) others have tried to identify the circumstances under which organizations can be expected or predicted to "internalize" environmental uncertainties, that is: to prefer *internal* transactions over external or spot market transactions. Specialization of assets, recurrent transactions among small numbers of participants and the risk of opportunism or free-rider behavior are said to belong to these circumstances: the higher the risk of opportunism and the more specialized the knowledge or other skills of one's partners, the stronger the propensity to internalize market transactions (Williamson 1975, p. 29).

Unfortunately the polar types of market-exchange on the one hand (i.e., competitive relationships) *versus* intra-firm exchange on the other hand (i.e., hierarchical relationships by substituting authoritative devices for competitive market transactions, as in the case of mergers), do leave an intermediate type unmentioned: inter-firm agreements. This type of alliance "may (. .) be more attractive to European firms than alliances with non-European firms to the extent that they, firstly, involve less risk, secondly, permit firms to take advantage of economies of scale in one or more of their production processes while remaining separate entities, and thirdly, are rendered relatively less costly by the existence of programs such as ESPRIT" (Mytelka and De la Pierre 1987, p. 233). Analyzing the inter-firm linkages that emerged through ESPRIT, Mytelka and De la pierre find that both the number of participating firms and the number of alliances between them have grown. Figure 5 presents an overview; the digits between brackets represent the number of agreements linking pairs of firms.

The authors impute two major roles for ESPRIT in the strategies of the (big) 12 firms: ESPRIT is a *complement* to existing alliance patterns and ESPRIT serves to *reinforce* the European orientation of the firm. (Mytelka and De la Pierre 1987, p. 247). However, the program appears to serve the latter purpose for only four of the "big 12" (Bull, GEC, AEG and STC). The other eight are still predominantly outwardly directed; for them ESPRIT seems to be merely complementary, in the sense of broadening or "completing" their existing alliances (Mytelka and De la Pierre 1987, p. 249). What "completing" means, remains to be seen.

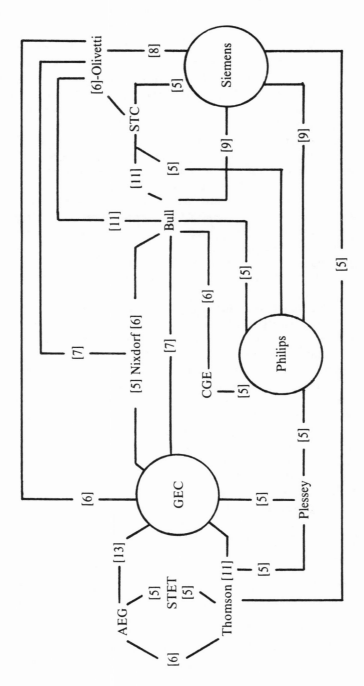

Source: Mytelka and De la Pierre (1987, p. 248).

Figure 5. Intra-EC Cooperation Agreements Through ESPRIT:
The European IT-Clan Extended

By functionally differentiating the 193 agreements of their study Van Tulder and Junne find an interesting difference, parallel to Mytelka and De la Pierre (1987, p. 240) between intra-EC and EC-U.S.A/EC-Japan partnerships: the former are oriented far more towards knowledge production than are agreements between EC and American firms; in addition, the pattern of Euro-Japanese deals "reveals that European multinationals follow a similar strategy in Japan as Japanese multinationals in Europe, which primarily is aimed at facilitating their internationalization process by using alliances to enter foreign markets that are, in many cases, protected" (Van Tulder and Junne, 1988, p. 244). Van Tulder and Junne's analysis suggests that there are more reasons for the formation of strategic alliances than the sole rationale of technology transfer. Kreiken (1986), borrowing from another industry (civil aviation, or more particularly the Airbus-case) but general enough to be useful in the interpretation of developments in the IT-industry as well, offers such a list of potential rationales (Kreiken 1986, p. 289): R&D efforts may be distributed among the partners, thus reducing risks; partners may want to avoid parallel production in competing programs; similar and dissimilar programs may be joined to gain access to know-how and know-why or for more collusive purposes; furthermore, alliances facilitate the access to international markets where demand for products is often accompanied by protective policies such as the associated demand for compensation orders. Last, but not least, cross border partnerships may facilitate the access to foreign or supranational public funding of R&D, production and sales promotion.

Whatever the rationales, the question that still waits to be answered is to what extent intra (regional) versus extra-European (global) cooperation have to be considered as mutually exclusive or conflicting strategies. As far as third party alliances (Euro-United States or Euro-Japan) are intended to create a leverage for competition vis-à-vis other European firms, the global and the regional components of the mosaic are in conflict. However, there may be equally good reasons to believe that intra-communautarian alliances are complementary as far as European cooperation can be regarded as a prerequisite for global alliances, in the sense of increasing Europe's attractiveness as a prospective partner or avoiding the risk of being excluded from international technology transfers. Considered this way, intra-communautarian cooperation is neither necessarily in conflict with, nor a complete substitute for global partnerships.

C.   Unanswered (European) Prayers

Whatever the plausibility of the motives and arguments listed above, there should be a less *ad hoc* explanation for the "irrational" ambiguities of intra-European *versus* global alliance strategies. Missing the link that explains the gap between Euro-centered prayers and non-Euro-oriented practices, complicates an unabated appraisal of Europe's efforts at industrial-technological integration.

Mytelka and De la Pierre do not seem to be overoptimistic about Europe's capacity to design, let alone to stick to, a coherent strategy-mix:

> ... the accelerating pace of technological change in the IT industry, and the major advances being made by Japanese and American competitors in computers, semiconductors and fibre-optics, puts into question the ability of a programme such as ESPRIT to build and maintain an independent European technological base. R&D partnerships with world leaders and access to global markets will continue to exercise a *counter*weight to a European-oriented alliance strategy for many firms in the IT industry (1987, p. 251, italics added).

Van Tulder and Junne speculate about the reasons of the pro-United States/ pro-Japan bias of European IT-multinationals. One of their findings is that European MF's are more diversified and are therefore used to solve their problems in-house. The diversity of technologies within a "representative" multidivisional firm usually covers more than just a single stage on the path of development. Second, European firms often acquired U.S. technology through U.S. foreign investment, and have therefore no experience (like the Japanese) in licence agreements. Third, European firms experienced a smoother growth of exports, thus mitigating the risk of anti-reactions (as against the Japanese) and diminishing the need for cooperative agreements to penetrate foreign markets. For one or more of these reasons:

> the threshold for European companies to enter a cooperation agreement may just be somewhat higher than for American or Japanese companies. This may be one of the reasons why European companies reach more agreements with American or Japanese partners than with other European firms. Negotiations with an American or Japanese prospective partner may be more straightforward and less filled with mutual mistrust than is the case with two European prospective partners. Negotiations between European firms can also be more difficult because their markets may overlap to a larger extent. As a result competition may dominate in their relationship leaving little room for cooperation (Van Tulder and Junne 1988, p. 221).

Yet, as documented above, intra-European interfirm connections are by no means totally absent. Consequently, we are left with a couple of intriguing questions:

- How to explain the specific *mix* of communautarian, regional and global alliances?
- Given such a mix, what to say about the "net" impact of official Community policy objectives (as exemplified by ESPRIT)?
- Is ESPRIT a stimulus for the formation of regional alliances or just a temporary "brake" on the European eagerness to enter into global alliances?

In order to answer these questions we have to say something on another type of moves and motives in alliance behavior, which went thus far unnoticed: preemptive or preventive tactics. Three rationales can be distinguished within this behavioral category. First, organizations join up with rivals to be able to monitor the actions of others in the industry. Second, to prevent being "left behind" it may prove worthwhile to team up with other firms: if a firm does not join, certainly another will, causing the former to lose a, yet to be established, advantage over the latter or losing a potential entry option to a "privileged group" *in spe* (Olson 1975, pp. 48-50). Third, joining up with the (friend[s]) of) "the enemy of your enemies" (Fennema 1982, p. 167) may sometimes neutralize potential first mover advantages of the initial or main "enemy." These rationales introduce a totally different arsenal of key-concepts in our analysis of cooperation among firms and non-market organizations. The "European" way in which Plessey, a *British* electronics firm, summer 1989 mobilizes the tactical support of a prominent *French* rival, Thompson, to defend its would-be autonomy against a combined *German-British* take-over attack by Siemens-GEC, gives an instructive impression of the key-concepts we should think of: the growing, rather than waning role of opportunism in the reproduction of the "European" network; the role of sequential triadic tactics rather than dyadic exchange relationships between strategically interdependent firms; the politics of discrediting reluctant "partners" rather than building trust among "opponents" for more constructive purposes—amounting to a type of interorganizational regime that might be summarized as the evolution of order out of incomplete antagonism.

Tactical motives for selecting, forming and breaking *strategic* alliances for preemptive purposes—call them the politics of antagonistic cooperation or reciprocity—clearly belong to a framework of interorganizational bargaining games (in which the logic of opportunism happens to play a prominent and *enduring* role). On the other hand, maneuvers of this kind do not fit well into the (over-)rationalized theories and equilibrium seeking notions of cooperation and integration quoted extensively earlier (in which the logic of opportunism-*suppression* plays a larger role than seems warranted, logically as well as empirically). By taking elements from the "economics of flexibility" (referring to the bases of market power) and the politics of flexibility (relating to the uses of market power) and integrating these notions into one conceptual framework, we hope to offer a more convincing, or at least: a less *ad hoc* explanation of the phenomenon we discussed in Section III: the dualistic nature of network competition in the European IT-industry. Formulated in a summary fashion: *whatever competitive ambition proves too hot to handle within the communatarian web of interlockings, will be lifted out into a web of global alliances, eventually used as a leverage to settle or to control conflicts of interest in the regional part of the mosaic of power.*

IV.   A NEGOTIATED CONTINGENCY APPROACH

In this section an interpretation will be offered of the apparent contradictions between the frontstage norm of Euro-centrism (Section II) and its "empirical" counterpart: the backstage praxis of Euro-opportunism (Section III). A central place in this interpretation has to be reserved for the unintended consequences of the intendedly rational strategies and tactics of European firms combining ESPRIT-related partnerships with non-European alliances. The contradiction can be summarized as follows: where official R&D policies follow the logic of European integration and market-oriented partnerships follow the logic of global competition, the latter tend to interfere with the former by generating competing R&D-partnerships of a non-European signature.

One may wonder how far the two logics can be kept apart; or, alternatively, whether MFs somehow succeed in neutralizing the self-denying potential of the two logics. The descriptive literature on the feasibility (short term) or the viability (long term) of European IT-strategies is exclusively based on an assessment of external *strategies* based on *inter*organizational relationships. *Tactical* moves and motives based on *intra*organizational power relationships, not only in the private but also in the public domain, are left out. Some, reasoning from this one-sided frame of orientation, describe the "imbroglio" of external relationships (see for instance Figure 4) as unmanageable; others expect a kind of uncontrolled "technology race" (fought with various weapons, ranging from patents to complete tradewars between the economic blocs). The question remains, however, what should be called "strategy" and what "tactics"—apart from the intriguing question what should be called "intended behaviour" and, looking at the overall dynamics of the game, what should be seen as the "unintended outcomes" of intendedly rational strategies and tactics. Tactics may be completely at variance with "grand" strategies. Tactical aims may appear to have unintended strategical consequences. It becomes crucial, then, to understand where, apart from strategic choice, *tactical* choice precisely comes from.

The manageability of this uneasy mix of intentions and outcomes will depend on two conditions: first on the distribution of power *within* organizations (e.g., a marketing versus a research department inside firms; or the contrasting priorities between ministries with their respective client-systems inside national governments; or the budget-game between directorates general inside the Brussels administration, and so on). Second, the power distribution *among* organizations (like firms, interest-groups, governments of the EC-member states, as well as between these entities and the Brussels administration) will determine the manageability and the final outcome of this mixed-motives and multi-level game.

A. Bargaining Power

The bargaining power of an organization, essentially speaking, is based on two conditions: the amount of its external *maneuvrability* and the extent of its internal *cohesion*. The interplay between maneuvrability and cohesion determines an organization's overall or "net" *respectability* as a bargaining partner.

Maneuverability in negotiations is defined by the entry and exit conditions and the degree of concentration of the dominant alliances *between* organizations. (Leaving other things out: the higher the concentration ratio and the higher the entry and/or exit barriers in an interorganizational network, the less room for maneuvring.) Cohesion, a necessary condition for an organization's internal mobilization and decision making potential during negotiations, is defined by the rate of turnover and the degree of centralization of dominant coalitions *within* organizations. (Again leaving other things out: the higher the rate of elite turnover and the more decentralized organizational leadership, the lower an organization's directionality.) The interplay of maneuverability and cohesion produces bargaining power—where bargaining power can be defined as the cost to an organization of imposing a loss on another organization. Losses can be expressed in terms of a reduction of an opponent's exit or entry opportunities and/or an increase of an opponent's internal discord. By mentioning the cost to *oneself* of imposing a loss upon another, the relational character of bargaining power is accentuated: in situations of strategic interdependence the imposition of will is rarely, if ever costless. Figure 6 summarizes the argument.

Note that the concept of organizational "respectability" is a somewhat ambiguous one, in theory as well as in practice. It is useful to distinguish between an organization's respectability and its *credibility* in bargaining situations. Though we have said that respectability necessarily presupposes bargaining power and, therefore, is functionally related to external mobility (by defining the degree of stability of a partnership) and to internal mobilization (by defining an organization's accountability or reputation as a coherent actor), bargaining power is not a sufficient precondition for bargaining credibility. For instance: bargaining power increases with asymmetries in exit opportunities, but credibility may decrease under the same circumstances. Conceptual (though not necessarily practical) ambiguities will disappear when we specify the opposite commitments actors are condemned to or may opt for in negotiations: maneuvrability increases the credibility of *threats* (a fortiori in case of high cohesion such as organizational militancy), but diminishes the credibility of *promises* (a fortiori in case of reduced cohesion such as organizational strife).

Consequently respectability should not be mistaken for trustworthiness or loyalty or even less for legitimacy. Organizational credibility refers to the

Bargaining power =

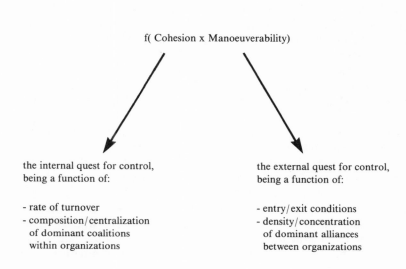

f(Cohesion x Manoeuverability)

the internal quest for control,   the external quest for control,
being a function of: being a function of:

- rate of turnover   - entry/exit conditions
- composition/centralization   - density/concentration
  of dominant coalitions   of dominant alliances
  within organizations   between organizations

Figure 6.   The Production of Bargaining Power

readiness or preparedness of the opponent to take the negotiator's threats *and* promises serious. In concreto, this implies that a credible negotiator has to give up, demonstrably, some of his exit opportunities. Certainly, one may add that a firm or a governmental agency enhances its respectability if its conduct is based on trust or legitimacy. However, what matters in negotiations, ultimately, is the predictability of the opponent's conduct. When bargaining power is seen as a potential based on the parameters of external mobility (maneuverability) and internal mobilization (cohesion), we must say that predictions on the factual use of that potential will depend on the (a)symmetries in mobility and mobilization among the players. Trust and so forth, in this a-moral universe, is seen as derivative of the former conditions.

1.   Strategy Formulation as a Bargaining Process

The ESPRIT experience suggests that the effectiveness of the uses of public and private bargaining power depends on the skills to *demonstrate* one's bargaining potential, and to test the potential of one's counterparts, already in stages preceding actual negotiations. Lobbying can serve that purpose.

Lobbying is negotiating-in-disguise: the preparatory act of exploring the faculties and the facilities of others. Negotiating, then, turns the results of explorative lobbying into "definitive" commitments. Lobbying aims at the creation of shared expectations and coordinated aspirations; it is the process by which collective symbols are (re)produced, like for instance the Japanese or the American "drive for hegemony" or the creation of a "truly European mission" for ESPRIT. Symbols, though belonging to the texture of normative understandings, often play a useful role in the management of the web of empirical commitments. An informative example of the symbolic uses of politics in the material uses of resource dependencies, is the largely rhetorical use of the concept of "national champions": dismissed by multinationals themselves as a rather narrow minded, while outdated nationalistic device, they nevertheless still consider the symbol as a very useful entry to their respective national treasuries.

The "goodness of fit" between understandings and commitments will vary according to:

- the degree of interdependence between the stakeholders due to their differential access to the global, the regional and the community reaches of the mosaic of power (the *arena*);
- the amount of ambiguity due to the unstable articulation of public and private interests at stake (the *agenda*); and
- the time needed to coordinate interests by synchronizing commitments (the *timing* specifying the time-bound character of the agenda and the arena).

2. Arena, Agenda, and Timing

Arena, agenda and timing are interrelated. Timing—for instance the relative speed of substituting the regional for the community setting, or substituting the global for the regional setting, and *vice-versa*—qualifies the impact of interdependence and ambiguity of interests. Applied to industrial policy making this means the following. Effective strategy formulation may be defined as the art of exploiting the opportunities and minimizing the constraints of ambiguity and interdependence by manipulating—as far as within one's reach—the conditions of maneuverability. The most crucial aspect of strategic choice appears to be the right *timing* of mobility from one level of the mosaic of power to another (see again Figure 1).

Making strategic choices is not enough: choices have to be implemented. Under conditions of interdependence, implementation means lobbying and negotiating. Assuming a modicum of shared interests among firms, politicians and public officials in reducing ambiguity—reinforced by a sense of strategic interdependence but relaxed by differences in entry and exit opportunities— effective lobbying alias negotiating means: the art and science of securing a modicum of *understanding* between two or more interdependent actors that are trying to maximize their *individual outcomes* by finding a more or less acceptable balance of *commitments*.

3. Retaliation and Fragmentation: On the "Recycling" of Alliances and Coalitions

A special note should be made on the explicative status of so-called "individual outcomes." As argued before, bargaining power has to do with (a)symmetries in entry and exit opportunities among the players. Density, concentration and mobility determine the risk of interorganizational retaliation: the higher the degree of interorganizational density and concentration and the more unequal the entry and exit opportunities, the higher the cost to the relatively immobile of not giving in to or imposing a loss on the relatively mobile. However, in order to produce respectable commitments, actors have to be internally cohesive. Cohesion—an internal asset—supplements external negotiation power. In that sense effective bargaining requires the control of the *interplay* between internal faculties (the stability of intra-organizational coalitions) and external facilities (the stability of inter-organizational alliances). Intra-organizational and inter-organizational bargaining are of equal importance. The interplay of both determines the ultimate respectability of the resulting commitments. Sometimes, as in the case of ESPRIT, the ambiguity of the bargaining agenda and the instability of the policy arena(s) and, consequently, doubts about the time-horizon (timing, timeliness and duration) of concluded commitments, are due to the *intra*-actor ambiguity of so called "individual" goals or interests—rather than to *inter*-actor controversies or conflicts of interest. Strategic ambiguity and partnership dilemmas originate from external as much as from internal sources, that is: from *intra*-actor fragmentation or rivalry, generating unreliable responses to critical inter-actor interdependencies and *vice-versa*. It is wise to keep in mind that not only governmental organizations, but also business firms and interest groups are *themselves* political coalitions and that the executive in a bureau, a pressure group or a firm is a political broker. The behavioral point of view adopted here leans on the unorthodox work of organization theorists and researchers as Cohen, Cyert, March and Olsen (Cyert and March 1963; March and Olsen 1976), pithily paraphrased by March, the "dean" of this *intra*-organization school of thinking: *The composition of the firm is not given; it is negotiated. The goals of the firm are not given; they are bargained.*

Interpreting the composition and the goals of a firm as contingent or dependent on the composition of an organization's dominant coalition, rather than as data or independent variables, is bound to lead to a critical reappraisal of the conceptual and empirical merits of the transaction costs approach to strategic partnerships as a means to control environmental ambiguities (see Section III.B). Just as an interorganizational bargaining approach purports to take the risk of external *retaliation*, rather than the control of opportunism, as a key explanatory variable in the management of environmental uncertainty, it also urges to grant a more prominent status to the risk of emergent opportunism *within* organizations, that is, the risk of internal *fragmentation*—precisely *because of* the internalization of external adversities or opportunities—in the explanation of organizational responses to external contingencies. It is the latter phenomenon, that is: the immanent risk of internal dissensus or disorientation and its crucial impact on the selection and the degree of "internalization" of external allies, that is conspicuously missing in transaction-cost or neo-institutional approaches to organizational reactions on environmental uncertainty.

Summarizing: an interorganizational model taking bargaining power as the co-product of the conditions of maneuverability and cohesion, treats the decision of organizations whether or not to incorporate environmental uncertainty (the risk of opportunism not excluded) as a strategic choice indeed, that is: as a pain-staking *trade-off* between the risk of retaliation externally *versus* the risk of fragmentation or discord internally. By internalizing external contingencies, organizations sometimes succeed in averting an Olsonian "prisoners" dilemma (see Olson [1975, pp. 11-43] on the self-destructive potential of distrust, opportunism and tit-for-tat stratagems *among* organizations) only to discover that they became entrapped in an Allisonian "guerilla" (see Allison [1971, pp. 144-184] in the tradition of many others (Sapolsky 1972; Halperin 1974), on the multiplier of discretionary power, trench-warfare and control-deficits *inside* large, bureaucratic organizations).

Conceptualizing the politics of organizations in controlling their environment as the ambition to control the interplay between internal coalitions and external alliances, introduces an unexpected connotation of "other-directedness" in our discussion: more often than not effective lobbying and negotiating comes to imply securing understandings and fixing commitments by accommodating to or manipulating the internal cohesion and decision making power of one's *counterpart(s)*. (See Figure 7 for a graphic illustration of the "recycling" of internal coalitions and external alliances.) What insight does this approach offer when applied to ESPRIT?

B. The Logic of the Actors

We started our analysis of the "European" answer to the dynamics of the international IT-arena with the distinction of a global, a regional and a communautarian setting. The complexity of this mosaic of powers raised several questions: how rational is the decision to invest or not to invest in the communautarian part of the mosaic of power? How to coordinate one's strategic choices across the different settings of the mosaic of power? And what about the actors differential freedom to choose at all? To answer these questions, however tentatively, we should learn at least more about the logic of the respective actors.

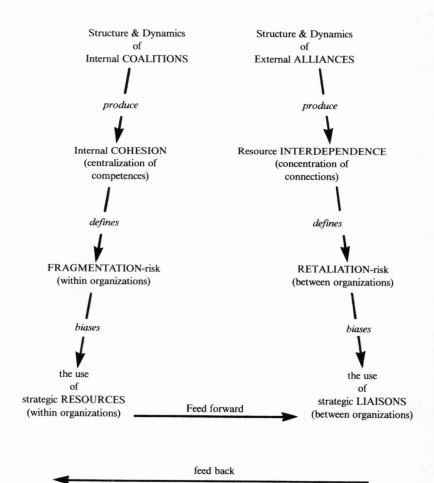

STRATEGIC AMBIGUITY AND
PARTNERSHIP DILEMMAS
as a function of

Structure & Dynamics
of
Internal COALITIONS

Structure & Dynamics
of
External ALLIANCES

produce

produce

Internal COHESION
(centralization of
competences)

Resource INTERDEPENDENCE
(concentration of
connections)

defines

defines

FRAGMENTATION-risk
(within organizations)

RETALIATION-risk
(between organizations)

biases

biases

the use
of
strategic RESOURCES
(within organizations)

Feed forward

the use
of
strategic LIAISONS
(between organizations)

feed back

Figure 7.   The Relation Between Strategic Ambiguity/Partnership Dilemmas
and the Characteristics of the Internal and External Environment

1. The Strategic Triangle

In case of strategic interdependence rational organizations—public and private alike—may be expected to follow a simple behavioral axiom: increase one's own limited liability and promote or maintain one's counterpart's reliability. In terms of Section II (on the *three* Triad power settings): actors will try to maximize their chances of free entry and exit in any bargaining setting—keeping their position as flexible as possible by avoiding long term commitments—while hoping or promoting that the opposite will hold for their bargaining partners. Asymmetries in commitments make life much easier, but not necessarily more stable. There is a clear trade-off between the desire for flexibility and the quest for stability. Much of the actual behavior of the partners in ESPRIT, but even more relevant: much of the future behavior of the partners and of the future outcome of the private/private as well as private/ public alliances in this context, depends essentially on the question how the partners in ESPRIT will cope with a typical dilemma in "nested" power games: how much loss of flexibility or administrative discretion should one allow on the communautarian level in exchange for how much gain in competitive capability in the other (the global and the regional) reaches of the mosaic of power?

As argued before, the answer to that question will vary with the degree of internal mobilization and external mobility, that is, with (a) the internal cohesion and resolution of the respective actors, and (b) the freedom to switch from one part of the mosaic of bargaining power to another. MFs, COs and PMs differ significantly in terms of their respective cohesion or decision-making power and in the degree of mobility within and outside the different settings. Needless to say that, in their mutual anticipations, the respective actors or partners-to-be will take into account the knowledge they have (or think to have) about their counterparts' cohesion and maneuverability. The interplay of cohesion and maneuverability leads to commitments or agreements (credible threats and promises). Agreements may serve several purposes (see also Winham 1979, p. 133):

- to *resolve* disputes (e.g., about cooperative market agreements vis-à-vis anti-cartel legislation or competition policy of the European Commission);
- to *demonstrate* values (e.g., restoration of European economic "sovereignty" or self-reliance vis-à-vis other economic powers);
- to *distribute* resources (e.g., the allocation of funds for ESPRIT among industries, sectors, member states and so on); and
- to *administer* rules and roles (e.g., consultation by means of the ESPRIT Management Committee, revision of the rules of partner-selection, redefinition of performance criteria, and so on).

More often than not negotiating and lobbying involve more than one purpose. The specific mix varies again with the structure of interdependence determining the *maneuverability* of the respective players (the "arena"), the stakes or interests articulated by negotiations and agreements and delineating the rules of *accountability* of the respective players (the "agenda") and the time required, or preferred, to reach agreement and to monitor the consummation of commitments; the latter determines the *time span of feedback* on the first two variables: maneuverability and accountability.

Figure 8 summarizes the interrelationships between actors' maneuvrability, accountability and their time span of feedback in the form of a "strategic triangle." The triangle should be seen as a *dynamic* model of power: changes in maneuvrability will entail (changes in) accountability, just as (changes in) the time span of feedback on actors' conduct—that is, the exploitation of differences in maneuvrability—will result in a revaluation of these bases of power.

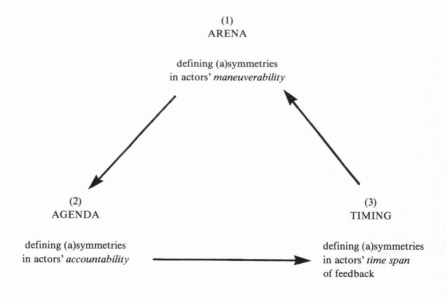

(1)
ARENA

defining (a)symmetries
in actors' *maneuverability*

(2)   (3)
AGENDA   TIMING

defining (a)symmetries   defining (a)symmetries
in actors' *accountability*   in actors' *time span*
                                                                   of feedback

Figure 8.   The Strategic Triangle

The strategic triangle has a double heuristic value: it may help to arrive at a better understanding of the *trans*actional logic of the individual stakeholders of ESPRIT as well as provide an explanation of the *inter*actional momentum of the program as a whole. The specific configuration of maneuverability, accountability and timing governs the decision of each actor whether or not to invest in the ESPRIT program. Assuming that (1) *rational organizations will look for predictable/accountable partners while preserving as much as possible their own maneuverability;* and assuming that (2) *the respective actors differ in terms of handicaps or facilities as summarized in the strategic triangle*—we may characterize the essence of ESPRIT as:

- a highly unstable mix of heterogeneous motives, interests and faculties;
- buttressed by unequal power relationships;
- between allies with different conceptions of the appropriate timing of commitments. (For instance: the higher a player's bargaining power in terms of manoeuvrability and cohesion, and the greater his wish for limited liability, the shorter his preferred time-horizon will be.)

In such a setting it is not the official mission of ESPRIT, but rather the aggregate or interactive outcome of the transaction logic of the actors—that is, as summarized in Figure 7, their differential responses to the risks of retaliation and/or fragmentation —that will explain the resulting momentum of ESPRIT.

2. Conditions for Integrated Concertation

Reviewing the literature on strategy formulation and policy making in 'organisation sets' or networks, the reader can conclude that close public/ private concertation will occur most likely in policy/strategy arenas where interdependence is shared by small numbers of governmental agencies and organized interests. Thus, integrated "participation" prevails where (Olsen 1981, p. 510):

- societies segment into functionally autonomous sectors, especially sectors characterized by small numbers of well-defined, *stable interests*;
- for each policy topic it should be easy to specify *stable rules* about which organizations can participate, which problems and solutions are relevant, and which rules of the game are legitimate; and
- *specialised systems* prevent policies from becoming large garbage cans, from becoming fortuitous results of the intermeshing of loosely coupled processes.

Empirical findings suggest that integrated participation occurs where "predictability, certainty, compromises, recognition, role differentiation, and effective representation outwards offer high benefits, and where the costs are low of commitment and rigidity" (Olsen 1981, p. 510). Besides the requirement of non-ambiguity concerning the extent and the character of interdependence and power between organizations, Olsen mentions a stable division of intraorganizational labor and power, reasonably well articulated orderings of interests and preferences in a situation where organizations know how much of the attainment of one goal they are prepared to sacrifice in order to attain other goals somewhat more fully. In short, close and stable public/private concertation can be expected where (Olsen 1981, pp. 510-511, italics added), "*the causal world is well understood, where decisions have predictable consequences, and where it is easy to know who has competence and expertise.*"

In the case of ESPRIT none of these intra- and extra-organizational conditions seem to be fulfilled. The section on "the cast" of ESPRIT (see Section II.B) does not reveal the presence of a "small organisation set of governmental agencies and well-organized interests" with stable rules about insiders and outsiders, stable and unambiguously defined interests, consensual rules of the "European game" and a clear conception of the scope of interdependence. This assessment refers not only to (inter-)governmental relationships (see next section), nor exclusively to public/private asymmetries in maneuvrability and accountability, but also to inherent ambivalences, not to say contradictions, between European firms that are supposed to cooperate within the communautarian setting.

The available literature suggests that cooperative agreements, even in a "precompetitive" make-up, as in ESPRIT-related research and development projects, are fragile and unstable constructions confronted with various difficulties, leading generally to early breaking ups, buy-outs or mergers. The situation is aggravated where the majority of R&D arrangements are multicountry and where divergent objectives, strategies, domestic regulations, and institutions often combine with socio-psychological factors such as nationalistic feelings and attachment to familiar working methods. Jacquemin and Spinoit (1986, pp. 492-494) distinguish three major obstacles undermining the reliability of this type of interfirm agreements:

(First), a cooperative agreement is a compromise between a desire for collaboration and an intention of maintaining independence, so that the organisational structure reflecting such an ambiguity is usually complex. Various clauses of the legal structure express this concern and imply heavy transaction costs of negotiation, especially for transnational ventures. Partner selection and the possibility of defining well-balanced contributions is the first barrier. An especially important fear is that one partner will be strengthened by the cooperation in such a way that it will become a dangerous competitor. This situation is of course more probable for horizontal agreements than for vertical ones. In the latter case, complementarities allow the benefits to be distributed according to the respective activities and products. In the case of cooperation between competitors, a geographical partition is the most obvious system of trying to solve the problem but has a side effect on existing competition.

(Second), the management of existing cooperative agreements is also costly, especially in R&D where technological conditions are changing rapidly and unpredictably. As it is not possible to maintain complete control over the functioning of the cooperation, it is necessary to construct complex contracts containing explicit clauses concerning confidentiality and transmission of information; and patent, trademark and copyright licenses. In fact, in joint R&D, there are fundamental limits on the ability to protect intellectual property, especially when technology advances at a rapid pace and competitors can invent around existing patents.

(Finally), it is not easy to divide the benefits of a cooperative agreement in R&D given that scientific knowledge has many aspects of a public good and that its results are not often easily incorporated. Disputes about joint appropriation, exclusivity and sharing (*ratione loci* or *ratione materiae*) of the results are often the source of disagreements.

All of these elements suggest that even in the context of a very tolerant antitrust policy, without positive public actions, European cooperation in R&D will remain a limited and unstable phenomenon.

The limits and instabilities of interorganizational cooperation are intensified rather than mitigated by the logic of opportunism when some appear to use the regional and/or the global setting as a tactical leverage for controlling the evolution of cooperation within the communautarian setting (and *vice-versa*). In addition, one may question the stability of public/private commitments based on such a fragile regime of interfirm relationships and attitudes. Yet ESPRIT exists. How to explain the miracle?

3. ESPRIT's Raison d'Etre

Part of the passion of public *Eurocracy* for the takeoff of new policies can be found in old frustrations: the credibility, and hence the prestige, of the Community were eroded by such diversities as the economic crisis, uncontrollability of the agricultural budget, disappointing results of the reorganization of ailing sectors like the steel- and shipbuilding-industry, demonstrations of persistent protectionism of the member states, and so on. In the epiphany institutional and psychological state of readiness such as of the American/Japanese Challenge had to be welcomed as an inspiring common cause.

Second, seen from the perspective of the credibility and the prestige of the European top of private *industry,* part of the passion for ESPRIT can be found in the intended and expected "side payment" of a European Commission's preparedness to adopt a more friendly attitude vis-à-vis cartel-like behavior of European firms. The most important part of the miracle of the "impossible" flair of ESPRIT lies to my opinion in the condition that multinational firms may *win* as much, or more, as they say to lose from the contradictions of European "intergovernmentalism" (see the next section).

Furthermore the existence of ESPRIT is based on the potential of a double strategy for the MFs involved: the "normative" network provides the rationalization and legitimation of European chauvinism, resulting in access to European funds plus clemency in the interpretation of the anticartel rules of the Treaty of Rome, whereas the "empirical" network serves as a European backing for global and regional guerilla purposes, resulting in *ad hoc* EC/Japan and EC/U.S. partnerships.

At one side, one may expect that organizations are less likely to participate in issue-areas that are experiencing major changes, and during periods when the organizations themselves are experiencing changes in values, perspectives, priorities or resources: "organisations remain reluctant to participate until priorities and resources, and thus their interdependencies, become clearer" (Olsen 1981, p. 511). At the other side, the stakes of the game do not allow for waiting. Even more importantly: the only effective way to test priorities, resources and the structures of interdependence, is participating in ESPRIT *as long as one does not give up one's freedom to move,* simultaneously or sequentially, *from the communautarian setting to other parts of the power mosaic.* As we have seen, this is exactly what the MFs practice. Mytelka and De la Pierre's documentation can be used as a perfect illustration of this dualism. Their data indicate the presence of a tight knit network inside the European IT-clan. It would go too far to speak of a centralized leadership within MF-clan, but combining the cumulative partnerships of GCE, Philips and Siemens (to mention only the biggest linkers, see Figures 3 and 5, the encircled items) with the spectacular growth in importance of research projects linking the big-12 firms to a web of non-big-12 firms (see Table 4) suggests clearly the presence of a centralized *two-tier architecture* of resource-dependencies among the key players and a web of satellites.

Table 4.   ESPRIT-Projects Involving Big-12 Firms,
non-Big-12 Firms and Either Research
Institutes or Universities or Both

Year	Number of projects[a]
1983	8
1984	36
1985	44

Note: [a]The share of this type of projects has risen sharply from 32 percent in 1983 to 56 percent in 1985, while "big-12 projects" dwindled from 36 percent to 6 percent ("non-big-12 projects," excluding the "big-12" but including research institutes and/or universities, increased from 32 percent to 37 percent in the same period).

Source: Computed from European Commission (1986).

In spite of the high degree of centralization and concentration of bargaining power in the IT-arena, the game as such remains a highly ambivalent game indeed. On the one hand it is perfectly clear why the big-12 firms practice the politics of *respectability* or "competitive self-restraint" inside the ESPRIT-arena: the density of linkages depicted in Figure 5, and reinforced by a web of project-bound satellites (Table 4) have had the undeniable effect of increasing the "costs to A of imposing a loss upon B" *directly*. However, the emerging European discipline based on this insight is *indirectly* eroded through American/Japanese partnerships initiated or welcomed by each of the same key actors. It is this duality that eventually debouches into a self-denying "European prophesy."

This practice has far reaching consequences for the distribution and the uses of bargaining power when we decide to look at the other side of the public/ private interface of industrial policymaking. Looking at this side reinforces our doubts about how typically *European* the final outcome of the "sovereignty game" will be. Member state politicians (PMs) and may be even more saliently, community officials (COs) neither have the facilities (external entry and exit opportunities and degree of concentration) nor the faculties (internal cohesion and degree of centralization) of their private counterparts (MFs), as a short overview of the contradictions of "intergovernmentalism" may clarify.

4. Cohesion of the European Community

The strategic alliances concept of European cooperation, the rise of intergovernmentalism and the decision procedure of the Community itself clearly indicate that the member governments remain the ultimate source of formal policymaking. National governments even decide effectively on most of the Commissions budget and on the Commissioner's appointments. On external matters they decide which issues are to be regulated through traditional diplomatic channels, summits, or community institutions. In spite of a general European commitment several inhibiting features have emerged or intensified as matters of concern during the seventies, a period of slower economic growth and persistent high unemployment levels: narrow national interests dominating high policy objectives, increased European discrepancies in economic development and political stability, member state firms competing (with governmental assistance) for external markets, raw materials and energy supplies, and the persistence of anti-EC sentiments in the political organizations representing those strata in Europe that feel disadvantaged by the present mode of integration (e.g., the British and French working classes and small entrepreneurs).

Highly relevant, in the case of ESPRIT, are the differences in philosophy on trade and industrial policy between the member states. Merlini (Merlini 1984) from whom we borrowed the preceding assessment of persisting nationalistic sentiments, summarizes the intra-Community variety on trade and industry policy matters as follows. In general the official positions of France, Germany and the United Kingdom represent the three different groups into which member governments of the Community divide on trade and industrial policy matters. The virtues of free trade are extolled in Germany but doubted in France. British policy aims to maintain the present degree of openness in world trade. It is accepted by member governments and by the Commission that Europe is protectionist, though no more so than the United States and Japan. There is disagreement as to whether in this situation Europe should become more or less protectionist. Commission officials would like to achieve a reduction in European protection, but believe that it would be unwise to steer a naively free-trade course.

The *French* government is keen to see internal barriers lowered but does not want to expose the economy to the gaps it sees in the Community's external protection. Hence it argues that increased external protection should accompany reduced internal protection. The German administration cautiously welcomes the French position on internal market policy but regrets the connection being made between this and the demand for a more robust external-trade policy. For successive British governments, lowering internal barriers has been a major objective. The French approach—consonant with J.J. Servan Schreiber's assessment of some 20 years ago—is most radically inspired by the belief that in most advanced-technology sectors' Europe is not competitive with the United States and Japan. To rectify this will require a domestic market larger than that of any single member state. Hence industrial cooperation at the European level is essential, internal barriers should be brought down and temporary external protection may be necessary. The memorandum proposes that to make cooperation between European firms more attractive, member states should channel more of their R&D expenditure through the Community for the financing of joint projects. Cooperation should also be made easier by revising national company and competition legislation.

In *Germany* the contention that Europe is lagging behind the United States and Japan in advanced technology is more accepted than it was, but not as widely acknowledged as it is in France. The French position is viewed with mixed feelings. Severe criticism is directed at proposals that are seen as reducing competition, whether in the domestic market through increased government intervention or in the external market through increased protection. German officials agree that there should be more cooperation in basic research but believe that Community financial support should be confined to projects of a European dimension in which Community action would yield greater benefits than national action, and that it should be kept *as far as possible from production and from the market*. Cooperation between European firms is welcome if the firms take the initiative. The role of government is to provide a climate conducive to innovation and investment by firms. German competition policy gives priority to maintaining a competitive situation in the German market; the suggestion that the community is the relevant market is resisted. The German administration favors liberalization in technical standards and public procurement. It dismisses the case for protecting infant industry. This might seem useful in the short run, but temporary protection tends to become permanent, and in the long run it would be very damaging. Attitudes toward inward investment are generally more positive than in France.

The *British* government has for some time been perturbed by the failure of its high-technology industry to keep pace with those of the United States and Japan. It attaches importance to making community action in research innovation and new technologies more effective, particularly in facilitating cooperation between firms, though it emphasizes the need to control costs. It favors joint European ventures and has pressed for the removal of impediments to them, and it advocates directing competition policy towards promoting industrial developments as well as preventing distortion of competition. Proposals to open up the internal market are received warmly in the British administration, though there are reservations about measures designed to benefit other member states but not third countries. As in Germany, temporary strengthening of external protection is rejected. Although a good deal of convergence on internal liberalization can be observed at the approach of "1992"—be it accompanied by a clear revival of protectionist sentiments for the community as a whole—no fundamental change seems to have occurred in this (Merlini 1984) comparative portrait of the competition and industrial policy-philosophies of the three leading member states of the Community.

With the exception of the supranational orientation of the European Commission, most of the European officials participating in the functional committees coordinated by COREPER (the committee of "permanent representatives" of the member-state governments; see Section II.B), are instructed by their national governments and cannot depart significantly from their briefs. They are there, for the most part, to defend, rather than to bargain concessions freely. The net result of this mushrooming of intergovernmental committees is to produce hard and prolonged bargaining among governments rather than creative interchange between the Commission, national officials and interest groups (Webb 1977). Strategy formulation and policy implementation are the subject of ongoing intra-organizational bargaining within a conglomerate of functional committees. In some respects multinational firms will feel handicapped by the ambiguities of this political and bureaucratic pluralism. But they may profit as well as from the administrative discretion stemming from intra-bureaucratic rivalry and the intergovernmental lack of consensus or sense of direction in matters of European industrial policymaking as sketched above. However, whether this blessing in disguise is used by European firms in such a way that, more particularly, *Europe's* competitive capabilities are improved and its "sovereignty" saved, remains to be seen. The logic of the resulting game does not have to correspond with the rational intentions and the factual use that the actors make, according to their individual logic of transaction, of their respective faculties and facilities. The earlier presented summary of empirical findings on the extra-European bias and the built-in instability of resulting interfirm cooperative agreements, does not inspire great confidence. The next paragraph sketches the potential odds between the macro or interactive logic of the game (Section IV.C) against the micro-rational or transaction logic of the individual architects of that game, as sketched in this section.

C.   The Logic of the Game

Organization-environment politics, whether practiced by firms, bureaucrats or politicians, can be defined as the process that takes place when actors attempt to structure a situation of interdependence in such a way that their individual goals are promoted. In terms of the "strategic triangle" (see Figure 8, par. 3.2) the capacity of an actor to impose his definition of the situation on the other(s) does not depend on his moral qualities—though the perceived legitimacy of goals, interests and sentiments related to "external threats" or "common adversaries" do play an auxiliary role in the creation of shared symbols, in the manufacture of credibility of resulting commitments and in the maintenance of respectability. However, the capacity to impose one's definition of what should be done depends rather on the structure of interdependence and on the effective *timing* of the use of facilities flowing from the symmetry or asymmetry of that structure of interdependence. As argued before, the effective timing of the use of power depends on the internal characteristics of the actors—that is, on their internal cohesion and sense of direction. It is here that we have to look for the origin of possible deviations between the logic of the actors—"trying to maximize their outcomes by finding a more or less acceptable balance of commitments" (see Section IV.A.2)—and the logic of the game—"failing to find an acceptable balance of commitments."

The foregoing paragraphs have shown that the international politics of economic concertation can be usefully conceived as a four-level game: at one side the national game where domestic groups (national champions with affiliated interests) seek to maximize their interests by pressuring their own governments to adopt favorable policies, and politicians in search of power and prestige by constructing or responding to alliances among those groups; at the other side the international game, to be subdivided into three, more or less substitutable but clearly separate games: the global, the regional and the communautarian sub-games. At the international level, national governments seek to maximize their own freedom to satisfy domestic pressures, while minimizing the adverse consequences of foreign developments.

The four games are played simultaneously, so that national policies are in some sense the resultant of both the domestic and the international parts of the mosaic of power sketched in Section II. Neither of the respective games can be ignored by policymakers, so long as their countries remain interdependent, yet sovereign democracies. National political leaders appear at least at the national, the communautarian and the regional ("dyad plus one") game boards. Across the international table sit his foreign counterparts, and at his elbows sit diplomats and other international advisers (e.g., the Task Force, the ESPRIT advisory board, the ESPRIT Management Committee as mentioned in Section II.B). Around the domestic table behind him sit spokesmen for the large domestic ministries and representatives of the "natural champions" with *their* supporters or clients.

The strategic essence of this multi-level game is that moves that are rational for a player at one board (such as supporting a "national champion" or subsidising a bi-national "competitive advantage") may be quite irrational for that same player at the other board (such as promoting a "communautarian program" or welcoming "strategic alliances" between European firms and third country competitors). Nevertheless, there are powerful incentives for attending each of the games and monitoring their outputs—for instance for testing asymmetries in maneuvrability and for learning about differences in accountability based on differences in the time span of feedback at the respective game boards.

Putnam (1984) commenting on the "staggering complexities" of this kind of "multi-level games," observes a built-in conservative mechanism: "each national leader has already made a substantial investment in building a particular coalition at the domestic board, and he will be loathe to try to construct a different coalition simply to sustain an alternative policy mix that might be more acceptable internationally" (Putnam 1984, p. 50). Conversely, each MF having invested in international joint ventures (European or otherwise) will refuse to dissolve his alliance simply to accommodate nationalistic or communautarian critics.

Even in theory there is no guarantee that any solution exists that will simultaneously satisfy the needs of the core players, and if such a solution exists in principle the uncertainties of practical politics may prevent the players form reaching it (Putnam 1984).

There is no "superbrain" coordinating or accommodating the contradictions between level-specific optima specifying each actors' preferred ratio between his own limited liability and others' unlimited reliability. What *de facto* rules the game of "finding an acceptable balance of commitments" may be called the *dynamics of myopia*: organizations, confronted with uncertainty about the maneuvrability (*arena*), accountability (*agenda*), and time preferences (*timing*) of other organizations on which they feel strategically dependent scrutinize the nearest links of the chain of interdependence but will thereby lose control over the chain-as-a-whole as far as the players are not in a position to oversee the ramifying web of—preexisting or would-be—commitments of their partners or rivals (the reader, wishing to promote his understanding of the "rationality of myopia," should inspect again Figure 4, on the ramifications of Siemens/Philips-deal; I borrow the label for this mechanism, as an *organizational* extension, from Olson's "rationality of ignorance" in individual citizens' voting behavior [Olson 1986]). The typical (defensive/opportunistic/ short term) reaction to these limits of "knowledgeability"—a mix of bounded rationality *and* bounded legitimacy—is the propensity to use the global or the regional "parts" of the four-level game to correct for a loss of maneuvrability (or the increase of liability) incurred by participation in the communautarian "part" of the game. It is from here that the actors—not in spite of their individual logic of transaction but precisely *because* of that micro- rationality—happen to lose their control of the logic of the game as a whole. The loss of control has to be interpreted as a mechanism of circular causation: regional games, initiated for correcting prisoners' dilemma-situations on the Community-level, produce global games, but *once produced* the global games start to restrain or even to *dictate* the rationale of the regional (and the communautarian) games—in the paradoxical sense of becoming the *prime mover* of their own causal antecedents (Elster 1978, pp. 121-122, 1986, pp. 202-210, 217-218; Giddens 1979, p. 211).

1.   Rational Choice versus Strategic Choice

At first sight, the outcome of the perplexities of the four-level game comes close to what Scharpf, characterizing the developments of European policymaking since the mid-sixties, labelled as "frustration without disintegration and resilience without progress" (Scharpf 1985, p. 40):

> In ongoing joint-decision systems, from which *exit is excluded or very costly*, non-agreement would imply the self-defeating continuation of past policies in the face of a changing policy environment. Thus, pressures to reach agreement will be great. The substance of agreement will be affected, however, by the prevailing style of decision-making. In its ability to achieve effective responses to a changing policy environment, the 'bargaining' style is clearly inferior to the 'problem solving' style. But the preconditions of 'problem solving'—the orientation towards common goals, values and norms—are difficult to create, and they are easily eroded in cases of ideological conflict, mutual distrust or disagreement over the fairness of distribution rules. Thus, reversion to a 'bargaining' style of decision making [. .] seems to have been characteristic of the European Community ever since the great confrontations of the mid-sixties. The price to be paid for that is not simply a prevalence of distributive conflicts complicating all substantive decisions, but a systematic tendency towards sub-optimal substantive solutions.

Perhaps this assessment should be called an understatement in the case of industrial and technology policy problems confronting Europe, if for multinational firms and, to a lesser degree, national politicians exit from the communautarian framework appears *not* to be excluded or if the costs of exit from the communautarian setting are compensated by the benefits of investment in other (global or regional) industrial policy games. The substantive results will be worse than sub-optimal if the micro-rationality underlying the corporate strategy of multinational firms, incidentally supported by national politicians interested in protecting their "national champions," drives out the meso-rationality of industrial policies on the Community level. The disappointing results of that substitution process, while not providing adequate answers to the problem of excess capacity and other competitive *dis*advantages mentioned earlier (see section II.A), may inspire to a second substitution effect: endless series of short term trade guerilla tactics driving out long term, structural industrial policies and corporate strategies. The net outcome in that case might be frustration *and* disintegration.

The presence of (1) the perplexities of the four-level game—complicated by asymmetries in internal cohesion and the unequal distribution of bargaining power among the participants due to unequal barriers to entry and/or exit for each of them—coinciding with (2) a horizontal orientation in the prevailing policy programs—intending or pretending cooperation among the main competitors in the European arena—is apt to produce misalliances and trained incapacities. Misalliances in general arise from situations in which defensive tactics have to conceal a lack or impossibility of offensive strategies. Those situations may be expected in the area of new technologies, that is, in areas where the conditions of strategic interdependence and uncertainty about the symbiotic or competitive nature of interdependence prevail. Looking at some recent illustrations, misalliances with concomitant supplanting of strategy by tactics can be expected when, more precisely, one or more of the following conditions hold: uneven levels of commitments, changing strategic objectives, a world moving faster than one's partners do, big-firm small-firm mismatches, inadequate internal structures and incentives for cooperation, insufficient executive attention, misjudging distribution capabilities, overestimating the technology and underestimating the rivalry, power struggles and power vacuum and, finally, lack of an internal sense of direction and consensus.

2. Frustration without Disintegration

What may be expected from ESPRIT in such a setting? "Some witnesses expressed great hopes for Esprit," say the minutes of a 1985 hearing in which officials and captains of industry were consulted by a special Committee of the British House of Lords (Select Committee on the European Communities 1984-1985, par. 112).

> The Committee fear that these [hopes] may be exaggerated. Although it is always possible that there will be an unexpected breakthrough, the Committee believe it is unrealistic to talk of leapfrogging the Japanese and Americans. It will prove extremely difficult even to catch up. Europe is starting off so far behind; there is much ground to make up; and the competition is not standing still. The committee agree with the witness from British Aerospace who said that ' . . . the genesis of ESPRIT is a reaction and as a reaction it is always going to be one step behind the thing which caused it.' [. .] Nor is it commercially

realistic to think of selling on a large scale in the American market. The distribution network
and service backup needed cost too much: the equivalent of ten years' return [. .]. So
it is unlikely that any European manufacturer will win a large slice of the American market
for European companies. What ESPRIT can hope to do is to help win back a sizeable
part of the European market for European manufacturers, and thereby reduce the adverse
balance of payments in IT. This is certainly well worth aiming for. ESPRIT can help by
building on areas of strength and by limiting damage where Europe is lagging behind. By
building a portfolio of technologies where Europe is strong, a better basis will be established
for negotiating in areas where Europe is weak. The Committee agree that ESPRIT can
provide a stronger basis for that negotiation.

Maybe part of the reported mood of the Lords has to be related to Britain's
specific stance on trade and industrial policy matters as indicated in section IV.B.4.
But the last sentence of the quote—hinting at the usefulness of a portfolio of
technologies where Europe is strong as a base for negotiating in areas where Europe
is weak—suggests a more promising interpretation. In that interpretation not only
Europe's industrial structure but even the peculiarities of its political and
administrative infrastructure could be seen as an asset rather than as a liability.

V.   CONCLUSIONS

Two conclusions may be drawn from this case study: one relates to the
contradictory nature of "network competition" eventually inducing a self-defeating
European prophesy in response to the American/Japanese *défi*; the other relates
to the merits of the "negotiated contingency"-approach as explanatory framework
for the phenomena described above: so-called strategic partnerships, their
rationales and their unintended or latent deficiencies. The conclusions will be
topped off with a note on what one may expect for the future of ESPRIT.

A.   European/Non-European Commitments

In the second section of this chapter it has been shown that despite the
intended promotion of intracommunautarian cooperation a large number
of so-called strategic partnerships of European firms is concluded with
nonEuropean firms. The conflict between the "normative" and "empirical"
faces of ESPRIT has to be interpreted as a tactical response to the unintended
consequences of the logic of *trans*action of the actors: on different levels of
the mosaic of power, the actors generate a self-propelling logic of *inter*action
for ESPRIT as a whole that even tends to escape from the control of its
very supporters. The economics of flexibility (referring to the changing
characteristics of international competition, see Section III.A) lead European
MFs to choose for non-European partners, whereas the politics of flexibility
lead them to profess support for and participate in ESPRIT. The paradox
condensed: access to communautarian funds is used to conclude preemptive

alliances with *extra*-European rivals in order to win the intra-European battle; the selfdefeating potential of the logic of this game may be losing the Triad Power-game proper.

B. The Negotiated Contingency Approach

To come to the above conclusion on the logic of European/non-European partnerships, we placed the ESPRIT experience in an interorganizational context (for understanding the *structures* of interdependence) and interpreted the paradoxical findings with a negotiated contingency theory (for understanding the strategical and tactical *uses* of interdependence). The approach demonstrates its use in reconstructing the mixed motives and multi-level character of the "nested" power games in industrial policymaking. Besides, the approach describes the coexistence of two different institutional arrangements—frontstage versus backstage—and, more interestingly, it helps to explain the miracle of the *lasting* character of their coexistence. A sociological or *strategic* choice-theory on interorganizational search and bargaining behavior seems especially productive in institutional environments where, as quoted in the introduction, "uncertainty, struggle and motion rather than [. .] careful calculations over well-defined choice-sets" predominate. Such a paradigm offers a useful alternative to *rational* choice- and game theoretical assumptions about pre-defined/well-articulated pay-off matrices.

C. Esprit Revisited: A Sorcerer's Apprentice?

The negotiated contingency approach strongly favors an assessment of strategies and tactics in terms of the competitiveness of concrete *clusters* of organizations, rather than of either individual firms or for aggregate "sectors" and abstract combinations of "technological trajectories" (Dosi 1982, p. 152). As argued in the introduction and leaving nationalistic peculiarities out, the "spirit" of ESPRIT proper appears to be contingent on the strategies and tactics pursued in two other settings: the global "triad" and the regional "dyad-plus-one" settings of industrial policymaking.

There is no formal or institutionalized platform to confront, let alone to coordinate authoritatively, understandings and commitments made *across* these three settings. The only operative principle of integration is the type of respectability that one may expect in situations of strategic interdependence: *antagonistic reciprocity,* based on a complex web of interlocking strategic partnerships of multinational firms that somehow manage to participate simultaneously in global, regional and communautarian alliances. Firms form the nexus of the overall mosaic of power. Their bargaining power, not only vis-à-vis their public partners but also vis-à-vis their private partners, rests on their superior *mobility:* they may move from one setting to another (and back) following the principle that they participate only in some form of concerted action if the inducements they receive or hope to receive in one setting are better than what they would get elsewhere.

Yet the preceding reconstruction learns that there are limits to mobility. Politicians have their prisoners' dilemmas; entrepreneurs have their deal busters. Both may have their doubts about the long term stability of firm-to-firm and firm-to government commitments. Under those conditions it becomes probable that short term tactical considerations (may be primarily in order to consolidate internal coalitions among the stakeholders of the firm) drive out long term strategic aims. The result of the officially sponsored "sovereignty game," mentioned in the introduction of this chapter, may be some sort of uncontrolled technology race (Roobeek 1988). A rational, albeit largely hypothetical response should echo somehow Toynbee's antidote against "anarchic parochialism" (Toynbee 1949, p. 59): "a system of international economic interdependence could only be made to work if it could be brought within the framework of a system of international political interdependence: some international system of political law and order which would place a restraint upon the anarchic parochial sovereignty of the local city-states." The anarchistic potential tends to increase, and the quest for sovereignty to become illusionary, when the lead is not longer played, as in Toynbee's reference, by territorially restricted city-states but rather by modern multinational nomads that try to control their (self-made) risks of antagonistic cooperation by playing off the "city-states" against each other.

It remains difficult to prove, but maybe one should relate the remarkable optimism reported in the Mid-Term Review of ESPRIT (European Commission 1985b) primarily to the merits *tactical* trade-off between the industrial politics of intra-European *versus* global containment. If understood correctly, that orientation may turn out to be a risky gambit when triggering a more or less uncontrolled industrial arms race. Especially the mechanism whereby "city-states" and multinational firms try to catch up with or to undo the competitive advantage of their rivals by *imitating* them, in combination with the ineluctability of long term investments required by participation in the high-technology race, may turn out to be an explosive mechanism. How will organizations—private as well as public—react when entrapped in counter-productive alliances?

D. Hors Concours/Postscript

Medio 1991 the European majors in the IT-industry show again signs of strong nervousness. So does the European Commission, be it more about the unmistakeable revival of protectionist passions in the industrial establishment. The statistics are even grimmer than when Viscount Davignon assembled the "big 12" for the first time: Europe is now underrepresented in key-areas such as semiconductors (10.5% of the world production by the EC as against Japan 49.5% and 36.5% for the United States), computer peripherals (15% EC, 40% Japan, and 25% of United States) and consumer electronics (20% EC, 55% Japan). The resulting European trade-deficit in electronics (more than $35 bln. in 1990 as against a Japanese surplus of about $65 bln. and a U.S.-surplus of $8 bln.) asks for a radical shift in the philosophy and the composition of the European network—in short, a shift in the *negotiated order* of industrial policymaking.

Until now the thrust of the ESPRIT program has been directed at a *horizontal* Pax Europeana, that is, at the politics of *containment* of oligopolistic rivalry by promoting a web of cooperative ventures between "the big 12." This predilection is reinforced by the substantial administrative discretion of the ESPRIT Management Committee (see Section II.B on the less than strict rules and roles of "pre-competitive" conduct). Even Directorate General-IV's former chief executive and the later competition Commissioner, Peter Sutherland, who was reportedly ready to institute a more pragmatic regime by exempting *en bloc* all small and medium sized enterprises (SMEs) collaborating in R&D programs from Article 85 of the Rome Treaty (European Commission 1985c, p. 238) can not be seen as a serious counterforce against this horizontal bias. On the contrary, the horizontal bias tends to be intensified as long as the majority of SME-participation in ESPRIT appears to be embedded in projects administered by the "big 12" (see Section IV.B.3, Table 4).

Without wanting to underestimate the merits of the ESPRIT-1 program as aptly summarized in the Mid Term Review, one important actor is missing in the scenario: launching customers promoting the uses of IT innovations (on which Japan's and United States strength are based) in sectors and activities where Europe's strengths are situated. "Strength for strength" rather than "strength copying strength," could be the message. Large government R&D and capital spending subsidies, especially if they are for me-too, copycat programs aimed at steering Western resources into head-on competition with the "unbeatable Japanese good," especially once the Japanese have already occupied such a market segment, are certainly a mistake. It would be far better to promote the diffusion and application in more sophisticated uses of (cheap) Japanese/ United States hardware (cf. the United Kingdom micro-electronics application program). It is one thing to understand, and support, European Information Technology (IT) firms' immediate interest in restoring global competitive balances. But there are several avenues that lead (back) to Rome. One of them would be a joint effort to exploit more thoroughly one of Europe's unique managerial capabilities—unfortunately considered currently as a major *handicap*—namely: its ability to cope, however reluctantly, with a multicultural, disjointed and pseudo-anarchistic environment. Such an environment is an ideal setting for acquiring a high tolerance for ambiguity. Organizations accustomed to operate without panicking in a highly ambiguous environment are better equipped, "by nature," to create multi-purpose/multi-environment software applications of hardware innovations (possibly generated elsewhere) than organizations accustomed to live in a habitat of homogeneous mass markets. Europe should reflect somewhat more on the trained incapacities of its counterparts, rather than to rush to match the latters' capacities.

One may take, by way of concluding illustration, Japan's "non-challenging" sectors as an example—that is, the sectors in which Europe still has its considerable strengths. What structures of interdependence and strategies of negotiating would MFs, COs and PMs need to gain control over the sophisticated *soft*ware uses of IT-hardware in such vital sectors as listed in the Appendix?

An imaginative answer to the question how to preserve and to vitalize these sectors—a matter of strategic choice—would be a fair dowry for the second stage of ESPRIT. The reasons why a strategic switch from European cooperative R&D-efforts (ESPRIT-1) to the promotion of cross-cultural and cross-sectoral applications of IT-hardware (ESPRIT-2) represents a multiple competitive advantage, will be clear:

1.   Europeans are better informed than the Americans or the Japanese about the subtleties of the sectors and industries listed in the Appendix (a strong asset in times of a selective return to "core businesses");

2.   complementary relationships (i.e., vertical and diagonal supplier-customer linkages) are substituted for competitive relationships (i.e., horizontal linkages between competing firms and competing governments, apt to breed or to reinforce distrust);

3.   the prevailing zero-sum game of lending priority to sunrise over sunset industries is redefined into a non zero-sum game linking the two (reducing opportunism and enhancing trust);

4.   the conditions for a return from a "bargaining" to a "problem solving" style of policy making (cf. section IV.C.1) are enhanced because of a closer approximation of the prerequisites deemed necessary for "integrated concertation" (cf. Section IV.B.2);

5.   conversely, the risks of a fatal me-too industrial arms race, supplanting industrial policy strategies by trade warfare tactics, are reduced; and

6.   last but not least: the (justified) scepsis about European/non-European partnerships may disappear while the international logic of comparative and competitive advantage moves again to the center of strategy formulation and policymaking.

Europe experiments with new types of industrial cohabitation. Given the still unquestioned standing of a range of typically European sectors, the promotion of intelligent producer/user linkages in a complementary, strategic mode deserves special incentives,—that is, something more lasting than dubious returns from the search for excellence in purely tactical and defensive *marriages de raison.*

APPENDIX

Japanese Non-Challenges or Sectors In Which Europe Still Shows Strengths (As of Early Eighties)

Industries or Industry Segments of Major Japanese Weakness

Aerospace (airplanes, engines, launchers,
  satellites, avionics, radar, etc.)
Food processing
Paper and products
Non-ferrous metals
Agricultural machinery
Large construction machinery
Industrial chemicals
Oil exploration and logistics
Oil services
Heavy-duty commercial vehicles
Flavors and fragrances
Custom machine tools and dies
Hybrid electro/hydraulic or electro/mechanical
  machinery
Precision and scientific instruments
Jewelry
Custom and hybrid integrated circuits
Computer software

Industries or Industry Segments of Japanese Presence But No Significant Lead Over Western Competitors

Pharmaceuticals
Bio-technology
Process plant construction
Civil engineering
Construction
Rapid and mass surface transport (high-speed
  trains, subways, buses)
Heavy electrical equipment (nuclear and
  conventional power
    plant, turbines, generators, transmission
    equipment)
Computers
Telecommunications
Microwave apparatus

Source: Franko (1983, p. 4).

REFERENCES

Allison, G.T. 1971. *Essence of Decision–Explaining the Cuban Missile Crisis.* London: Scott, Foresman & Co.

Carnarca, G.C., Colombo, M. G. and S. Marriotti. 1988. "Accordi tra imprese nel sistema industriale dell'informacione e della communicazione." (Business Agreements in the System of Information and Communication Industries) Rappotto Interno, No. 88-039. Milano: Politecnico di Milano, Departemoneto di Elettronica.

Caty, G.F. 1984. "Le Programme ESPRIT." *Futuribles,* 26-36.

Cecchini, P. 1988. *1992, The European Challenge.* Wildwood House.

Coase, R. 1937. "The Nature of the Firm." *Economica* 4(16)386-405.

Coombs, R., Saviotti, P. and V. Walsh. 1987. *Economics and Technological Change.* Houndsmills: Macmillan.

Cyert, R.M. and J.G. March. 1963. *A Behavioral Theory of the Firm.* Englewood Cliffs: Prentice Hall.

Dosi, G. 1982. "Technological Paradigms and Technological Trajectories—A Suggested Interpretation of the Determinants and Directions of Technical Change." *Research Policy* 11:147-162.

The Economist, November 24, 1984.

Elster J. 1978. *Logic and Society.* New York: Wiley.

Elster, J. 1986. "Further Thoughts on Marxism, Functionalism, and Game Theory." Pp. 202-220 in *Analytical Marxism,* edited by J. Roemer. Cambridge University Press. Editions de la Maison des Sciences de l'Homme, Cambridge, Paris.

European Commission. 1985a. *Fourteenth Report on Competition Policy.* Brussels, pp. 196-198.

European Commission. 1985b. *The Mid-Term Review of ESPRIT.* Brussels.

European Commission. 1985c. *Official Journal* (19-9-1985).

European Commission. 1986. *Esprit Project Synopses.* Brussels (April).

Fennema, M. 1982. *International Networks of Banks and Industry.* The Hague: Martinus Nijhoff.

Franko, L.G. 1983. *The Threat of Japanese Multinationals, How the West Can Respond.* New York: Wiley.

Giddens, A. 1979. *Central Problems in Social Theory.* London: MacMillan.

Halperin, M.H. 1974. *Bureaucratic Politics & Foreign Policy.* Washington: Brookings Institution.

Jacquemin, A. and B. Spinoit. 1986. "Economic and Legal Aspects of Cooperative Research: A European View." Pp. 487-519 in *The Annual Proceedings of Fordham Corporate Law Institute.* New York: Matthew Bender & Co.

Kreiken, E.J. 1986. "De Coalitiestrategie: Creatieve Coöperatieve Competitie." (The Coalition Strategy: Creative Cooperative Competition.) Pp. 285-294 in *Ondernemingsstrategie: Theorie en Praktijk,* (Corporate Strategy: Theory and Practice.) edited by J. Bilderbeek. Leiden: Stenfert Kroese.

LAREA/CEREM. 1986. *Les Strategies d'Accords des Groupes Européens Entre la Cohésion et l'Éclament:* Nanterre: Université de Paris-X, .

March, J.G. and J.P. Olsen. 1976. *Ambiguity and Choice in Organizations.* Tromso: Universiteitsforlaget Bergen, Oslo.

Merlini, C. (ed.) 1984. *Economic Summits and Western Decisionmaking.* London: Croom Helm.

Mytelka, L.K. and De la Pierre. 1987. The Alliance Strategies of European Firms in the Information Technology Industry and the Role of ESPRIT." *Journal of Common Market Studies* 26(2): 231-253.

Ohmae, K. 1985. *Triad Power: The Coming Shape of Global Competition.* New York: The Free Press.

Olsen, J.P. 1981. "Integrated Organizational Participation in Government." Pp. 492-516 in *Handbook of Organizational Design,* Vol. 2., edited by P.C. Nystrom and W.H. Starbuck. Remodeling Organizations and Their Environments. Oxford: Oxford University Press.

Olson, M. 1975. *The Logic of Collective Action, Public Goods and the Theory of Groups.* Cambridge, MA: Harvard University Press.

Olson, M. 1986. "Supply-side Economics, Industrial Policy, and Rational Ignorance." Pp. 245-269 in *The Politics of Industrial Policy*, edited by C. E. Barfield and W.A. Schramba. Washington, DC: The American Enterprise Institute for Public Policy Research.

Putnam, R. 1984. "The Western Economic Summits: A Political Interpretation." In *Economic Summits and Western Decisionmaking*, edited by C. Merlini. London: Croom-Helm.

Roobeek, A.J.M. 1988. *Een race zonder finish* (A race without a finish). Amsterdam: VU Uitgeverij.

Sapolsky, H. 1972. *The Polaris System Development.* Cambridge, MA: Harvard University Press.

Scharpf, F.W. 1985. "The Joint-Decision Trap: Lessons from German Federalism and European Integration." *Discussion paper IIM/LMP 85-1* (May). Berlin: International Institute of Management.

Schattschneider, E.E. 1957. "Power: Intensity, Visibility, Direction and Scope." *American Political Science Review* 51 (December).

Select Committee on the European Communities. 1985. House of Lords, Session 1984-1985, 8th Report, *ESPRIT*, with Minutes of Evidence, London: Her Majesty's Stationary Office.

Servan Schreiber, J.J. 1967. *Le Défi Américain* (The American Challenge). Paris: Denoël.

Toynbee, A.J. 1949. *Civilization on Trial.* Oxford: Oxford University Press.

Tulder, R. van. 1990. "Samenwerken krijgt een nieuwe dimensie; meer LAT-relaties in het bedrijfsleven" (Cooperation assumes a new dimension: more LAT-relationships in industry). *De Ingenieurskrant*, (10)25.

Tulder, R. van and G. Junne. 1988. *European Multinationals in Core Technologies.* Geneva: Wiley.

U.S. Dept. of Commerce. 1983. International Trade Administration, *The Telecommunications Industry*, (April) Washington, DC: U.S. Government Printing Office.

Webb, G. 1977. "Decision Making in the EEC." In *Policy Making in the European Communities*, edited by H. Wallace. Chichester: John Wiley.

Williamson, O.E. 1975. *Markets and Hierarchies. Analysis and Anti-trust Implications.* New York: The Free Press.

Winham, G.R. 1979. "Practitioner's View of International Negotiation." Pp. 111-135 in *World Politics.*

THE EUROPEAN CASE OF JOINT R&D ACTIVITIES IN CORE TECHNOLOGIES

Michiel Roscam Abbing and Jos Schakenraad

I. INTRODUCTION

Since the sixties the state of Europe's competitiveness has always been on the agenda of politicians and managers. In the sixties and seventies most Western European governments supported their "national champions" through financial aid, procurement policies, or protection of the market. Shelter based policies dominated. Meanwhile, technology was becoming recognized as one of the most important inputs to gain or ensure a high level of international competitiveness. Throughout the seventies and eighties an increasing amount of support was given to the development of technology.

Whereas direct national support to firms for research is still very important, support has also become a major element of the industrial policy of the Commission of the European Communities (CEC). Industrial policy on the EC-level is an effort to harmonize the different industrial policies of the member countries in order to profit fully from the creation of one large single market at the end of 1992. Besides internal forces to establish a common industrial policy it is also formulated as a response to increasing pressure from outside

Research in Global Strategic Management, Volume 2, pages 203-237.
Copyright © 1991 by JAI Press Inc.
All rights of reproduction in any form reserved.
ISBN: 1-55938-277-5

Europe, caused by severe international competition and rapid technological changes. A stronger technology base in Europe should impose higher entry barriers on third country firms.

One of the measures taken by the CEC that started in 1983 is the promotion of cooperation in research with potential industrial applications, mainly in the strategic field of information technologies. A number of technology-programs were initiated, and a large number of separate national governments agreed on launching the EUREKA-program in 1985.

The policy of the CEC is to give direct support to firms. This provides the Commission with a severe policy dilemma: on the one hand it feels that European industry has to be supported in the development of strategic technologies, and on the other hand, in order to do so effectively, the synergy of a large technological potential is needed. Promotion of combined technological research thus stimulates a process of industrial concentration, creating a fertile environment for oligopolistic behavior.

A related policy dilemma is that, through its policy, the CEC makes the European IT sector more attractive for take-overs or mergers with American or Japanese firms as is shown by the majority shareholding deal of Japan's Fujitsu in Britain's ICL.

In this chapter we present some empirical evidence on the "oligopolistic networks" that are being created by firms through the European technology programs. We focus our research on the role of several large European firms (especially those in the sector of information technology).

In the first section we show that the CEC plays its part in the international phenomenon of increasing collaboration in R&D through the initiation of technology programs that subsidize private research.

Following van Tulder and Junne (1988) we assume that information technology (IT), biotechnology (BT) and new materials (NMT) are core technologies. Core technologies lead to a large number of new products and processes and are applicable across a large number of economic sectors.[1] In other words, they contribute essentially to the competitiveness of firms. We therefore focus our attention on the technology programs that are aimed at developing these core technologies. We further limit our research to programs through which firms are directly financially supported. These programs are: BAP, BRITE, EURAM, ESPRIT and RACE from the European Communities, and EUREKA. In this section we look at different motives of firms to collaborate privately or to collaborate in the cost-sharing programs. We further explore the aims of the CEC to set up cost-sharing technology programs and the difficulties the Commission meets in doing so.

In the second section we look more closely at the different technology programs. We explore the financial weight of the technology programs, recent changes in the policy, and we compare EUREKA with the EC-programs.

In the third section, overall empirical results of collaboration in European co-financed R&D projects are presented. We also compare the involvement of firms in information technology in the "European" and in the "private" networks of collaboration and focus on the role of twelve major European IT firms. We conclude with some remarks on an oligopolistic network in the European IT-sector.

II. THE EUROPEAN CASE OF JOINT R&D ACTIVITIES

A. Motives for Firms to Participate in Joint R&D Projects

Fast technological development, rising R&D costs and the internationalization of markets lead firms to seek new cooperative strategies. See for instance Contractor and Lorange (1988) for an overview of cooperative strategies that facilitate a reduction in costs, risks and uncertainties. One such new strategy is to pool the complementary technologies of the partners. The high risks that can be involved in research projects are often illustrated by examples such as the development of successive generations of memory chips. The costs of developing a new generation of memory chips is estimated at more than three billion dollars, and no single firm is expected to be able to bear these costs (and related risks) on its own.

It may therefore not be surprising that the decade of the eighties is characterized by an increasing importance of inter-firm collaboration, on a national as well as on an international level (Hergert and Morris 1988). Firms organize joint efforts in technology development in different ways. In Hagedoorn (1990) six different modes of co-operation based on the MERIT/CATI database are given: joint ventures and research corporations; joint R&D; technology exchange agreements; direct investment; customer-supplier relationships; and one-directional technology flow.[2] It appears that the share of private joint R&D agreements has been increased significantly over the years. Of all six modes of co-operation in 1985-1988 the share of joint R&D represented 33.7 percent, compared to 9 percent in 1972. Joint R&D has in the second half of the eighties indeed become the most important form of partnership; more important than the joint venture.[3]

In order to compare financially supported links with those that are privately established, we limit our analysis to the joint R&D-form of cooperation.[4]

Hagedoorn and Schakenraad (1990) listed the following motives for joint development of R&D in biotechnology, information technologies and new materials on the basis of the MERIT/CATI database. Their research excludes the government or EC supported partnerships.

1. Expansion/new markets;
2. Reduction of innovation lead time;
3. Technological complementarity;
4. Influencing market structure;
5. Rationalization of production;
6. Monitoring technological opportunities;
7. Specific technological opportunities;
8. Basic R&D; and
9. Lack of financial resources.

Undoubtedly these motives play a role when firms decide to engage in cost-shared projects. Although to our knowledge no studies have been published that explore and weigh the different reasons of participation in co-financed projects, we were able to deduct several additional motives.[5] The following additional motives to participate in cost-shared projects are used here merely for illustrative purposes.

1. Financial support from the EC or the national governments in the case of EUREKA;
2. Enlargement of the relative strength through networks of collaboration;
3. Higher status of the firm;
4. Involvement by standardization;
5. Preparation for Europe 1992;
6. A way to increase international activities;
7. A way to contact other firms, institutes or researchers through EC- or EUREKA channels;
8. Easier access to university-research;
9. A way to gain more bargaining power versus other cooperative activities.

B.   The R&D-Objectives of the European Communities

The European Commission plays its part in an overall tendency of increasing international collaboration rather successfully. Its aim is to keep the inter-firm collaboration as European as possible, to stimulate the exchange of technical knowledge and to prevent duplication of expensive research. These aims almost necessarily lead to a concentration of R&D. The European Commission finds itself in a situation of balancing between the economic benefits of increased collaboration and the possible dangers of oligopolistic behavior for the individual consumer.

The legal basis for the European Commission to implement an R&D policy is to be found in the Single European Act (SEA). In February 1986 the SEA was signed by the governments of all 12 member states of the EC. Along with other parts of the SEA this section, on "Research and technological development" was added to the original EEC Treaty from 1957, which contained no special requirements concerning Community research or a common research policy.

From article 130f of the SEA one learns that "the Community's aim shall be to strengthen the scientific and technological basis of European industry and to encourage it to become more competitive at international level." In order to achieve this the Community "shall encourage undertakings including small and medium-sized undertakings, research centres and universities in their research and technological development activities; it shall support their efforts to cooperate with one another, aiming notably at enabling undertakings to exploit the Community's internal market potential to the full, in particular through the opening up of national public contracts, the definition of common standards and the removal of legal and fiscal barriers to that cooperation." There are four main activities to pursue these Community objectives (article 130g). First, the implementation of research, technological development and demonstration programs, by promoting cooperation with undertakings, research centres and universities. Second, the promotion of cooperation in the field of Community research, technological development and demonstration with third countries and international organizations. Third, dissemination and optimization of the results of activities in Community research, technological development and demonstration. Fourth, stimulation of the training and mobility of researchers in the Community.

Through the SEA it thus has become a major policy aim to promote inter-firm relationships at the European level. The principal instrument to reach these objectives is a multi-annual framework program. The First Framework Program (1984-1987), in which the improvement of industrial competitiveness in Europe was explicitly mentioned among the objectives, however, was already implemented a few years before the SEA was signed. From 1983 onwards programs such as ESPRIT, BRITE, RACE and BAP have been initiated.[6]

A crucial question is whether direct financial support for private R&D is in conflict with the basic competition rules outlined in the EEC Treaty (articles 85-94). R&D Agreements, Patent Licensing and Know-how Licensing are exempted by block on basis of Article 85(3) from the competition rules.[7] There are good grounds for these exemptions, for example, joint R&D and joint exploitation of the results are believed to promote technical or economic progress. The question remains, does subsidizing affect competition within the Common market (article 85) and does the subsidizing process stimulate a process of concentration in which one or more firms become able to influence the market by independent action (article 86). Furthermore, in principle all government aid to business is forbidden (article 92), but the Commission makes a general exemption for R&D state aid to firms.[8]

C.   Pre-Competitive versus Commercial Research

The European Commission emphasizes the pre-competitive nature of shared cost research projects, because it fears that inter-firm collaboration could be interpreted as a step towards the creation of a European oligopoly of high-tech firms.[9] The difference between pre-competitive and "competitive" research is, however, hard to define, because in the end all knowledge is meant to be used for marketable products.

Many participating firms in the EC technology programs even expect short-term commercial results. Half of the participating firms are said to profit already in an early stage from commercial spin-offs. As many as 85 percent of the Dutch firms with 100 to 1000 employees report that co-financed R&D collaboration leads to a reduction of the innovation lead time.[10] And the "Report of the ESPRIT Review Board" remarks that the results of ESPRIT research only lie partly in the pre-competitive sphere. A significant number of respondents to their questionnaire claimed that ESPRIT-projects contributed to existing products (35%) or new products (45%).[11] This would hardly be an argument against subsidizing R&D if access to developed knowledge would be relatively easy for other firms. But in reality the dissemination of knowledge is slow and difficult. According to the ESPRIT Review Board, knowledge transfer among ESPRIT projects is poor,[12] let alone the transfer of knowledge among ESPRIT participants and interested non-participants.

Unfair competition seems to be stimulated, because (1) access to results of EC co-funded research is very difficult for non-participating companies (whether or not participating in other EC co-funded projects), and (2) the barriers for small companies to become participants in a cost shared project are relatively high. Small firms do not have the same lobbying capacities, experience and bargaining power as the larger firms.

D.   Participation of European Community-Firms versus Non European Community-Firms

The European Commission emphasizes the "European" nature of the technology programs by focusing on both European competitiveness and fair trade within the Common Market. However, firms that are based in the EFTA-countries can easily participate in the projects.[13] Within the framework of EUREKA there are no differences between the EC and the EFTA countries. The EC programs are in principle open to all industrial enterprises, universities, research institutes and other interested organizations in the EC and EFTA countries, but firms based in EFTA-countries are faced with some special conditions.[14]

The governments of the EFTA countries expressed their willingness to participate more in Community R&D activities and to contribute to the financing of the entire framework program on the basis of their GNP. It is very likely that further EFTA participation in EC-programs will depend on the outcome of negotiations that started in the beginning of 1990 between the EC and the EFTA about the establishment of a European Economic Space (EES). These talks are aimed at the establishment of a common market of 350 million people (EC and EFTA together). Eastern European countries may also enlarge such an EES in the long run.[15]

In addition to firms from the EFTA countries different firms from the USA and Canada can participate in the EC research programs and EUREKA, most of them via European subsidiaries. Such participation is often legitimized with the expectation that the European partners gain more technology from (than they loose to) the American firms, or that both gain because of synergies, but it makes the European nature of the programs doubtful.

In EUREKA, 13 "organizations" from non-member countries were recorded in 1989, among which at least one from Yugoslavia.[16]

III. THE TECHNOLOGY PROGRAMS: AN OVERVIEW

A. The European Community-Programs: ESPRIT; RACE; BRITE/EURAM; BAP/BRIDGE

1. ESPRIT

In the beginning of the eighties there was a growing consensus among top managers of several European IT-firms about the necessity to collaborate on technology development. In 1982 the European electronics firms had only 11 percent of the world market for information technologies against more than 60 percent for the U.S. and 22 percent for the Japanese firms.[17] The European Commission invited 12 large firms in the information sector to a series of Round Table discussions. These firms were AEG (now Daimler), Bull, CGE, GEC, ICL (now STC),[18] Nixdorf, Olivetti, Philips, Plessey, Siemens, STET (part of IRI) and Thomson. The aim of the Round Table meetings was to agree on the way European electronics firms could reverse the deteriorating trade balance in Europe's electronics industries through cooperation and standardization. The Round Table defined the first research areas and goals for the European Strategic Programme for Research and Development in Information Technologies (ESPRIT).

Adopted in 1984, ESPRIT was conceived for a 10 year period under direction of DG XIII (Telecommunications, Information Industries and Innovation) with three main objectives: to help provide European IT industry with the technology base it needed to meet the competitive requirements of the nineties;

Table 1.   EC Funds for Joint Development of Technology

Program	Duration	EC Contribution (in MECUs)
First Framework Program	1984-1987	3.750
Second Framework Program	1987-1991	5.396
Third Framework Program	1990-1994	5.700

The following programs are part of the first or second framework program:

ESPRIT I	1984-1988	1.500
ESPRIT II	1988-1992	1.600
RACE	1987-1992	550
BRITE/EURAM	1989-1992	499,5
BAP	1985-1989	75
BRIDGE	1990-1994	100

Sources: EC Research Funding (1990), and other publications from the European Commission.

to promote European industrial cooperation in IT and to contribute to the development of internationally accepted standards. Of all EC technology programs ESPRIT is the largest (see Table 1).

Two hundred and twenty six projects were launched in the first phase, each containing at least two industrial companies from different EC member-states. In June 1990 some five hundred projects had been launched since the beginning of ESPRIT.

In May 1989 the ESPRIT Review Board published The Review of ESPRIT 1984-1988 and estimated that "in the vast majority of projects trans-European cooperation has been a success and resulted in significant benefits for the participants." These benefits went for a large part to the twelve information-conglomerates. According to the same report the twelve received 50 percent of the total budget of ESPRIT I and were involved in 70 percent of the projects. See Figure 1 on the allocation of the funds of ESPRIT I. The big twelve not only received 50.7 percent of the ESPRIT budget, but also give a distribution among the twelve (see Hare et al. 1988). The share of Thomson is the highest with 6.9 percent of the total ESPRIT budget, followed by Philips and Siemens both with 5.9 percent.[19]

2.   RACE

RACE is a kind of spin-off program of ESPRIT. The big twelve played, together with a number of national PTT-companies, again a dominant role

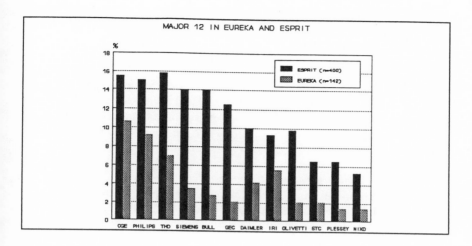

Source: The Report of the ESPRIT Review Board (1989, p. 17).

Figure 1. ESPRIT I Funding Allocated by Sector.

when RACE (Research and Development in Advanced Communications Technologies for Europe) started in 1987. The program, under direction of DG XIII and with a budget of 550 MECUs, deals mainly with technologies that are required for an integrated broadband communications network. Such a network is to be implemented throughout the Community. RACE is one of the elements of the Commission's "Telecommunications Action Programme" that aims at the creation of a common market for telecommunications services and equipment.[20] By combining the expertise of telecommunications researchers, manufacturers, administrations and broadcasting stations across Europe an attempt is made to create a climate for cooperation between the telecommunications administrations and the industry.

3. BRITE/EURAM

The BRITE/EURAM program will continue on the basis of the separate BRITE (Basic Research in Industrial Technologies for Europe) and EURAM (European Research on Advanced Materials) programs for the 1989-1992 period. The program is aimed at industrial manufacturing technologies and advanced materials applications. Most of the funding of 499.5 MECUs is used to the development of five technical areas: advanced materials technologies; design methodology and assurance for products and processes; application of manufacturing technologies; technologies for manufacturing processes; and specific activities related to aeronautics.

4. BAP/BRIDGE

Both biotechnology programs, BAP and BRIDGE, are under direction of DG XII (Science, Research & Development). The essential objective of BAP, which started with a budget of 55 MECUs, and increased to 75 MECUs, is to develop the Community's capacity to master and exploit the applications of biotechnology into agriculture and industry. BRIDGE includes research and training activities (90%) and collaborative activities (10%). The research and training program includes information infrastructures, enabling technologies, cellular biology and pre-competitive research. Collaborative activities will cover a range of monitoring, information and partnership activities.

In contrast with the information sector, large multinational companies are hardly involved in the Community's biotechnology programs. According to some observers a coherent policy on biotechnology in Brussels has been hindered by internal European Commission battles. Although 83 percent of the 1989 worldwide investment in biotechnology came from European sources, not more than 3 percent of these funds was allocated to R&D projects inside the EC.[21]

B. The Financial Weight of European Technology Programs

The German firm Siemens spent almost 2.5 billion ECU on R&D in 1988. Siemens is without doubt the firm with the highest expenditures on R&D in Europe. The R&D expenditures of this single firm are 7.7 times higher than the yearly EC contribution to ESPRIT II, which amounts to 320 million ECU.

Total EC-expenditures in 1988 were only four percent of the total civilian R&D-expenditures of all EC-countries together. These figures indicate that the financial support from the different programs is of a minor importance to large firms.[22] Mytelka argues, for instance, that the ESPRIT funds that Bull (France) acquired in 1986 as a participant in 32 projects was just over 5 percent of Bull's own R&D expenditures.[23] It is therefore expected that the amount of money given by the European Communities is not the major incentive for large firms to join European projects. Instead their central position in the network seems to be more important.

The financial support could be, of course, of much more importance for the R&D-activities of smaller firms. Leaving out the universities, only 6.7 percent of the ESPRIT participants interviewed by an ESPRIT evaluation committee reported that funding accounted for more than 25 percent of their R&D expenditures; 18.4 percent estimated that it accounted for between 5 and

25 percent, and 49.1 percent reported that it accounted for less than 5 percent of total R&D.[24] It is without doubt that the largest twelve companies are among the 49.1 percent and that 6.7 percent represent the smallest companies.

C. The Third Framework Program (1990-1994)

The total budget of the Third Framework Program is 5.700 MECUs, only slightly higher than the budget of the Second Framework Program (see Table 1). Compared to the Second Framework Program it foresees a number of significant changes:[25]

1. A regrouping of activities around three strategic areas covering six R&D sectors: information and communications technologies; industrial and materials technologies; environment; life sciences and technologies; energy; human capital and mobility. While the Second Framework Program counts over 30 specific programs, the Third will have 15 separate programs.
2. Support for energy research has declined; support for information and communication technologies and new materials has been kept on the same level, while support for environmental research, biotechnology and "mobility of researchers" has been increased, albeit the greatest part of the budget will be devoted to "enabling technologies" as information and telecommunications.
3. Closer cooperation with third countries, in particular with countries from EFTA and Central or Eastern Europe.
4. The new Framework Program will allow the Community to run programs that only involve some Member States, and to associate the Community with national initiatives and EUREKA projects.

IV. EUREKA

EUREKA (European Research Coordinating Agency) is a separate technology program in which 19 countries (EC, EFTA and Turkey) participate. The program was initiated in early 1985 by the French as a direct response to President Reagan's Strategic Defense Initiative (SDI). The initiative was originally more politically than economically motivated. First, because the Americans at that time tried very hard to incorporate European research into the SDI or Star Wars research-program. Second, the larger European countries were not satisfied with their relatively weak position in determining the priorities of R&D-cooperation at the European level through EC-programs, in which smaller and larger countries have an equal voice. The EUREKA initiative was officially accepted at the European Council meeting in Milan,

June 1985.[26] Many policy makers in Brussels at that time were convinced that EUREKA was launched because the European technology programs were either too slow, too bureaucratic or too narrowly defined.

Due to its launching initiative, France was the first to generate large-scale funding for French participants. By the end of 1986 French companies participated in two thirds of the projects.[27] France remains the country with the highest participation in EUREKA projects; in 1989 France was involved in 135 EUREKA-projects, Western Germany in 108, the United Kingdom in 87, Italy in 87, Spain in 85, and the Netherlands in 73.

The main objective of EUREKA, according to the Declaration of Principles of November 6, 1985, is "to raise, through closer cooperation among enterprises and research institutes in the field of advanced technologies, the productivity and competitiveness of Europe's industries and national economies on the world market, and hence strengthen the basis for lasting prosperity and employment."[28] These advanced technologies are classified into 9 areas (see Table 2).[29]

The 295 projects listed in Table 2 have a total estimated cost of 6.517 MECUs and involve more than 1500 participants (700 larger companies, 300 SMEs, 450 research institutes, 80 other organizations, and 13 organizations from non-member countries).

Table 2. Areas and Projects in EUREKA

Area	Number of Projects	Budget (MECUs)
Medical- and Biotechnology	55	542
Communications	19	1194
Energy Technology	14	526
Environment	32	607
Information Technology	50	1512
Lasers	13	271
New Materials	24	159
Robotics and Production Automation	67	1115
Transport	21	591
Total	295	6.517

Source: EUREKA Annual Project Report (1989).

A. Declining Complementarity between EUREKA and the European Community-Programs

The main aims of EUREKA and the EC programs largely overlap, namely the promotion of cross-border cooperation in research and technology and the strengthening of the European technology base. However, there are also differences between the two. The two ways to set up European projects for joint technology development are different and complementary, at the same time:

1. EUREKA does not exclude any technology area: the companies and research institutes that are involved select the research-areas, while project proposals for Community co-financed research must fit the criteria of the specific research programs.
2. Not only the EC-member countries can participate under the same conditions in EUREKA, also the EFTA-countries and Turkey can.
3. National governments decide whether and how much financial support is given within the EUREKA framework. The high rate of French participation in EUREKA, for instance, can be explained by the generosity of the French Government.
4. Most EUREKA projects lead directly to marketable products, whereas the majority of projects within the EC research programs are concerned with basic, pre-competitive research.
5. EUREKA can provide an additional framework for the continuation of the work started in EC projects.[30]

Since the Hannover Declaration of Principles (November 1985) the European Community (represented by the Commission) can participate as a partner in EUREKA. EUREKA is (now) fully supported by the CEC and seen as part of the framework of institutional mechanisms, Community objectives and policies, and particularly in light of the implementation of the internal market in 1992. EUREKA is considered to be an integral part of the Community Programs. The support of the CEC takes the following forms:[31]

1. Direct participation in EUREKA projects. The European Commission participates among others financially in EUREKA project JESSI (development of 64-Mb memories and their applications). The CEC also participates directly in several EUREKA projects through the Joint Research Centres of the European Communities, and contributes to the EUREKA Secretariat in Brussels.
2. The technical objectives of EUREKA-projects are taken into account by community programs like ESPRIT and RACE, and vice versa.

3. Supportive measures, for example relating to HDTV (European standard for High Definition TeleVision), where the CEC has supported the promotion of HDTV by funding a studio.

EUREKA provides additional funds and possibilities for European (research) cooperation for enterprises. In fact, it is even suggested that EUREKA can finance projects refused by EC-research programs (provided that they fit the criteria for EUREKA-status).[32]

The EUREKA-program has become almost an integral part of the EC technology policies. EUREKA provides more funds for firms and more flexibility for governments to pursue national and international industrial policy aims.

V. PARTICIPATION IN EUROPEAN COST-SHARING TECHNOLOGY PROGRAMS: EMPIRICAL RESULTS

A. Overall Participation

We now turn to the empirical analysis of firms and their (subsidized) cooperative behavior. We decided to investigate all projects stemming from pan-European programs aimed at the development of one of the core technologies: BAP, BRITE, EURAM, ESPRIT and RACE from the European Communities, and EUREKA. Table 3 shows all established projects for these technology programs we analyzed until January 1990. We found 920 projects meeting our criterion that at least one industrial or software company should participate in a project.[33] In the Biotechnology Action Program (BAP) this criterion has brought us a surprisingly low number of 33 remaining projects. Even within these projects the average number of participating firms is just over one (see the last column of Table 3 representing the average participation rate of firms). Apparently, universities and institutes dominate in almost all 200 BAP projects and hardly any link between companies can be found. If all European biotechnology projects are taken into consideration, thus both from BAP and EUREKA, the total number of projects with at least one company is 92 (see Table 7). An inspection of participating firms reveals an almost complete lack of large pharmaceutical and (petro)chemical corporations in the biotechnology programs.

A quite different situation appears in the information technology program RACE. There are very few universities or institutes in RACE projects, and there are no projects without participating firms. Participation in RACE projects is relatively high, running up to more than 24 partners in a project such as RACE 1046 on "specification and programming environment for communication software." The mean participation within RACE is 6.5, which

Table 3. Number of Projects and Average Number of Participating Firms for Different European Cost-sharing Technology Programs

Program	Total Number of Projects	Selected Projects Number (%)	Mean Number of Participating Firms
BAP	200	33 (17)	1.1
BRITE	91	89 (98)	2.7
EURAM	85	67 (79)	1.9
ESPRIT	449	400 (89)	3.8
RACE	47	47 (100)	6.5
EUREKA	410	284 (69)	3.8
Total	1282	920 (72)	3.6

Source: MERIT/CATI.

is the highest for all programs we analyzed and which is explained by the high number of standard setting projects. About 15 percent of all ESPRIT projects and several projects in EUREKA are also concerned with standardization efforts.

In order to see which companies are most involved in the technology programs, we have taken parent-companies instead of subsidiaries. Thus, to give an example, we registered Philips Videowerk GmbH in Austria, PKI in Germany, and French or Belgian national Philips organizations all as Philips NV of the Netherlands. We counted altogether 1,233 independent firms participating in all selected technology projects.[34] A rather high percentage of these firms participate in one project only (865 out of 1,233, that is 70%).[35] The most collaborating firm is French CGE, which is involved in 108 different projects. See Table 4 for a ranking of the firms, participating in most ventures.

Table 5 represents an overall view of the participation of independent firms per country. France has the most firms that join the EC programs and EUREKA, followed by West Germany and the United Kingdom.

Many non-EC firms like to participate in the European technology projects. There are hardly any barriers for firms that are based in one of the EFTA countries. Although the European policy aims to counter American and Japanese competitiveness, no less than 38 U.S. and Canada-based firms are engaged in one or more projects. Most of these firms participate through European subsidiaries. In Table 6 we listed the firms that participate in at least two European technology projects.

Table 4.   List of Companies With Seven or More Projects in BAP, BRITE,
ESPRIT, EURAM, RACE and EUREKA Together

Firm	Country	Number of projects
ABB	SWI	11
Aérospatiale	FRA	15
AKZO	NET	10
AT&T	USA	7
Babcock	UK	8
Bertin	FRA	16
Bosch	FRG	31
British Aerospace	UK	16
British Shipbuilders	UK	14
British Telecom	UK	42
BULL	FRA	60
CAP Gemini Sogeti	FRA	36
CGE	FRA	108
CISE	ITA	9
CISI	FRA	7
CRI	DEN	13
CTNE	SPA	23
Daimler	FRG	68
Degussa	FRG	9
EFIM	ITA	7
ENI	ITA	18
Ericsson	SWE	12
Ferranti	UK	8
Fiat	ITA	36
Framatome	FRA	9
France Télécom	FRA	40
GEC	UK	77
GHH	FRG	12
Hoechst	FRG	13
IBM	USA	8
ICI	UK	16
IMEC	BEL	29
INI	SPA	11
IRI	ITA	63
Krupp	FRG	17
Logica	UK	11
Matra	FRA	18
Nixdorf	FRG	25
Nokia	FIN	12
Océ Nederland	NET	8
Olivetti	ITA	43
Péchiney	FRA	12
Philips	NET	99

(*continued*)

Table 4.   (Continued)

Firm	Country	Number of projects
Plessey	UK	39
PSA	FRA	12
PTT Nederland	NET	21
Renault	FRA	19
Rhône-Poulenc	FRA	9
SAGEM	FRA	14
Sema CAP	UK	18
Siemens	FRG	77
Société Générale	BEL	8
STC	UK	37
SYSECA	FRA	13
Televerket	SWE	12
Thomson	FRA	88
Thorn-EMI	UK	14
Vickers	UK	11

Source: MERIT/CATI.

Table 5.   Participation of Independent Firms per Country in BAP, BRITE, ESPRIT, EURAM, RACE and EURKEA Together

Country	Number of firms	(Percent)
(Unknown)	73	5.9
Austria	24	1.9
Belgium	49	4.0
Canada	4	.3
Denmark	53	4.3
Finland	23	1.9
France	185	15.0
Germany	175	14.2
Greece	17	1.4
Iceland	1	.1
Ireland	12	1.0
Italy	123	10.0
Luxembourg	7	.6
Netherlands	60	4.9
Norway	35	2.8
Portugal	16	1.3
Spain	94	7.6
Sweden	43	3.5
Switzerland	36	2.9
Turkey	1	.1
United Kingdom	164	13.3
United States	38	3.1
Total	1233	100.0

Source: MERIT/CATI.

Table 6.   United States- and Canada-based Firms that Participate in at Least Two European Cost-sharing Technology Projects

Name of Firm	CP	BAP	ESPRIT	RACE	EURAM	BRITE	EUREKA	TOT
Alcan Aluminum	CAN	—	—	—	—	—	2	2
AT&T	U.S.	—	2	4	—	—	1	7
Computer Sciences	U.S.	—	2	—	—	3	—	5
Digital Equipment	U.S.	—	3	—	—	—	1	4
Foxboro	U.S.	—	1	—	—	—	1	2
Hewlett Packard	U.S.	—	3	1	—	—	—	4
Honeywell	U.S.	—	1	—	—	—	1	2
IBM	U.S.	—	3	3	—	—	2	8
Merck & Co.	U.S.	—	1	—	—	—	1	2
Rockwell International	U.S.	—	—	—	—	2	—	2
United Technologies	U.S.	—	1	—	—	—	1	2

Source: MERIT/CATI.

The U.S. authorities would like to intensify transatlantic R&D collaboration. Negotiations on this matter were ongoing at the time of writing this chapter in 1990. Another increasingly important issue is to open the respective programs for Eastern European firms in the near future. It is very likely that these firms may participate either directly or through joint ventures with firms of Western Europe. However, up until January 1990 there were no firms from Eastern European countries involved. Neither did we find any participating Japanese firm. The take-over of ICL by Fujitsu, however, raises the question whether ICL, one of the founding fathers of ESPRIT, may continue to participate in the programs. Through this purchase, Fujitsu gained full access to the knowledge ICL acquired by joining European technology projects. It illustrates the difficulties of the policy to increase Europe's competitiveness in IT.

B.   The Predominance of the IT Sector

For two reasons we concentrate our further analysis on the information technologies sector. First, an overwhelming part of all projects appears to be concerned with IT. To show this we labelled all projects as being aimed at one of the three core technologies : biotechnology, information technology, and new materials technology. An additional category comprises projects that could not be related to one of the core technologies, for example, the development of laser technology or energy- and environmental-related projects. The cross tabulations of core technologies and number of projects and distribution of funds are shown in Table 7 and Table 8 respectively. Sixty-four percent of

Table 7. Number of Projects by Core Technology for Different
European Cost-sharing Technology Programs

Program	Bio-technology	Information Technology	New Materials Technology	Other Projects	Total Number
BAP	33	—	—	—	33
BRITE	—	—	89	—	89
EURAM	—	—	67	—	67
ESPRIT	—	400	—	—	400
RACE	—	47	—	—	47
EUREKA	59	142	24	59	284
All	92	589	180	59	920
(%)	(10)	(64)	(20)	(6)	(100)

Source: MERIT/CATI.

Table 8. Distribution of Funds (In MECUs) by Core Technology
for Different European Cost-sharing Technology Programs

Program	Bio-technology	Information Technology	New Materials Technology	Other	Total
BAP	350	—	—	—	350
BRITE/ EURAM	—	—	999	—	999
ESPRIT	—	6.200	—	—	6.200
RACE	—	1.100	—	—	1.100
EUREKA	542	3.821	159	1.995	6.517
All	892	11.121	1.158	1.195	15.166
(%)	(6)	(73)	(8)	(13)	(100)

Source: MERIT/CATI.

the projects takes place in the framework of IT, while IT seems to absorb 73 percent of all funds.

A second reason to shed light on information technologies is that twelve large European IT firms stood at the beginning of the first and largest cost-sharing European technology program: ESPRIT. Top management of these firms were and are clearly in favor of collaboration efforts, whereas firms in other sectors are far less engaged.

C. A Comparison between the Cost-Sharing and the Private Network in IT

From Table 9 we learn that the overall comparison between cost-sharing and private collaboration in IT is based on 589 cost-sharing and 429 private projects.[36] At first sight it seems that more firms are collaborating in cost-sharing projects than in a private context (761 against 345). To explain this difference one might argue that the European programs have attracted a number of relative small companies that cooperate for the first time internationally in R&D. To a limited extent, this certainly happened. However, there are three reasons why the number of firms participating in subsidized projects is biased upwards with respect to the private sector joint R&D.

- First, the 761 firms that cooperate in subsidized IT projects originate from the group of 1233 independent firms participating in all selected projects. This number is biased upwards because, following the ECHO-data, in some cases it is not clear whether a participant is an institute or a firm.
- Second, the number of privately cooperating firms is open to a fierce underestimation.[37]
- Third, the low number of privately cooperating firms results partly from different definitions of joint R&D.[38]

From the 345 different firms that are engaged in private IT alliances, we found 201 that are also collaborating in European cost-sharing IT projects. This is an overlap of 58 percent. If we change our point of entry to dyads or couples of collaborating firms, it appears that 482 of all 661 dyads are unique (73%). Thus there are 482 unique direct links or paths among firms. 191 (or 40%) of these unique private joint R&D links also turn up in the co-financed sphere. Due to the incompleteness of the private part of the database we expect that the cross-section as indicated by the percentages of 58 (for firms) and 40 (for couples) is in reality higher.

On the basis of our data it is very difficult to judge whether co-financed collaboration precedes or follows private collaboration. In other words, are the authorities subsidizing existing partnerships, or are they generating the basis for future private collaboration. Generally, large and medium-sized firms were

Table 9. The Involvement of the Major Twelve European IT Firms
in Three Different Cost-sharing Programs and in Private R&D
Collaboration in Information Technologies

	EUREKA	ESPRIT	RACE	All Cost-sharing R&D	Private R&D
Number of Firms	395	461	92	761	345
Number of Projects	142	400	47	589	429
-involving one of 12	52	262	38	352	269
Mean Firms/Project	4.3	4.3	6.8	4.5	2.2
Mean Duration (in months)	48	40	29	41	25
Number of Dyads	1538	3532	1288	6358	661
-among the 12	30	517	134	681	157
-major 12 - other	280	1341	560	2181	248
-among non-twelve	1228	1674	594	3496	259

Source: MERIT/CATI.

already collaborating before they got involved in the European technology programs. In our opinion, during the eighties, they simultaneously established both private and co-financed alliances.

Although some pilot ESPRIT projects started as early as in 1983, significant subsidized cooperation began no sooner than 1985 or 1986. Very few projects are yet being successfully terminated. Based on the estimated duration, only 19 IT projects from a total of 589, that is only 3 percent, are considered to be finished before 1990.[39] Private follow-up projects are therefore limited until now. We can only expect that these subsidized partnerships will generate more private ones in the near future. The main conclusions are threefold.

- First, the European technology programs probably have attracted some relatively small firms, cooperating for the first time, which very often are engaged in projects with at least one major IT firm.
- Second, a substantial share of firms and research couples in privately established joint projects are also working together in subsidized projects.
- Third, whether or not the subsidized network follows the private network, there are no major differences between both networks except for the density. They largely overlap.[40]

D. The Dominance of the Major Twelve European IT Firms

The ESPRIT program, as well as the RACE and EUREKA programs, provide a platform for the major actors in the European IT-field to decide how they can jointly meet competition from the United States and Japan, and how they can synchronize their strategies. The programs are said to be very helpful in harmonizing and integrating the still highly fragmented European IT market. Listed alphabetically, the firms that formed the Round Table of ESPRIT are AEG, Bull, CGE, GEC, ICL, Nixdorf, Olivetti, Philips, Plessey, Siemens, STET, and Thomson.[41]

Table 9 compares the participation of the major twelve in cost-sharing programs with their involvement in privately established R&D links.[42] Attention is paid to differences with respect to numbers of projects (and dyads resulting from it), participating firms, and the mean participation rate and duration of projects.[43]

It appears that in 60 percent of all subsidized alliances at least one of the twelve companies is engaged. Although an exact comparison between the private and subsidized joint R&D is precarious, the dominance of large IT companies in both cooperation spheres seems to correspond (63% for the private sphere).

Table 9 also shows that the twelve of ESPRIT are involved in 53 percent (= 15 + 38) of all inter-firm linkages of all European cost-sharing programs in IT. The big twelve must have received at least 34 percent (=15 + ½ .38 percent) of all ESPRIT I and II-funds. This percentage is in reality certainly higher, as Figure I indicates, but our information is biased because we did not include the number of linkages between the twelve and universities/ institutes. On the other hand the dominant role of the twelve may have declined relatively, due to a larger number of small and medium sized firms in ESPRIT II.

In Table 10 (A-D) we show the joint collaboration of the big twelve in respectively, ESPRIT, all cost-shared IT-programs, EUREKA and the private R&D IT-projects. First, we can see that there is a very high network density. One hundred percent in the cost-shared programs and 80 percent (53 of the 66 possible links) in the private projects. The different numbers in the four tables indicate how often specific firms collaborate. Besides a large number of mutual links among the major twelve, these firms have single links with a large number of different partners, the latter being often relatively small firms, but also well-known established companies of which the main activities lie outside information technology. Bull for instance has links with 107 different IT firms outside the other 11 founding firms of ESPRIT (Table 10-C). One third of all 118 firms, listed in the Appendix, have more than one link with Bull.

Table 10.   Joint IT Collaboration of the Major Twelve in
ESPRIT (A), EUREKA (B), ESPRIT, EUREKA and RACE
Together (C) and In Private Joint R&D (D)

A.   ESPRIT

	AEG	BUL	CGE	GEC	ICL	NIX	OLI	PHI	PLE	SIE	STE	THO	N
AEG	X												100
BULL	5	X											115
CGE	11	10	X										156
GEC	10	13	10	X									99
ICL	1	6	5	4	X								46
NIXDORF	3	14	8	6	2	X							55
OLIVETTI	6	19	6	8	3	11	X						51
PHILIPS	11	11	11	8	5	5	5	X					118
PLESSEY	3	2	3	6	4	2	1	9	X				25
SIEMENS	6	21	12	10	10	9	14	16	6	X			126
STET	8	7	12	6	2	6	2	8	2	5	X		98
THOMSON	8	8	11	14	11	4	4	16	11	12	9	X	94
	A E G	B U L	C G E	G E C	I C L	N I X	O L I	P H I	P L E	S I E	S T E	T H O	

B.   EUREKA (IT)

	AEG	BUL	CGE	GEC	ICL	NIX	OLI	PHI	PLE	SIE	STE	THO	N
AEG	X												38
BULL	-	X											8
CGE	1	1	X										86
GEC	-	-	-	X									10
ICL	1	1	1	-	X								10
NIXDORF	1	-	-	-	1	X							11
OLIVETTI	-	-	-	-	-	-	X						5
PHILIPS	1	-	-	1	-	-	-	X					37
PLESSEY	-	-	-	-	-	-	-	1	X				4
SIEMENS	-	-	-	1	-	-	-	2	1	X			11
STET	3	1	1	-	-	-	-	-	-	-	X		42
THOMSON	1	-	2	1	-	-	-	4	1	2	-	X	34
	A E G	B U L	C G E	G E C	I C L	N I X	O L I	P H I	P L E	S I E	S T E	T H O	

(*continued*)

Table 10.   (Continued)

C.   ESPRIT, EUREKA (IT), RACE

	AEG	BUL	CGE	GEC	ICL	NIX	OLI	PHL	PLE	STE	THO	N
AEG	X											125
BULL	5	X										107
CGE	15	11	X									238
GEC	14	13	20	X								119
ICL	2	7	10	7	X							57
NIXDORF	4	14	8	6	3	X						52
OLIVETTI	6	19	6	8	3	11	X					66
PHILIPS	15	11	20	15	7	5	5	X				139
PLESSEY	5	2	10	13	4	2	1	17	X			46
SIEMENS	6	21	14	12	11	9	14	22	10	X		126
STET	12	8	18	9	3	6	2	11	5	7	X	115
THOMSON	12	8	21	23	14	4	4	27	18	15	11	X	124
	A E G	B U L	C G E	G E C	I C L	N I X	O L I	P H I	P L E	S I T	S T E	T H O	

D.   PRIVATE R&D LINKS

	AEG	BUL	CGE	GEC	ICL	NIX	OLI	PHL	PLE	STE	THO	N
AEG	X											9
BULL	1	X										24
CGE	6	—	X									7
GEC	2	1	2	X								13
ICL	—	3	—	2	X							8
NIXDORF	1	2	—	1	1	X						4
OLIVETTI	—	7	2	—	1	1	X					351
PHILIPS	1	5	1	1	3	3	4	X				40
PLESSEY	—	—	2	6	2	—	—	2	X			14
SIEMENS	4	3	7	1	2	1	2	18	4	X		28
STET	1	1	3	3	—	1	2	3	2	3	X	11
THOMSON	1	2	6	3	—	—	2	10	2	5	2	X	20
	A E G	B U L	C G E	G E C	I C L	N I X	O L I	P H I	P L E	S I T	S T E	T H O	

Notes: AEG = DAIMLER; ICL = STC; STET = IRI.

     N = Number of different firms with which a link exists, excluding the 11 other founding firms of ESPRIT.

     Only IT projects of EUREKA are selected.

Source: MERIT/CATI database.

There is, however, a significant distinction between the involvement of the twelve large companies in ESPRIT and in EUREKA. In 66 percent of all ESPRIT projects at least one of the twelve is involved. And this is only the case in 37 percent of the EUREKA-IT projects. The network density of the twelve in EUREKA, shown in Table 10-B, is only 33 percent. In Figure 2 we show that the twelve IT-firms are more dominant in ESPRIT than in EUREKA. Also more smaller firms are participating in EUREKA.[44] This difference could be explained by the different nature of the programs. The twelve can probably exercise more influence in Brussels on the features of ESPRIT than they can on EUREKA, where they have to deal with different national authorities. Furthermore, the twelve probably have a larger interest in agreements on standards or production-systems (ESPRIT) than in collaboration in more market-led projects (EUREKA), where they are in more direct competition with each other.[45]

E.   An Oligopolistic Network

The amount of financial support the big twelve receive and the increasing number of links they have, indicate that these firms occupy dominant positions in the European IT-R&D network. This leads one to think that the ongoing process of collaboration is at the same time an ongoing process of integration

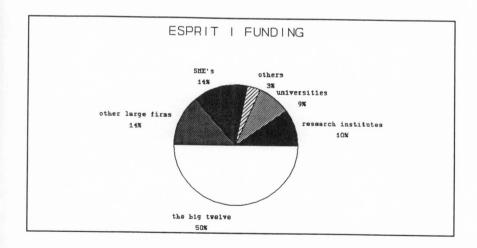

Source: MERIT/CATI.

Figure 2.   Involvement of Twelve IT Majors in ESPRITand EUREKA

and oligopolization. While oligopoly is usually associated with price setting behavior of a small group of firms and not with joint R&D activities, we assume that joint R&D activities and (standardization) agreements have a significant effect on opportunities for oligopolistic behavior.

We call networks in which a small group of firms have a dominant position "oligopolistic networks." As in the case with the twelve founding fathers of ESPRIT, there are strong links among the dominant firms and each of the dominant firms has links with many different, often smaller firms. Part of these smaller firms collaborate with more than one dominant firm or amongst each other.

The R&D networks stimulate oligopolistic behavior of the dominant firms. Tacit agreements on market share, prices, standardization, and so forth, are likely to increase through the multiplication of contacts especially between the dominant firms. The European integration program facilitates collusive arrangements within the common market. It implies a multiplication of contacts and of the number of markets in which firms operate.[46] The more firms meet on different markets and the more firms collaborate, for example on R&D, the more possibilities they have to coordinate their strategies.

Firms with a nodal position in the network have the best possibilities to influence the network and to gain from it. Unlike conventional economic textbook oligopolies the oligopolistic network is relatively open. First, the barriers to entry for newcomers in traditional oligopolies are higher than in oligopolistic networks. In networks, newcomers are not only potential competitors but also collaborators that can strengthen the oligopolistic structure as a whole. Second, diffusion of technology towards other firms is likely to go faster through oligopolistic networks than through traditional oligopolies. There is a technology flow from and to the dominant firms. But one can speak from oligopolistic advantages, because the dominant firms are better positioned to exploit the technology on the market than most of their less nodal partners.

Oligopolistic networks place authorities (national governments and in our case the CEC) before difficult dilemmas. Collaboration is often a first step in a take-over process. If collaboration is stimulated, mergers and take-overs may be triggered, leading to a process of oligopolization. Such take-overs or changes of control over firms' strategies may fit in the overall policy of strengthening the European industrial structure vis-à-vis the two other triad powers. But policy makers cannot prevent firms with a central network position to establish joint ventures worldwide or to be taken over by firms against whom the stimulation of collaboration was directed in the first place, as is demonstrated by the Fujitsu/STC deal concerning ICL.

VI. CONCLUSIONS

Of all core technologies, IT is most strongly represented in the European technology programs. In this sector life cycles of products and technologies are very short and investments in new R&D are very high. Firms try to reduce the high risks through collaboration with other firms or with research institutes. Agreement on standards is an important element to reduce the risks and the European programs provide an excellent way to agree on standards and synchronize strategies.

The Commission of the European Community (CEC) legitimizes the funding of the projects by stressing their "pre-competitive" character. A survey held among participants, however, stresses the importance of commercializing technology. The programs of course fasten the process of commercialization and this makes it difficult to differentiate between funding pre-competitive research and funding the development of marketable products. The latter is in principle not in harmony with EC-regulations.

The countries with an advanced IT-sector profit most from the projects (see Table 5). France has the highest number of projects (185 or 15%), partly because of the generous support of the French government for French EUREKA projects. One of the aims of all technology programs is to improve Europe's competitiveness. In fact, some European countries hardly profit at all from the programs (Portugal and Ireland have participation rates of respectively 1.3 and 1%). Some non-European countries, on the other hand, do better: United States- and Canada-based firms together represent 3.4 percent of the overall involvement in the programs.

The large multinationals that are involved in the IT technology projects, profit relatively more than the small and medium sized enterprises, simply because they are involved in more projects (108 for CGE, 99 for Philips, 88 for Thomson, etc., compare Table 4). Through these projects they have created a high number of inter-firm linkages. Bull has as many as 259 industrial links in ESPRIT alone. Furthermore, 856 firms (69.4%) have no or only one dyad. Among these 856, small and medium sized firms dominate. The more a firm participates, the more funds it receives, because for each participation a certain amount of money is given by the European Community.

Large firms also profit through the establishment of networks. An oligopolistic network is created in which these firms have central positions. There are strong links among the large firms (see Tables 9 and 10 A-D) and many links between individual giants and small and medium sized firms. In the Appendix all IT-partnerships Bull created through ESPRIT and EUREKA are presented as an illustration of the position of one central firm. Furthermore, many links with universities and research institutes are created, which we did not examine. The networks are not only used for monitoring (seeing what other companies are doing), easier access to additional technology and preparation for Europe 1992, but also give central firms opportunities for oligopolistic behavior.

During the eighties both the private and the cost-sharing European networks expanded and many joint R&D projects started more or less simultaneously in both networks. The cost-sharing European network for major IT firms or firms heavily investing in IT is, however, partly a replica of an already existing and privately financed network. In general, the absolute number of partners, projects and dyads have increased during the eighties. Although an exact comparison between private and subsidized joint R&D is precarious, a dominance of large IT companies in both cooperation spheres can be observed. A substantial percentage of the firms and research couples in privately established joint projects are also working together in subsidized projects.

The different research-programs certainly contribute to the level of basic research in Europe and the competitiveness of firms. Our data suggest that a relative small number of European firms profit most from the programs. The European technology programs imply a multiplication of contacts between the participating firms, which provides firms with more possibilities to coordinate their strategies and facilitates take-overs and further concentration in high technology sectors. Concentration (and oligopolization) in the IT-sector is, however, not a purely European phenomenon. Concentration takes place both in Europe (Plessey and Nixdorf for instance came under the control of Siemens) and worldwide (ICL under the control of Fujitsu). The possibility of large European firms being acquired by multinationals from the two other triad members (the United States and Japan) obviously raises important questions related to the effectiveness of European policies in the area of information technology.

APPENDIX

The Industrial Links of Bull
in European Technology Programs for
Information Technologies

Firm	Country	Links
SIEMENS AG	FRG	21
OLIVETTI SPA	ITA	19
NIXDORF COMPUTER AG	FRG	14
GEC PLC	UK	13
CGE	FRA	11
PHILIPS NV	NET	11
IRI	ITA	8
THOMSON SA	FRA	8
STC PLC	UK	7
CAP GEMINI SOGETI SA	FRA	6

(*continued*)

APPENDIX (*Continued*)

Firm	Country	Links
BRITISH TELECOM PLC	UK	5
CHORUS SYSTEMES	FRA	5
DAIMLER-BENZ AG	FRG	5
AEROSPATIALE (SNIAS)	FRA	3
BRITISH AEROSPACE PLC	UK	3
FERRANTI PLC	UK	3
FIAT SPA	ITA	3
FRANCE TELECOM	FRA	3
OCE-NEDERLAND BV	NET	3
RENAULT	FRA	3
SEMA CAP	UK	3
STOLLMAN & CO GMBH	FRG	3
SYSECA	FRA	3
TELEFONICA (CTNE)	SPA	3
APPLIED RESEARCH GROUP SPA (ARG)	ITA	2
BOSCH GMBH	FRG	2
COMPUTER RESOURCES INT A/S (CRI)	DEN	2
ENI	ITA	2
ENTEL SA	SPA	2
FA MEYER AG	FRG	2
IBM	USA	2
NOKIA OY	FIN	2
PLESSEY CO PLC	UK	2
SYSTEM AND MANAGEMENT SPA	ITA	2
2I INDUSTRIAL INFORMATION GMBH	FRG	1
ADDAX	FRA	1
ADVANCED MECHANICS & ENGINEERING LTD	UK	1
ASCOM HOLDING LTD	SWI	1
AT&T	USA	1
BAZIS	FRA	1
BMW BAYERISCHE MOTOREN WERKE AG	FRG	1
BRITISH SHIPBUILDERS	UK	1
CIRRUS COMPUTER LTD	UK	1
COMPUTER TECHNOLOGIES COMPANY LTD	UK	1
COMPUTER LOGIC	GRE	1
DATACENTRALEN	DEN	1
DATAMAT INGEGNERIA DEI SISTEMI SPA	ITA	1
DESARROLLO DE SOFTWARE	SPA	1
DIGITAL EQUIPMENT CORP	USA	1
ELEKTRONIK CENTRALEN	DEN	1
ELSA SOFTWARE	FRA	1
EPSILON SYSTEMS & SOFTWARE CO LTD	UK	1
ESPASA CALPE	SPA	1

(*continued*)

APPENDIX (*Continued*)

Firm	Country	Links
EUROPEAN SILICON STRUCTURES ES2	BEL	1
EUROPEAN COMPUTER INDUSTRY RESEARCH CENTRE	FRG	1
EUROSOFT SA	FRA	1
EXPERT SOFTWARE SYSTEMS NV	BEL	1
FHG AGD	FRG	1
FIAR	ITA	1
FRAMATOME	FRA	1
FRIEDRICH KRUPP GMBH	FRG	1
GENERICS SOFTWARE LTD	IRE	1
GESI SRL	ITA	1
GIE EMERAUDE	FRA	1
GIPSI SA	FRA	1
GIPSI-2	U	1
GRUPO APD SA	SPA	1
GRUPO DE MECANICA DEL VUELO SA	SPA	1
HARLEQUIN LTD	UK	1
HOESCHST AG	FRG	1
IMEC	BEL	1
INDUSTRIE-WERKE KARLSRUHE AUGS-BURG AG	FRG	1
INDUYCO/INVESTRONICA	SPA	1
INTECS SISTEMI SPA	ITA	1
KMK KREUTZ & MAYR	FRG	1
KNOWLEDGE LTD	GRE	1
LANGTON LTD	UK	1
LGMI	ITA	1
MANNESMANN GMBH	FRG	1
MATRA-HARRIS SEMICONDUCTORS	UK	1
MATRICI	SPA	1
MBLE ASSOCIATED SA	BEL	1
MCTS MICRO CONNECTIQUE	FRA	1
ÖSTERREICHISCHE INDUSTRIEVERWAL-TUNGS AG	AUST	1
PEUGEOT SA	FRA	1
PLANET SA	LUX	1
PRISMA INFORMATICA	ITA	1
PTT NEDERLAND NV	NET	1
QMC INSTRUMENTS LTD	UK	1
ROBOTIKER	SPA	1
RTE GMBH	FRG	1
RUTHERFORD APPLETON LABORATORIES	UK	1
SARIN SPA	ITA	1
SD-SCICON	UK	1

(*continued*)

APPENDIX (*Continued*)

Firm	Country	Links
SECRE	6RA	1
SEPT	FRA	1
SESAM	ITA	1
SIMULOG	FKA	1
SISMET	POR	1
SISTEMI E TELEMATICA	ITA	1
SOBEMAP SA	BEL	1
SOCIETE FRANCIASE DE GENIE LOGICIEL (SFGL)	FRA	1
SOGEI-SOC. GENERALE D'INFORMATICA	ITA	1
STAF	FRA	1
SUPRENUM GMBH	FRG	1
SYD SYNERGIE	FRA	1
SYNERGIA	ITA	1
TEAM SRL	ITA	1
TECNO T&G	SPA	1
TECNOPOLIS CSATA NOVUS ORTUS	ITA	1
TECOGRAF SOFTWARE	ITA	1
TELELOGIC AB	SWE	1
TELESYSTEMS	FRA	1
THORN EMI	UK	1
UKAEA ATOMIC ENERGY AUTHORITY	UK	1
VERILOG	FRA	1
VOLKSWAGENWERKE AG	FRG	1

Note: (U = Unknown)
Source: MERIT/CATI.

ACKNOWLEDGMENT

We are grateful for the participation of Geert Duysters and Paul Hollanders in our joint research project.

NOTES

1. Van Tulder and Junne (1988, Chapter I).
2. The MERIT/CATI database is a relational database which contains separate data files that can be linked to each other and provide disaggregated and combined information from several files. Up until 1990 information on nearly 10,000 cooperative agreements involving some 3,500 different parent companies has been collected. The database contains private as well as European cost-shared collaboration agreements.
3. Hagedoorn (1990, pp. 19, 20 [Table 2], 23).

4.   We included joint R&D in the framework of equity joint ventures and joint R&D resulting from minority holdings.

5.   These additional motives are for a large part deducted from Bureau EG-liaison (1989, Chapter 3).

6.   See for example, Commission of the European Communities (1987, Part I).

7.   Patent Licensing is published in *Official Journal* No. L 219 (August 16, 1984); R&D Agreements in *Official Journal* No. L 53 (February 22, 1985); and Know-how Licensing in *Official Journal of the European Communities* No. 61 (March 4, 1989).

8.   See, for example, Hitiris (1988, pp. 229-235).

9.   Mytelka (1988, p. 13).

10.   Bureau EG-Liaison (1989, p. 21-22).

11.   ESPRIT (1989, p. 27).

12.   ESPRIT (1989, p. 28). The report also remarks that "[T]he interchange and collaboration within projects was for the most part good and knowledge was transferred well both between industrial partners and between industry and academic partners. Difficulties sometimes occurred between large and small industrial partners, who sought more information than the larger partner was willing to divulge, but these instances were not numerous."

13.   The countries of the European Free Trade Association (EFTA) are: Austria, Switzerland, Finland, Iceland, Sweden and Norway. The EC member countries are: Belgium, Denmark, Federal Republic of Germany, France, Greece, Ireland, Italy, Luxembourg, the Netherlands, Portugal, Spain, and the United Kingdom.

14.   Firms from EFTA countries may be involved if an EFTA country is directly associated with a program as a result of signing an agreement with the EC, and, secondly, when specific decisions are made between the EC and EFTA countries. In the latter case 5.000 ECU has to be paid for general costs, and no financial EC support is given. See CEC (1990, p. 14).

15.   *Financial Times,* December 18, 1989. Any agreement between the EFTA and the EC is not likely to involve a rewriting of the Treaty of Rome or let the EFTA-countries participate in the decision making process in Brussels.

16.   EUREKA ("Annual Project Report 1989," p. 5). We found only one from an Eastern European country: the Boris Kidric Institute of Nuclear Sciences from Belgrade (Yugoslavia) participates in EU-294.

17.   Hitiris (1988, p. 255).

18.   STC announced July 30, 1990 the sale of 80 percent of its computer subsidiary ICL to Fujitsu.

19.   Hare, Lauchlan, and Thompson (1988) as cited in Hobday (1989, p. 163).

20.   Commission of the European Communities (1984).

21.   *Financial Times* (July 4, 1990).

22.   Compare Table 1 on EC funds for joint development of technology.

23.   Mytelka (1988, p. 15).

24.   *Evaluation intermediaire du Programme ESPRIT* (1985, p. 64). Recorded in Mytelka (1988, p. 15).

25.   DG XIII, *Newsletter,* Vol. 11/1, February 1990, p. 1,2.

26.   Cf. for example, Sharp (1987).

27.   Van Tulder and Junne (1988, p. 231).

28.   Cited in : EUREKA (s.a., p. 18).

29.   EUREKA ("Annual Project Report 1989.")

30.   EUREKA ("Annual Project Report 1989.")

31.   EUREKA ("Annual Project Report 1989.")

32.   EUREKA-Bulletin (December 1988, p. 3).

33. Consequently, we excluded publishing firms, transport and airline companies, consultancy firms, and so forth. We recall that our research focuses on inter-firm alliances which implies that universities, research institutes, and government bodies lie outside the scope of this study. However, national (and regional) telecom organizations are kept in the analysis. A final comment regards EUREKA. Of all 410 EUREKA-projects we dropped 126 for different reasons: 55 because they have the status of being proposed; 56 because they are withdrawn; 6 have the status of "undecided." Lastly, we excluded 9 projects because the participating entities did not fulfil our criteria. Among these were projects such as EU-144, called ERTIS (European Road Transport Information Services) or projects in which only institutes or universities are collaborating such as EU-316 and EU-294. The remaining 284 projects are analyzed (see Table 3).

34. The total number of participating firms might be biased due to unclear data from the European Commission Host Organization (ECHO) databases. Mainly because of the use of abbreviations it is not always clear whether a participant is an institute or a firm. Thanks to some external sources we could identify many institutes. The fact that parent companies are not always known also causes some bias.

35. Some 166 firms are engaged in 2 projects, while 61 entered 3 projects, that is respectively 14 and 5 percent.

36. Private joint R&D projects are those IT projects in which at least two different European firms participate. The resulting 429 projects contain 661 dyads. To indicate the share of intra-European joint R&D links for IT, we mention that 661 out of 2986 dyads worldwide, that is (only!) 22 percent, are between European firms.

37. Primarily because of some largely unsolvable shortcomings of the "private" section of our database. Of particular interest are the lack of many small, low- profiled firms in general and a plausible underestimation of the role of Spanish and Italian firms to mention but a few countries.

38. As privately established R&D links we consider strategic partnerships which contain some arrangements for joint R&D. By definition, this applies to all joint development agreements, joint research pacts and research corporations, but also for a number of (equity) joint ventures and minority holdings. However, customer-supplier kind of relations, such as the co-makership, were left outside the sample because we do not consider these relations as being of strategic value, at least not for the dominant partner. Besides, it would require a considerable time effort to collect all co-makership relations. For example, Philips might have a 1000 of them worldwide. As cost-sharing alliances we have taken all ESPRIT and RACE projects supplemented with IT projects from EUREKA, regardless their specific contents. Consequently, "hidden" subsidized co-makerships disturb the comparison. The same applies to standardization projects that we have not included in the private alliances at all. All subsidized standardization projects are kept in the sample because it is very difficult to trace and remove them on the basis of the often vague project descriptions.

39. According to ECHO database information (which may give a wrong impression of the real number of successfully ended projects).

40. Because both time intervals in our analysis overlap (1980-1988 versus 1983-1989) we have to consider the possibility that the private and subsidized networks have been created simultaneously.

41. STET is part of IRI; in the first half of the eighties STC took over ICL, later Daimler got control of AEG. Although Plessey in fact lost control to a Siemens—GEC consortium, we prefer to keep Plessey apart. Since the time horizon of our analysis ends in January 1990, the acquisition of Nixdorf by Siemens later on is not taken into account, nor is the majority stake of Fujitsu in ICL in the summer of 1990.

42. In Roscam Abbing and Schakenraad (1990b) we also compared the involvement of the 35 largest European IT firms in cost-sharing and private joint R&D projects.

43. A dyad is defined as a single link between two independent firms. In order to count the total number of dyads, all alliances were split up in the following way: an alliance between two

partners (A and B) gives one dyad (A-B); a project with three partners, called A, B and C, results in three different dyads (A- B, A-C and B-C), and so on.

44. In the 142 EUREKA-IT projects we analyzed, 395 independent firms are participating, while a same number (461) of different firms in ESPRIT are engaged in almost three times more projects (400) (see Table 9).

45. Roscam Abbing and Schakenraad (1990a).

46. Van Witteloostuijn and van Wegberg (1990, p. 15).

REFERENCES

Bureau EG-Liaison. 1989. *Euro Technology, Strategic Effects of EC R&D-Programmes in The Netherlands.* The Hague: Bureau EG-Liaison.

Commission of the European Communities. 1984. *Communication by the Commission to Council on Telecommunications,* COM(84)277.

————. 1987. *Vademecum of Community Research Promotion.*

————. 1989. *European Community Research Programmes,* Catalogue of Research Programmes Within the Framework Programme of the European community 1987-1991; status 31 December.

————. 1990. *EC Research Funding,* A Guide for Applicants, Brussels, January.

Contractor, F.J., and P. Lorange. 1988. "Why Should Firms Cooperate? The Strategy and Economics Basis for Cooperative Ventures." Pp. 3-28 in *Cooperative Strategies in International Business,* edited by F.J. Contractor and P. Lorange. Lexington, MA: Lexington Books.

ESPRIT. 1989. The Review of ESPRIT 1894-1988, The Report of the ESPRIT Review Board, Brussels, May.

EUREKA. (s.a.). *Annual Project Report 1989,* issued by the Eureka Secretariat, Brussels.

EUREKA. (s.a.) Vade Mecum.

Hagedoorn, J. 1990. "Organizational Modes of Inter-firm Co-operation and Technology Transfer." *Technovation* 10(1):17-30.

Hagedoorn, J., and J. Schakenraad. 1990. "Inter-firm Partnerships and Co-operative Strategies in Core Technologies." Pp. 3-28 in *New Explorations in the Economics of Technical Change,* edited by C. Freeman and L. Soete. London: Pinter.

Hergert, M., and D. Morris. 1988. "Trends in International Collaborative Agreements." Pp. 99-109 in *Cooperative Strategies in International Business,* edited by F.J. Contractor and P. Lorange. Lexington, MA: Lexington Books.

Hitiris, T. 1988. *European Community Economics.* New York: Harvester Wheatsheat.

Hobday, M. 1989. "The European Semiconductor Industry: Resurgence and Rationalization." *Journal of Common Market Studies* 28(2):155-186.

Mytelka, L.K., and M. Delapierre. 1987. "The Alliance Strategies of European Firms in the Information Technology Industry and the Role of ESPRIT." *Journal of Common Market Studies* 26(2):231-253.

Mytelka, L.K. 1988. "New Forms of International Competition: Strategic Alliances and the European ESPRIT program." Paper prepared for the International Political Science Association XIV, World Congress, Washington, D.C.

Roscam Abbing M., and J. Schakenraad. 1990a, "Eureka Kent Weinig Overlap Met Esprit" (Eureka overlaps hardly with Esprit). *Ingenieurskrant* (August 2), p. 25.

Roscam Abbing, M. and J. Schakenraad. 1990b. *Joint R&D Activities of Firms in European Cost-sharing Programmes. MERIT-paper* (August).

Sharp, M., and C. Shearman. 1987. *European Technological Collaboration.* London: Chatham House Papers.

Sharp, M. 1989. "Corporate Strategies and Collaboration: The Case of ESPRIT and European Electronics." Pp. 202-218 in *Technology Strategy and the Firm: Management and Public Policy,* edited by M. Dodgson. Harlow.

van Tulder, R., and G. Junne. 1988. *European Multinationals in Core Technologies, series on multinationals Chichester: Wiley/IRM*

Watts, S. 1989. "ESPRIT Gives Brussels a Good Name." *New Scientist* (December 30).

Wiltgen, P. 1987. *Research & Development for High Technology by European Multinationals.* Amsterdam University-mimeo (December).

van Witteloostuijn, A. and M. van Wegberg. 1990. "Multimarket Competition and European Integration." Paper presented at the "Workshop on Global Strategic Management." European Institute for Advanced Studies in Management (EIASM) Brussels, May, 10-11.

PART IV

EUROPEAN ECONOMIC INTEGRATION
AND ITS IMPACT ON OUTSIDERS

THE IMPACT OF EUROPEAN ECONOMIC INTEGRATION ON OUTSIDERS' GENERIC STRATEGIES:

THE CASE OF CANADIAN MULTINATIONALS

Jean-Émile Denis and Tony Quon

I. INTRODUCTION

A survey of fifteen Canadian multinationals was undertaken with a view to investigate which strategies they intend to pursue with the advent of the Single European Market in 1992, and to identify the key determinants of strategic choice. Following Porter (1980), three generic strategies were taken into consideration: cost competition, differentiation, and cost and differentiation. The results provided by the logistic regression models used in this study indicate that strategic choice can be best explained in terms of market growth potential and Country Specific Advantage (CSA).

The European business community was slow in reacting to plans for the creation of a Single European market "an area without internal frontiers." Although this idea was first presented in a White Paper from the Commission

Research in Global Strategic Management, Volume 2, pages 241-251.

to the European Council in 1985, and in full form by 1986 (Bulletin of the European Community 1986), it was not until late 1987 that the business community took notice of the proposal (Quelch, Buzzell and Salama 1990), and began to assess its impact on their activities. The international business community has taken even longer to react. Prompted more often by fear than by a sense of opportunity, many non European firms rushed into mergers and acquisitions in an attempt to penetrate "Fortress Europe." They felt the necessity to protect their competitive advantage against a perceived European protectionist initiative, a view also shared by some members of the academic community (see for instance Bruce 1988). On the other hand, other authors have opined that the creation of a single European market would more likely result in economic gains for third countries (for instance Dunning and Robson 1988). More recently Rugman and Verbeke (1990) have expressed the view that the single market initiative is unlikely to create a "Fortress Europe" although some informal entry barriers could be imposed on third country firms. A growing body of publications has addressed the issue of the type of strategy that might be adopted by firms in order to face the European challenge; the options include market integration, industry consolidation, mergers and acquisitions, and strategic alliances. These themes have been documented, in particular, in the book edited by Quelch, Buzzell, and Salama which focuses on the type of marketing strategies adopted by European and non-European multinationals. Other authors such as Rugman and Verbeke have investigated the likely impact of entry barriers on corporate strategies. This paper focuses on the generic strategies adopted by Canadian multinationals[1] with the advent of the single market. The objective was to identify the variables affecting strategic choice, and the specific factors relating to the adoption of each generic strategy. Neither Canadian multinationals' perceptions regarding EC 1992 nor their intended entry strategies will be dealt with in this paper.

II. CONCEPTUAL FRAMEWORK

According to Porter's model (1980, 1985), the generic strategic choices open to firms are cost competition OR differentiation, and each of these basic options can be associated with a wide or narrow focus. Strategic choice is further affected by two sets of external and internal determinants.

A. External Determinants

Two variables are taken into account: accessibility and market potential. Following Porter (1980), and Buigues and Jacquemin (1988), accessibility is defined in terms of entry barriers (economies of scale, product differentiation, capital requirements, distribution channels, technological sophistication, product substitution, and industry profile [cost competition, and potential for differentiation]); level of competition; and localization of production (in the EC and/or in Canada). Accessibility is also constrained by government-controlled measures such as tariff and non tariff barriers. Market potential is defined in terms of both market size and market growth potential.

Corporate perceptions of market accessibility and of market potential were recorded using a five point scale, where 1 = very high, 2 = high, 3 = moderate, 4 = low, 5 = very low.

B.   Internal Determinants

Internal determinants include current EC activities (total and relative EC sales), Firm Specific Advantage (FSA, as defined by Porter [1980] and Rugman and MacIlveen [1985]), Country Specific Advantage (CSA), (see Rugman and MacIlveen 1985), and corporate goals.

FSAs covered in the survey were corporate strengths or weaknesses in such areas as product uniqueness and development, distribution network, marketing and selling organization, manufacturing operations, research and engineering, overall costs, financial strength, global organization, and general managerial ability.

CSAs were defined in terms of advantages (resulting from localization of the firm's headquarters in Canada) such as access to technology, to natural and financial resources, and to the North American market.

Corporate goals considered in this study are profitability, sales volume, market share, return on investment, and expansion of customer base.

Corporate perceptions of FSAs, CSAs, and corporate goals were also recorded using a 5-point scale.

III.   DATA COLLECTION

Data were collected on the above items through interviews conducted with the executives of firms listed among the Financial Post's top thirty exporting firms. Respondents were officers responsible for either European or international activities. They were either Vice Presidents of International Affairs or Vice-Presidents of Marketing and, occasionally, CEOs.

Usable responses were obtained from fifteen firms. These firms had 1988 sales amounting to 23 billion Canadian dollars including export sales to the EC of 3.2 billion. As a point of reference total Canadian exports to the EC stood at 9.3 billion in 1988.

These firms have between 2,000 and 40,000 employees. Their annual sales fluctuate between 130 million and 7 billion Canadian dollars, and their annual sales in the EC between 5 million and two billion. The share of their total sales made in Canada varies between 5 and 90 percent. Foreign ownership averages 20 percent.

Five firms belong to the high technology sector (e.g., telecommunications), four to the pulp and paper sector, and four to manufacturing (e.g., machinery).

The data revealed that firms adopted not only cost or differentiation strategies BUT ALSO a cost and differentiation strategy (in 47% of all cases). It was decided to investigate which factors were responsible for each of these strategic choices. Unfortunately, the sample size did not allow investigation of focus strategies. As a result, only two of Porter's four original generic strategies could be researched in this study, in addition to the cost AND differentiation case.

IV. PRELIMINARY SCREENING OF VARIABLES

A preliminary statistical analysis revealed that of all the determinants included in the survey only five emerged as being related to strategic choice (Cramer's V above .592). Contingency table analysis indicated that all the other determinants showed a weaker level of association with the strategies adopted by the firms (Cramer's V less than .300).

The first objective of this study was to verify whether these determinants do indeed fall into separate groups. For this purpose, a principal component analysis was performed on the five determinants.

The procedure yields satisfactory results (sampling adequacy = .511, Bartlett Test of sphericity, $p = .0242$). Communality measures indicate that all variables are well taken into account by three factors.

The factor loadings support the grouping of the variables into internal and external determinants. Factor 1 could be called the external determinant factor because entry barriers, competition, and growth potential have the highest loadings. Factor 2 would qualify as the internal determinant factor with the highest loading on EC sales and CSA. In factor 3, the highest loadings are on CSA and growth, indicating that these two variables are defined by more than one factor. In conclusion, although the factor analysis does not yield a simple structure, it confirms that internal and external determinants constitute fairly independent groups.

V. MODELLING THE CHOICE OF STRATEGY

The next objective was to explain strategic choice in terms of the internal and external determinants. For this purpose, three logistic regressions were performed, one for each strategy against the other two as the dependent variables, and with the five determinants as the independent variables. These models can be seen as discriminant functions dividing the firms into different groups defined by strategic choice. Classical discriminant analysis models are inappropriate here because the determinants are not continuous normal variables.

When a response variable has only qualitative outcomes, such as a firm's choice of a strategy, ordinary least square regression models are inappropriate. When the response variable Y is binary, however, we can interpret the mean response $E(Y)$, the expected value of Y, as the probability that $Y = 1$ rather than $Y = 0$. Because the probability measures must be defined on the unit interval $[0,1]$, the mean response $E(Y)$ must be modelled as a non linear function of the determinants or independent variables. A very general function that allows $E(Y)$ to be close to zero for values of each independent variable in a certain range, to be close to one for values in another range, and to be approximately linear for values between the two ranges, is the commonly used logistic function:

$$E(Y) = 1/\{1 + \exp[-(B0 + B1*X1 + B2*X2 + B3*X3)]\}$$

This is the equivalent to modelling the logit transformation of $E(Y)$:

$$\log[E/\,Y\big/[1-E(X)]$$

as a linear function of $B0 + B1*X1 + B2*X2+ \dots$ Another commonly used transformation is the probit transformation which is based on the cumulative normal distribution, rather than on the cumulative logistic distribution. However, the probit regression model cannot be extended to the use of more than one independent variable. To estimate the coefficients of the logistic regression model, maximum likelihood estimation is used based on the probability model of the response variable Y as a Bernouilli random variable. See Neter, Wasserman and Kutner (1989, pp. 578-616) for further details. The results indicate that only two variables have a statistically significant impact on strategic choice: growth potential and CSA.

Logistic regression models can be extended to response variables that take on more than two qualitative values, but these must be ordered categories to make sense. Because the three strategic choices are not necessarily ordered, we decided to examine three logistic regression models, each based on a response variable with two qualitative values. For each model i, we defined $Y = 1$ if the strategic choice was i, and $Y = 0$ if the strategic choice was not i. Only the growth potential and CSA variables were important in each of these models.

A. Cost Competition Strategy

In this model, we coded the response variable Y as 1 if the strategy chosen was cost competition; it was coded as 0 if the strategy chosen was one of the

Table 1.   Estimated Probability of Selecting a Cost Strategy

Growth Potential	Very High	High	Moderate
CSA			
Very Low	0	1.	1.
Low	0	0	1.
Moderate	0	0	1.
High	0	0	0
Very High	0	0	0

other two options. The resulting logistic model that estimates the probability that the cost-competition strategy is chosen is:

$$1/\{1 + \exp[-(42.285 + 15.476 * CSA + 32.106 * GROWTH)]\}$$

The estimated probabilities are given in Table 1 for the different characteristics of growth potential and CSA.

The cost competition strategy is strongly associated with moderate growth potential and very low to moderate CSA. The estimated model yields perfect prediction for the fifteen companies in the sample. Of the four firms choosing the cost-competition strategy, three firms fall in the moderate growth potential and very low CSA category, and one falls in the moderate growth potential and moderate CSA category. All of the other eleven firms choosing either the differentiation or the cost- and differentiation strategy correspond to categories of growth potential and CSA for which the estimated probability is zero.

B.   Differentiation Strategy

In this model, the response variable Y is coded as 1 if the strategy chosen is one of differentiation; it is coded as 0 if the strategy chosen is one of the other two options. The logistic model estimates that the probability of the differentiation strategy being chosen is:

$$1/\{1 + \exp[-(49.202 + 7.717 * CSA + 16.883 * GROWTH)]\}$$

The estimated probabilities are given in table 2 for different CSA and growth characteristics.

The choice of the differentiation strategy seems to be strongly associated with conditions of very high growth potential and very low to low CSA. The estimated model gives good predictions except for two firms with high growth potential and low CSA. The estimated probability that firms with these

Table 2.   Estimated Probability of Selecting a Differentiation Strategy

Growth Potential	Very High	High	Moderate
CSA			
Very Low	1.	1.	0
Low	1.	.5	0
Moderate	1.	0	0
High	0	0	0
Very High	0	0	0

characteristics will choose the differentiation strategy is 0.5. From the sample, one firm did choose this strategy, but another one chose the cost and-differentiation strategy. There were three other firms that chose the differentiation strategy. They all corresponded to the very high growth potential and very low to low CSA categories.

C.   Cost and Differentiation Strategy

In this model, the response variable is coded as 1 if the strategy chosen is the cost and differentiation (CAD); it is coded as 0 if the strategy chosen is one of the other two options. The logistic model estimates the probability of choosing the combined cost and differentiation strategy as being:

$$1/\{1 + \exp[-(6.047 + 2.960*CSA + .798*GROWTH)]\}$$

The estimated probabilities are given in Table 3 for the different CSA and growth potential characteristics.

The cost and differentiation strategy is strongly associated with firms with at least moderate to very high CSA. If we interpret an estimated probability greater than .5 as predicting a CAD strategy and less than .5 as predicting a cost OR a differentiation strategy, then the logistic model gives good predictions except for two firms in the sample. The model estimates the probability that a firm with moderate growth potential and moderate CSA would choose a CAD strategy at .6; however, from the sample, one firm chose the cost competition strategy instead. The model estimates the probability that a firm with high growth potential and low CSA would choose a CAD strategy at .15; however, from the sample, one firm did choose the CAD strategy.

The results of all three models can be synthesized in Table 4; this shows the most likely strategic choices based on growth potential and CSA characteristics.

Table 3. Estimated Probability of Selecting a Cost
and Differentiation Strategy

Growth Potential	Very High	High	Moderate
CSA			
Very Low	.0201	.0092	.0041
Low	.2841	.1516	.0744
Moderate	.8844	.7752	.6082
High	.9933	.9852	.9677
Very High	.9996	.9992	.9983

Table 4. Likely Generic Strategies in Relation
to Growth Potential and CSA

Growth Potential	Very High	High	Moderate
CSA			
Very Low	Diff	Diff OR Cost	Cost
Low	Diff	Diff OR CAD	Cost
Moderate	CAD	CAD	Cost
High	CAD	CAD	CAD
Very High	CAD	CAD	CAD

Given the limited nature of the sample and the somewhat subjective characterization of these variables on a 5-point scale, we offer the following interpretation of the results.

Firms with at least moderate CSA to very high CSA tend to opt for the combined cost and differentiation strategy if the growth potential is at least moderate. It should be noted that none of the fifteen firms in the sample expected a lower than moderate growth potential in the EC after 1992.

When CSA is low or very low, the choice is clearly for the differentiation strategy if the growth potential is also very high, but the choice is for the cost competition strategy if the growth potential is only moderate.

Overall, twelve of the fifteen firms chose strategies that are consistent with the above models. We have already discussed the ambiguity related to the high growth potential and low CSA category where two firms were wrongly predicted. In the moderate growth potential and moderate CSA category, one firm was correctly grouped with the cost competition firms using the first model, but incorrectly grouped with the CAD firms using the third model. There were no firms in the very low CSA and high growth potential category and therefore no way of deciding between the relative likelihoods of the cost competition and differentiation strategies. The ambiguity of choice prediction using the various models appears to exist only in border categories defined by the growth potential and CSA characteristics.

VI. CONCLUDING REMARKS

The results of the various statistical analyses performed in this study lead to the following tentative conclusions:

1. As far as Canadian multinationals are concerned, two factors appear to have an overwhelming influence on the adoption of a generic strategy, namely CSA (an internal determinant), and EC market growth potential (an external determinant);
2. With regard to the adoption of specific generic strategies, it appears, broadly speaking and in relative terms, that:

   a. firms are very likely to adopt a differentiation strategy when they have a very low to low CSA and enjoy a very high growth potential;
   b. firms are very likely to adopt a cost strategy when they have a low CSA, and when their markets present moderate growth potentials;
   c. firms are very likely to adopt a cost and differentiation strategy when their markets offer at least moderate growth potential, and when they enjoy a substantial CSA.

These patterns are understandable in terms of market growth conditions. One would indeed expect firms to adopt a differentiation strategy when growth potential is high, and a cost strategy when growth potential is moderate (see Doz 1986). These expectations proceed directly from the market/product life-cycle hypothesis.

The addition of the CSA variable adds a valuable perspective on strategic choice, in particular, with regard to the so called "stuck in the middle" position coined by Porter (1980).

According to Porter, firms adopting a cost and differentiation strategy are doomed. They cannot succeed because they are bound to be less effective than their competitors who reap the full benefit of a clearly defined strategy of either cost or differentiation. However, our data indicate that, in fact, firms enjoying a moderate to high CSA are the only ones to adopt such a strategy. A strong CSA may be just what it takes for a firm to afford to adopt a cost and differentiation strategy, and perhaps to be as successful as another company that does not enjoy such a CSA, and that opts for either one of the other two generic strategies.

Contrary to Porter's dictum (1985), the adoption of a cost and-differentiation strategy, based on having a substantial CSA may be a rational decision. The example of the Canadian multinationals included in this survey and claiming to enjoy such an advantage would support this view.

Clearly the limited size of the sample and the subjective nature of the responses hamper our ability to offer strong, unequivocal conclusions concerning the prediction of strategic choices made by Canadian multinational firms with respect to the European market of 1992. Given these limitations, however, the logistic regression models do result in some tentative conclusions beyond simple data description; moreover, these seem to be consistent with our understanding of the factors affecting strategic decisions.

Generic strategic choice would be expected to have an impact on the entry mode selected. Assuming rational behavior on the part of Canadian multinationals, entry strategies would proceed from generic strategic decisions. As was indicated previously, a cost- and differentiation strategy is associated with a strong CSA, which in turn favors production in Canada rather than in the EC. Other generic strategies would be more likely associated with production in the EC.

The evidence gathered in this survey does not allow to statistically test this proposition. However, it would appear that Canadian multinationals are planning to introduce major changes in their present patterns of entry into the EC market, regardless of their intended generic strategies.

The most prevalent mode of entry is now built on direct exporting and developing distribution networks. Direct investment, joint ventures, and licensing are much less frequently used. With the advent of EC 1992, firms intend to favor direct investment. The next options are direct exports and joint ventures, in that order. Altogether, 11 out of 15 firms intend to set up production facilities in the EC. We thus might see substantial production capacity move from Canada to the EC, regardless of the generic strategy being adopted (even when firms enjoy a strong Canadian CSA, and adopt a cost and differentiation strategy).

Just as do many of their American and Japanese counterparts, Canadian executives may feel that the best way to compete in Europe is still to be established there!

REFERENCES

Bruce, L. 1988. "1992: The Bad News." *International Management* (September): 22-26.
Buigues, P. and A. Jacquemin 1988. "Quelles stratégies pour les entreprises européennes?" (What Strategies for European Multinationals?) *Revue Française de Gestion* (juin-juillet-août:15).

"Completing the Internal Market." 1985. White Paper from the Commission to the European Council, June.

Doz, Y. 1986. *Strategic Management in Multinational Companies.* Oxford: Pergamon Press.

Dunning, J. and P. Robson, eds. 1988. *Multinationals and the European Community.* New York: Basil Blackwood.

Neter, J., Wasserman W., and M. Kutner. 1989. *Applied Linear Regression Models,* 2nd ed. Boston: Irwin.

Porter, M.E. 1980. *Competitive Strategy: Technique for Analysing Industries and Competitors.* New York: Free Press.

Porter, M.E. 1985, *Competitive Advantage: Creating and Sustaining Superior Performance.* New York: Free Press.

Quelch, J. A., R. Buzzell, and E.R. Salama. 1990. *The Marketing Challenge of 1992.* Reading, MA: Addison-Wesley.

Rugman, A. and J. McIlveen. 1985. *Megafirms Strategies for Canada's Multinationals.* Toronto: Methuen.

Rugman, A. and A. Verbeke. 1990. "Corporate Strategy After the Free Trade Agreement and Europe 1992." *Paper presented at the Joint Canada Germany Symposium on "Regional Integration in the World Economy: Europe and North America," Kiel, March.*

"Single European Act." 1986. *Bulletin of the European Communities,* Supplement (February).

AUTHOR INDEX

COMPANY INDEX

257

SUBJECT INDEX